Blundering for a Change

Errors & Expectations in Critical Pedagogy

Edited by John Paul Tassoni
& William H. Thelin

Boynton/Cook Publishers
HEINEMANN
Portsmouth, NH

For
James Berlin and Paulo Freire,
two people we wish we had known,
and Ira Shor,
one we are glad we do.

Boynton/Cook Publishers, Inc.
A subsidiary of Reed Elsevier Inc.
361 Hanover Street
Portsmouth, NH 03801-3912
www.boyntoncook.com

Offices and agents throughout the world

The editors and publisher wish to thank those who have generously given permission to reprint borrowed material:

"Doctoral Orals" by Jeff Sommers first appeared in *TETYC* 22.3 (1993): 87. Copyright © 1993 by the National Council of Teachers of English. Reprinted with permission.

Library of Congress Cataloging-in-Publication Data
Blundering for a change : errors and expectations in critical pedagogy / edited by John Paul Tassoni and William H. Thelin.
    p. cm.
    Includes bibliographical references.
    ISBN 0-86709-566-0 (pbk.)
    1. Critical pedagogy—United States—Case studies. 2. Teacher-student relationships—United States—Case studies. 3. English language—Study and teaching (Higher)—Social aspects—United States—Case studies. I. Tassoni, John Paul. II. Thelin, William H.

LC196.5.U6 B48 2000
370.11′5—dc21   00–042914

Editor: Lisa Luedeke
Production service: Lisa Garboski, bookworks
Production coordinator: Lynne Reed
Cover design: Joni Doherty
Manufacturing: Louise Richardson

Printed in the United States of America on acid-free paper
04 03 02 01 00 DA 1 2 3 4 5

Contents

Acknowledgments

We would jointly like to thank all of the contributors who put countless hours into meeting the demanding revision suggestions we put upon them. We also sincerely believe that those practitioners and theorists who sent us proposals, drafts, and revisions, but were ultimately not accepted for this volume helped us shape and understand our concept. We owe them a debt we cannot possibly repay. Finally, we are grateful to our institutions, Miami University at Middletown and the University of Cincinnati, for providing us with released time and the use of their facilities, and to Lisa Luedeke for her assistance.

Bill would like to acknowledge the sacrifices made by his wife, Leann, and his daughter, Katrina, so that he could have the time to devote to this project. He would like also to thank the professors at Indiana University of Pennsylvania and California State University at Northridge who contributed to the foundation of his education, and his parents, Howard and Vivien, who provided encouragement and all forms of support. He would be remiss if he did not also mention Michelle Worley and the other bartenders at The Cooker, who always poured him a mean cocktail when he needed one.

John would like to thank Beverly Compton, Donna Robinson, Karla Coffey, and Lois LaFayette for their expertise; Jess Hawk for researching the epigraph; Cynthia Lewiecki-Wilson and Gail Tayko for reading and commenting on the proposal; Tammy Allen, Tammy Alverson, Beth Boquet, Diane Delisio, Alexandra Muschelli, Mary Tassoni, Suzanne Tassoni-Lovejoy, and Margie Vagt for talking to him when his head was spinning; and Marty Stevens, his coordinator, for attending to all his other blunders while this project was underway.

Introduction

Blundering the Hero Narrative

The Critical Teacher in Classroom Representations

William H. Thelin and John Paul Tassoni

He who believes himself to be wise is but a fool; he who knows himself to be a fool is wise.

—William Shakespeare

I am so sure that the success of the whole depends on conversation being general that I do not wish anyone to join who does not intend, *if possible,* to take an active part. No one will be forced, but those who do not talk will not derive the same advantages with those who openly state their impressions and consent to learn by blundering, as is the destiny of [human beings] here below.

—Margaret Fuller

How can I dialogue if I always project ignorance onto others and never perceive my own?

—Paulo Freire

1

All English teachers make mistakes. In casual conversation, many seem willing to recount nightmarish experiences in the classroom—unproductive lesson plans, preparation problems, recalcitrant students, heat-of-the-moment comments that turn lively classes into stone. Few would deny encountering such difficulties. Yet, the narration of these mistakes remains within the confines of the coffee lounge or departmental offices, to be chuckled over or dismissed with the shake of a head. When mistake-driven narratives do surface in the public arena, whether in our journals or at our conferences, they typically appear to have use only as springboards to pedagogical innovations. In other words, English teachers will talk about a problem and then explain how they subsequently fixed it by isolating the cause and devising a technique as a remedy. Rarely have mistakes signified deeper tensions between the roles of teacher and student as they struggle for a culture of democratic authority.[1]

It seemed to us that practitioners of critical pedagogies, with their varying emphases on democracy and social critique, should have had especially poignant stories to recount. Student empowerment and challenges to the status quo obviously could not run seamlessly and still be what they claimed. Our own work with critical pedagogies, we have to admit, sometimes produced unwanted results: shouting matches; racist, homophobic, misogynistic term papers; botched collaborations. Some unpleasant outcomes seemed perfectly logical in retrospect but maddeningly perplexing at the time. And then there were the episodes that revealed the limits and possibilities of progressive teaching, those times when economic realities, academic hierarchies, and social assumptions collided in the classroom, making us wonder what we had done and what we could ever do. Surely others had experienced these less-than-successful teaching moments. We felt these occurrences—*blunders,* as we termed them—should be studied, not necessarily to find applied solutions, but to move toward a better understanding of blunders themselves and what they tell us about critical teaching and learning.

Thus, *Blundering for a Change* features English instructors who have blundered in their attempts at implementing democratic practices in their classrooms—graduate teaching assistants and tenured professors who have sought mutual authority with their students, who have scrutinized institutional and social forces that facilitate or curtail democratic aims, and who have arranged for their students' engagement with these forces both in and outside of classrooms. Together, they indicate what an amorphous concept blundering is. When they refer to blunders, they are talking about mistakes, but then again they are not. Their articles highlight what teachers learn from their own errors, but at the same time, they avoid the pat conclusions that seem to negate what errors may be telling the teachers. No contributor advocates blundering, yet they acknowledge the utility of blundering if instructors are ever to challenge the "same old, same old" of traditional education and advance their teaching toward democratic goals.

Grappling with the amorphousness of their blunders, contributors to this volume apply the term to varying teaching situations. Some of these situations fail miserably to accomplish much of anything, others cause teachers to pause and wonder about theory and research, others become knowledge in themselves, and still others force teachers to recognize the conditions under which they teach and the concomitant constraints imposed upon liberatory educators.

2

Following principles of Freire's dialogic pedagogy, critical teachers risk negotiations and changes with their students, and thus, will be more prone than traditional educators to see failure in the delivery or outcome. To be true to their theory, critical pedagogues—in many ways—must be blunderers, teachers who wind up in the middle of difficult, politically charged teaching situations. Blunderers find themselves wondering what happened on certain days or throughout particular courses, not because they are unskilled, but more often because they are not afraid to try new things in their classrooms, the consequences of which—given the complexity of interests and concerns of any group of students in any institution at any given moment—are often impossible to predict. The more decentered the classroom and the more the material challenges the status quo, the less the teacherly safety net of the tried and the true can be implemented. Empowering students means losing a certain amount of the order and control that characterize a traditional, banking-method classroom (see Freire 1970, 58), as student input is crucial to the direction of the course. To be fresh and relevant, texts and assignments that question the norms of society and the academy must constantly be changed, which prevents instructors from relying on their expertise of canonized material to assert stability during classroom activities.

These aspects of critical pedagogy, though, are not the lone or main contributors to blunders. Blunders occur due to many factors, including institutional expectations, political hegemony, the malaise of our educational system, cultural assumptions about teaching/learning, and, of course, instructor decisions/indecisions during any segment of the educational experience. In other words, several elements may contribute to the peer workshop that flops, the classroom brawl, the service learning project that produces disillusionment rather than social change. For instance, when students expect knowledge to be conveyed in a classroom under the lecture format, they are made uneasy by collaborative exercises and student-generated curricula. Many students feel frustrated because they do not know when to take notes or how to discern important information from the other conversations and activities happening during class time. Maybe the lack of authoritarian direction strikes them as too liberal or touchy-feely. Resistance crops up, leading to absences, unruly behavior, missed assignments, and generally unappreciated classroom sessions. Administrative intervention looms with the first complaint, either to discipline the student or to get the instructor back on track. Instructors may feel underprepared to negotiate with students and administrators due to the teachers' own lack of knowledge regarding students' personal and cultural backgrounds, their tenuous position within the academic hierarchy, their misunderstanding of liberatory practices, their complicity with conventional pedagogies, or even their fatigue resulting from teaching too many students in too many classes. The cause of most blunders, then, is often hard to pinpoint, as a network of factors contribute to these difficult and challenging occurrences. Identifying these factors, however, can often be teachers' first step toward democratizing the social, cultural, and institutional forces that confound their efforts.

To help our contributors identify their own blunders, we offered them the concept of the bungle as a point of departure. A bungle, we suggested, would be a classroom mistake that provided no insights for teachers. We suggested that, like blunders, bungles represented teaching moments antagonistic to democratic aims, only that bungles remained unrecognized in this regard. Sometimes through reflection, however, past bungles could become blunders, as critical teachers consistently reevaluate their aims and practices. Some contributors to this volume, Jeff Sommers and Brad Peters in particular, examine the fine line between blundering and bungling, but all of them (re)configure teachers as complex beings who can feel pain, make mistakes, be introspective, and change their minds—teachers whose experiences with particular students in particular classrooms continually shape and reshape what it means for them to be change agents in a democratic society.

Contributing to this volume, teacher-researchers make themselves vulnerable, expressing their misgivings and doubts in the context of actual classrooms. Some propose solutions to problems while others linger on the disjunction between theory and practice. Some suggest a second look at tenets of Freirian ideas, while others want to curb radical departures from process-based writing instruction. But they all share experiences that shook them up as educators and made them see what's at stake in their composition and literature classrooms. Our contributors are not confessing bungles as a means toward some public penance: They are blundering for change in society—and for a change, they represent critical teaching as a risky venture in which rewards are not always forthcoming.

3

The articles collected in *Blundering for a Change* stand in contrast to the most dominant narrative construction in education—teacher as hero. As Marguerite Helmers (1994) makes abundantly clear in *Writing Students: Composition Testimonials and Representations of Students,* the common image of teachers in writing classroom narratives and similar pedagogical re-creations found in journals and books displays the instructor in the role of undisputable knower/hero of classroom practice and the student as either listless or resistant, a figure in need of rescue (19). Typically, the narration involves teachers spotting a problem in the classroom, explaining the solution, and then showing how well they implemented that solution. The teacher might present herself as an experienced hand grown tired of the themes in her students' papers, or a conveyor of leftist insights, or a gatekeeper preventing the animals from overrunning the zoo, or even perhaps a novice who discards the regressive pedagogies taught to her in favor of listening to her students and uncovering their real needs. In all these narratives, the teacher promotes a pedagogy that will save students from a number of villains. Though these villains may change, the teacher remains the hero.

The teacher-student dichotomy found in these testimonials appears to be an outgrowth of the fictional hero plot that most English teachers learned in pursuing their degrees, as the structures appear remarkably similar. In the hero plot, the protagonist (conventionally male) must embark upon a quest or battle to save or liberate others. He will meet obstacles, implement strategies to overcome them, and ultimately succeed. The difficulty with this narrative pattern is that the "others," whether they be villains or victims, have no true perspective to offer to the plot. As Bakhtin (1987) conveys in discussing Dostoevski, the hero serves as a mouthpiece for the author and thus functions in a closed system as the vehicle for the author's own ideological position (6–7). The teacher-hero narrative, replete with its quest for better teaching methods against all obstacles—the students often cast in both the villain and victim roles—shows the same penchant for operating in a closed system. Within this narrative pattern, teacher-heroes remain unchallengeable authorities, and students are treated as objects for pedagogies to act upon, rather than speaking subjects developing skills and values necessary to citizens in a democratic society (see Giroux 1988, 6–7). Therefore, despite the implication that these narratives convey real pedagogy in a genuine teaching environment, all of these testimonials can be seen more or less as fictions of a monologic worldview. The teachers (rescuers) and the students (those rescued) are simply mouthpieces for the author in a preordained plot.

Clearly, then, the teacher-hero narrative flattens the complexity of classroom life. Yet, despite the challenge to conventional teaching inherent in the dialogic method, critical educators have continued to portray their classrooms within the constraints of the teacher-hero plot. Pedagogy scholarship, we believe, shapes our classrooms as much as classrooms shape scholarship. Consequently, we fear that the need to emulate the teacher-hero model compromises the very dialogic methods at the heart of critical pedagogy: those methods that allow students to teach as they learn and teachers to teach, but also learn (Freire 1970, 67). Obviously, there are heroic moments in the critical classroom, just as there are in many life situations, but to represent dialogic methods as accurately as possible, the errors need to be a bigger part of the story. Recounting these errors sheds light on learning and allows us to reconfigure teaching as an activity, not as a presentation nor as a script. Following what Robert P. Yagelski (1999) has urged, then, *Blundering for a Change* offers "a reimagining of teacher that doesn't allow [teachers] to ignore self-doubt even as [they] continue to believe in what [they] do" (46).

It could be argued that in exposing and—to a degree—creating the genre of the blunder narrative, this volume simply recasts the role of the hero, replacing the heroic virtues of action and resolution with tentativeness, doubt, sharing, reflectiveness, awkwardness, and disruption. We will not spend a lot of time disputing such a claim. However, these blunder narratives distinguish themselves from the teacher-hero variety in refusing to accept easy closure. Blunders indicate points of conflict for critical pedagogues between their aims as teachers, aims which they like to think as liberatory, and their practice. Blunderers avoid merely adjusting one or two factors to make a pedagogy work in deference to an understanding of the numerous agencies that lead to troubling results or disarming confrontations with students. Blunderers might be unsure of what to do next, but they know they've stumbled upon crucial sites for implementing change. Simply tinkering with application will not do. Instead, by revealing their blunders in this collection, our contributors hope to make situations more recognizable to other critical pedagogues, who, in turn, can help revise teaching, the academy, and culture in democratic ways. In this manner, the blunderer renames teaching and disrupts the hero plot.

Some might still be tempted to call the blunderer a hero, asserting that she is simply one with a tragic flaw—an educator who is not perfect but ultimately successful. If so, however, success needs to be redefined, as *Blundering for a Change* shows English instruction in the critical tradition as an ongoing quest to alter education, not as a mission completed. Answers produce more questions. Attempts at resolution bring up new issues. Blunderers are in a constant state of flux; their students do not automatically leave their courses transformed or otherwise saved. So blunderers might have heroic goals, but the hero plot unravels in unexpected ways, making blunderers continually revamp their strategies and reenvision their purpose. Blunderers are not heroes with or without tragic flaws. They are teachers forever struggling and sometimes getting lost on the way.

4

Given the complexity of factors that can attend blundering, it would be unfair to ask any of these contributors to have the last word on his or her own blunders. Demands of space and genre prohibit them from unpacking every cause and effect, every nuance of their situations, although the situations represented here surely do attest to complication. Thus, we've arranged this volume to help the articles speak to one another and to give full range to the array of issues immanent within each chapter.

At various times throughout the editing process we considered possible ways to group pieces into blundering subcategories: "Blundering Social Issues"; "Blundering Teacher Training"; "Blundering Classroom Practice"; "Blundering Service Learning"; "Blundering Student Revolt"; "Blundering Dialogics"; "Blundering Department Guidelines"; "Blundering Classroom Narratives"; etc. However, as we became more acquainted with concepts developed through the volume as a whole, we learned that such groupings only limited the range of issues each article could address. We found, for example, that Elizabeth Ervin's piece speaks as well to difficulties related to service learning projects as it does to issues in pedagogy scholarship and representation; that Brad Peter's chapter underscores the trials of writing program administration as much as it does tribulations inherent to computer-assisted instruction; and that Riché Richardson's piece highlights the precarious positioning of the teaching assistant as well as it does the preconditions necessary to make public discourses viable in literature and composition classrooms. The sections we developed (and ultimately discarded) weighted certain aspects of articles (a teaching practice, a student comment, a race, gender, or class concern, a Freirean concept) above others in ways that ironed over the complexities of classroom life displayed in each chapter and thwarted interplay amongst articles.

Our current arrangement of texts, we think, invites readers to accumulate interests and concerns about critical pedagogy and to bring those interests and concerns to bear on the various situations represented here. In other words, our arrangement invites readers to deepen contributors' considerations of their own blunders. So, in light of Laura Micciche's discussion of a working-class student's ways with anger, one might ponder, for instance, how class issues amplify the sexual and gender conflicts underlying student silence in Darrell g.h. Schramm's and Jeff Sommers' classrooms. Or one might find the student revolt that happens in Scott Hendrix and Erika Jacobson's composition class more understandable in relation to Douglas Reichert Powell's reflections on how place determines the meaning of blunders and in relation to Riché Richardson's scrutiny of her own positioning as graduate teaching assistant and its concomitant power struggles. A reader might find that similar power arrangements, in turn, confound Brad Peter's attempts to democratize his position as WPA, as well as attempts other teachers in this book undertake to share power with students, mentors, and administrators. Likewise, notions of *community* acquire layers of complication through Frances B. Singh's, Kevin Ball's, and Elizabeth Ervin's pieces, as authors respectively examine the term's usefulness in regard to institutional and cultural issues: institutionalized curricula, ethnic tensions, pedagogies that privilege "universal" concerns over the local and immediate, and forms of community (non)involvement that inauthenticate classroom exercises in civic participation.

In short, we think that *Blundering for a Change* should be read as a whole and that readers will find issues recurring throughout the volume in new and telling contexts. We hope that together these articles will enhance for critical teachers their understanding of what it means to challenge the status quo and possibly even point to further aspects of critical teaching ripe for blundering and for blunder narrative. As William Shakespeare's, Margaret Fuller's, and Paulo Freire's words at the beginning of this introduction would indicate, our investments in teaching and learning deserve as much.

Note

1. Overlapping with the concerns of this volume, texts that privilege discussion of error include K. Rose (1989), Tayko and Tassoni (1992), Tobin (1993), Hurlbert and Bodnar (1994), R. Miller (1994), Bishop (1997), Cooper and Lewandowski (1997), Zawodniak (1997), Clifford (1997), Bloom (1997), Fulwiler (1997), and Brock and Ellerby (1997). Notable full-length works include Power and Hubbard (1996), Dixon (1998), and Durst (1999).

1

The Story of the Story *Is* the Story

Placing the Blunder Narrative

Douglas Reichert Powell

1

So here I am, sitting in a small room in southwest Ohio in the summer of 1999, trying to remember back to the fall of 1995 and a group of people whose names I can only just recall, in a city, Boston, that I have left behind. Memory is both friend and enemy to me, both requirement and obstacle. I've got to try to put events in order here, to tell the story I have to tell accurately and honestly. So I hope my memory works well.

But I hope my memory doesn't work too well. I don't mean that I want to forget things—rather, I hope I won't forget selectively, which is one of the things memory does when it works the way it's supposed to. We forget the bad things, the painful things, the problems, the mess, the difficulty. We may not do so voluntarily, but we do it on purpose, I believe. Memory, acting on instructions from culture, tends to tidy itself up. I don't want to do that. So I hope that part of my memory isn't working well.

One way memory tidies up is to reduce things to just facts and figures, raw information—data. This story isn't about data. I don't know a mathematical, discrete, empirical way you could describe my ENG 1013 (Basic Writing) class, meeting in 42 Cahners Hall, Fall of 1995, beyond the numbers I just gave you, and maybe a couple more: Twenty students began the class, of which eighteen were still enrolled at term's end, and of those, thirteen were authorized to continue on to ENG 1110. Eighteen were men, two women; eight African American (one of these also Latino), two Asian, ten Anglo European. Somewhat surprisingly for a basic writing class, almost all the students were around the eighteen-to twenty-age range of traditional college kids.

This sketch seems like "the facts," the cold-hard part, but it's not. The sketch is not the class itself but the product of a particular way of looking at a classroom, at a group of students, at a period of time. I think mostly it's an administrative kind of way—the gradebook from which I got this (admittedly limited) information is the text I make in my administrative, institutional capacity, the role I savor least. It's certainly not the capacity in which I want to speak to you, nor, I imagine, the language in which you would prefer to be addressed (if I am guessing rightly about the folks who will read this book).

Don't worry. I'm not going to go any farther down the data road. I believe we need to pause at this crossroads, though, to think for a minute about data and the students that I am going to talk about. As basic writing students, they have not only been data-ed by way of being placed in this class, they have, many of them, been in some ways the victims of data for a while before arriving here. GPAs and test scores have limited their opportunities for participation in various facets of their public lives—employment, extracurriculars, advanced placement classes, to say nothing of university admissions (see Shor 1997).

So data is important to this story, but not sufficient in itself to explain what happened. This chapter is a narrative: subjective, constructed, didactic (but hopefully not pedantic). However, one kind of narrative, the legend, represents another strategy the memory uses to tidy itself up. The narrativization of messy experience involved in the making of a legend means cutting out the parts that don't fit with the plot structures we've all internalized from our cultural history (see White 1978, 70–99).

Legends have to be produced, paced, plotted, measured, i. e., tidied up. In this respect they are not unlike data in that they are, once again, the product, not the process, of observation. Teaching narratives in particular seem to get sanitized pretty thoroughly—and do a little teaching themselves: They teach teachers how to make good teaching stories. Movies like *Dead Poets Society* get rid of the social dimensions of the mess that educational practice usually is: Schooling becomes a matter of New Age personal conflicts, inner crises, personality matters, "finding yourself." (As I pointed out above, my students have already *been found,* statistically located with a fairly brutal determination.) The *Blackboard Jungle* genre, still thriving in modern-day inheritors like *Dangerous Minds, seems* to tackle social and political problems but almost invariably ends up solving them through the salvific power of white-middle-class values; the problem, it usually turns out, was incomplete assimilation on the part of the students. Then there's the bare-knuckle reactionary teacher-tale like *The Substitute,* where it turns out that education only lacks ass-kicking teachers to show their colleagues how to assimilate fascism. In all of these movies the teacher— whether guru, savior, or commandante—is the central character, the students a motley supporting cast reflecting back their leader's glory.

Most of the teachers I have worked with know better than to emulate any of their celluloid colleagues. But these genres probably do influence, if not classroom practice, then the way that we talk about our classrooms. We learn the forms and the principles and we use them, building on the most basic formula, in which the dullard students come to knowledge through the timely intervention of the teacher. The "Once upon a time" for this story goes, "Well, in *my* classroom. . . ."

Even though that opening line sounds pretty specific, it really isn't much more factual than its fairy-tale counterpart. "The Classroom" is a no-place of a sort. Usually it's not meant to refer to the physical space of the room itself—you never hear anyone say, "Well, in 218 Sheidler Hall . . ."—but to some general kind of pedagogical space under the proprietorship of the speaker (It's always "my" classroom). I've noticed too that teacher stories that use this formulaic beginning are generally told in a perpetual present, just as fairy tales exist in a static past—"In my classroom we *do* [insert wonderful thing that we do in my classroom]."

So in some ways this representation of classes and teaching is just as reductive as the statistical approach—it takes the specific experience of particular students and particular situations and abstracts them from their contexts. Most teachers, however, myself included, are much more comfortable with and much less self-conscious about these practices of representation than they are of the stats approach because this strategy is one that we share with our colleagues in meetings and hallways rather than one we perform on orders from administrative offices and officers with whom—especially in writing programs, it seems—our relationships tend to range from indifferent to antagonistic. Even those fleeting hallway conversations, in other words, are largely a part of our disciplinary lives rather than our institutional lives, even if they are more covert and less "authorized" than most other disciplinary practices, especially those of research and publication.

But if we think of the university's institutional discourse as objectifying and decontextualizing, so our disciplinary practices also have a tendency to pull our thinking, writing, and talking out of specific places and into a kind of intellectual no-place, the Universe of Ideas. We often think of and talk about the institutions that sustain our disciplinary activities not in terms of the specific constituencies they serve and the communities of which they are a part but instead in terms of their relative prestige as part of the peerage of institutions. Journals and conferences are thought of as "places" in and of themselves— where did you *place* that piece? (Is a journal really a "place?") Are you going to MLA? (Not, we note, to Chicago.) And indeed, the work of journal publication and conference organization does take place in physical space and time, but that's not what we think of. The material process and the physical context of the production of knowledge in these sites is best for us when it is not a factor at all, when the journal shows up without complication and on time, when the service at the Grand Hotel of the Great Big Conference does everything right and disappears into the woodwork (see Reynolds 1998).

Data and legend—they're part of a range of forces in our profession pushing folks out of place into the Big Nowhere of Academia: job markets that demand not only travel (and cutting classes, ditching duties at home) to interviews in hotel rooms that look like other hotel rooms, to get a job who knows where, and getting a job means being willing to go there; hiring practices that require the belief that displacement is a virtue—fresh perspectives can't be had from the locals; and finally the campus, a landscape that cuts off the institution from the rest of the city into a little green zone of tranquility, exempt from the rest of the world (see Cushman 1996). Now we're all the way back around to the institution again.

Appropriately enough—these pressures, cultural, disciplinary, institutional, to say nothing of personal and psychological, don't come in discrete little bundles—even if they each pressure us to think of ourselves as the function of only one of these forces at any given time. When we English teachers step into real, live classrooms, specific rooms with real material forms and noisy air conditioners or no windows or whatever, all these forces are intersecting, along with all the forces that intersect in our students' lives, producing a specific context for our work that despite all the forces working to the contrary, obscuring or trying to invalidate each other, we have to work hard to take into account. This accountability is no simple matter, not just a problem of paying better attention or thinking harder.

Being accountable to the specific places of our work is in part a matter of acknowledging, examining, and learning from our mistakes—the larger argument of this volume. But how do we do that in light of the many pressures that take us out of space and time when we meditate on our professional practice, when those pressures encourage us to clean up, conceal, repress, forget the untidiness that our work necessarily involves? What I've learned, and what I'll try to illustrate in the narrative that follows, is that without careful attention to the specific places where our work occurs, an attention that pushes back against the various forms we are tempted to ease our experience into, we can't really learn to develop new tactics out of old errors.

What I am trying to do, in short, is help create a body of lore. Lore lacks data's claims to empiricism and also eschews legend's attempts to enfable, to narrativize. Lore instead dramatizes—a distinction that transfers interpretive agency to the listener, the reader of the lore (see North 1987, 19–56; Harkin 1991; Staiger 1996). By dramatizing my own experience here, I hope to impart some information, ideas, questions, and problems that you can bring to your own place, not as a narrative template to lay atop it, nor as a rational analysis to test it against, but as some more-or-less useful perspectives that might cohere around your own problems and priorities. The story that follows is not a tool, but a set of tool-like problems, as an old office-mate of mine used to say of critical theory.

Lore is always tied crucially to specific places, to the interaction of particular people across a particular landscape at a particular point in history—but you have to do the tying. My tale is rooted in the experience of my specific places, but it might in some way shape the practices of you and your students in whatever specific place and time you inhabit. If it does, though, it will be you that is doing it, changing your place, by drawing connections between places near and far (see Hayden 1995, 1–81).

2

In the fall of 1995, at Northeastern University in Boston, I was teaching a basic writing class that one student described at an early meeting as "a cross between *Dangerous Minds* and *Welcome Back Kotter*": a rowdy, multiethnic, male-dominated group that fit, in appearance, the media stereotypes they used to describe themselves. I had come a long way, in more ways than one, to the classroom I found myself in—but perhaps not as far as I should have, in terms of experience, anyway. I had been teaching for just two and a half years when I walked into that room, having come from a semester of TAing and another year of adjuncting in upper East Tennessee. Though I had taught only one section of basic (still called "developmental") writing in that time, I had taught basic writers, to be sure. At both the community college and the regional university where I cut my teeth, many students were the first of their family to attend college, many were nontraditional and working class, many were underprepared by poorly funded rural school systems. But like most TAs and adjuncts I had almost no training in teaching writing—and none specifically in teaching basic writing. During my year of adjuncting I learned mostly how to drive very quickly between four different teaching sites.

And, besides, this class in Boston was *different*. Don't get me wrong; my students in Tennessee brought a remarkable range of abilities and experiences to the classroom—their collective identity was crisscrossed with lines of difference in class, in gender, in sexual orientation, in age, and (less frequently) in race. But I had grown up in Tennessee, so the students I was teaching there were home folks—in one section I even had a high school classmate of mine (a whole different kind of weird experience). My Northeastern class, though, was—for a big white boy out of the southern mountains—a lot more like the Other.

Yet these students were also strangely familiar. I recognized, and as the comment I mentioned above indicates, my students recognized as well, that this class was the image of those cultural narratives we all knew. Even the classroom itself, the physical setting, was almost like a set: the basement classroom of an aged and decrepit building (a former gymnasium) on the fringes of campus, with windows that pointlessly opened onto brick walls six inches away, noisy radiators, intermittent supplies of chalk and no a/v support. (Fortunately—and unlike most "urban education" stories—I was able to finagle a room change— though that only happened when construction on an adjacent building caused clouds of choking dust to fill our classroom on a daily basis, making it not just unacceptable but outright uninhabitable.) And here was the fresh-faced, new-in-town teacher, short on training and long on enthusiasm. I was ready to have my own little pack of Sweathogs.

And lo and behold, the students seemed to crave this kind of dynamic them-selves. They were a pack of students made for the role of underrated, energetic, scrappy urban students, each with distinctive, neglected talents but each playing a particular role in the whole. There was Willie, who took a couple of excused absences to attend the Million Man March, and who again and again emphasized to me his interest in eloquence, saying "I want to be a Writer" (you could just hear that capital letter in there). Gerry, who went by "G," a white suburban kid who emulated his urban African American counterparts and tried to impress them by being the class clown. Pham, who confounded his classmates' Asian stereotypes with his extraordinary interest in and knowledge of cars. Vlad, the Russian immigrant, who looked about twelve and loved heavy metal. Raymond, a handsome African American jock, who had been recruited to a suburban high school from his Dorchester home to play football. Bill, a surfer dude, and Julie, the hippie girl, were the most outspoken of the class' white minority. There was Andrea, an extremely intelligent and striking mestiza; her looks garnered her a lot of unwanted attention in this predominantly, sometimes overwhelmingly male classroom, but her quick wit and perceptible self-assurance, surely honed by lengthy experience in these situations, usually kept wolves at bay.

Then there was Nick, an Italian American kid, who was a favorite of mine, and even though he doesn't figure largely in the main incident of this story, he's worth a little more attention. He was the classic "slipped through the cracks" kid, loaded with skills and insights that the placement instruments and univer-sity standards couldn't detect. He was from a bilingual working-class family in a vintage, ethnic working-class neighborhood and brought those class politics to his work in streetwise but often astute ways. We bonded when we discovered we shared a love of Italo Calvino, whom I was reading in translation for a gradu-ate seminar and he had read in high school, it turned out, in the original Italian. Once he knew I was into that kind of thing—socialist fabulism—his writing became much more adventurous, elaborate, and bizarre. I was tickled pink, but even with—perhaps because of—his skills, he was still a stranger to univer-sity culture. One time I had to call him at home, getting him on the line only af-ter a difficult pidgin conversation with his grandma. The next day he told me how excited she was to talk to "a real college professor."

She may have thought I was real, but I wasn't so sure. Fortunately, my lim-ited experience as a basic writing instructor was propped up by my growing in-terest in critical pedagogy, which in turn was facilitated by an exceptional amount of latitude in course design permitted by the department. Back in Ten-nessee, the standard developmental syllabus I was handed was a dismal, not-even-current-traditional affair: skills and drills all the way. I knew I wanted to do something more, but I didn't have the knowledge or the training to do it. At Northeastern I not only had a little more training and another year of teaching under my belt, but also a seminar in composition studies that had me thinking in a much more serious and thorough manner than I ever had before about the role of teaching in my professional life. I also began to develop stronger opinions about the role of politics in academic writing and in college teaching more generally. This syllabus was the first I ever constructed with a little Freire (and hooks and Giroux and company) in my repertoire, and I tried hard to work with my students to create what I thought a democratic classroom was supposed to be.

I was (I still am) a very imperfect democratic educator, however. My inexperience and my unfamiliarity with the setting I was working in often made me timid. Fall quarter was only just underway when the O. J. Simpson verdict came in—just an hour before our class meeting. Having stood in the student center and seen how emotional reactions to the announcement of the verdict split directly on racial lines, from cheers to expressions of disgust, I sat out by the Back Bay Fens and worked out a few strategies for making the controversial moment the subject of the class. I felt so conjunctural, contemporary, engaged. Then I walked into the classroom and the first thing I heard was Bill, on one side of the room, proclaiming, "They ought to execute that guy." Meanwhile Raymond, on the other side, announced "If they found O. J. guilty, I was ready to RIOT." And I chickened right out. We talked about effective sentences or something. Or I did, anyway.

Often, though, this class was able to harness its remarkable range of experiences and viewpoints and the students' incredible energy to produce some really exciting intellectual work. Northeastern sits across the street from the Museum of Fine Arts in Boston, and students are admitted free, so a trip to the MFA was a staple of almost all of my writing courses. Usually it had something to do with interpreting images, tackling the intertextual writing task of translating color and design into written language, arguing an interpretation; this class engaged instead in a rough-and-tumble school of political criticism. My African American students talked about being tailed by security, shushed by docents; this opened the door for working-class students to talk about the inhospitability of the class trappings of the museum; even the hippie and the surfer—normally great defenders of the pious romanticist, solitary-genius idea of art—noted that the museum defined a passive, spectatorial role for its visitors. We realized the geographical organization of the museum balkanized world cultures, so you could stay in the museum for hours without ever encountering African or Asian art. We considered factors like these in a discussion of why such a vast majority, based on our observations, of museum visitors was white in our diverse city—especially when the museum sits adjacent to Boston's largest African American neighborhoods.

A couple of class meetings later we had developed a revised floor plan for the museum, organized chronologically rather than geographically, including interactive exhibits where visitors would be encouraged to make as well as view art—in short, a new vision of what a museum is and who it is for (see Anderson 1992, 163–185). In class meetings like these, my students gave me an energy and a courage, a new set of approaches to old material.

On the other hand, the class often teetered on the brink of total chaos, and I had to bite my tongue to keep from yelling at them to shut up. This was the very last thing I wanted to do. For one thing, I knew from their own testimony that formal schooling for many of the students, especially the African American men, had consisted primarily of being yelled at to shut up. I certainly didn't want to duplicate that authoritarianism, especially when they had so much to bring to the table, when the best-case scenario was, as in the case of our MFA discussion, so good. And furthermore, I was reluctant to ever tell a class to *stop* talking, having spent so many pained hours squeezing conversation out of reticent classes. My underprepared students in Tennessee tended to express their unfamiliarity with the college classroom with uncomfortable silence, and everywhere I've taught I've encountered aversion even by well-prepared students to extemporize in front of a crowd. This group had no such reluctance: Everyone wanted to talk, and under this pressure, the collective class disintegrated into multiple, fragmentary audiences.

Sometimes, indeed, many times, they really were talking about the material; other times, their discussion groups veered quickly well beyond the task at hand. I felt like the old circus performer trying to keep plates spinning on top of poles as I dashed from group to group, trying to steer them back on course, to keep that energy channeled into writing projects. I had to learn a whole new classroom style and fast, and I'd leave our meetings drained but also exhilarated, riding the wave of their enthusiasm, excited about the potential of this disorderly, democratic classroom—like the ones I was reading about, imagining, as I became more involved with critical pedagogy. But I was cautious about the tenuous coherence of the class and hence the course as a whole.

So here is where the class is supposed to gel, where we all learn how to talk to one another and see the importance of radical critique in our daily lives or whatever. I wish. Instead, one day in the midst of this generative turmoil, something suddenly snapped: Raymond, the charismatic African American football player, suddenly upped the ante in his private debate with Andrea, one of two women in the class and the only woman of color. I still don't know what they were arguing about; they had bickered back and forth for weeks already. He often pulled a bossy, macho, "listen-here-woman," kind of thing on her, putting on a show for his male classmates, but she was always quick and smart with a put-down, so to be honest, I usually just let it slide. Today was different.

All of a sudden, Raymond shouted, "WHY DON'T YOU SHUT THE FUCK UP!" Andrea responded by slapping his face, packing up her things, and storming out of the room, followed by several white male students, led by Bill the surfer, in apparent protest.

3

Narrative logic, plain-old "good storytelling," demands that this be the big scene. This is act three, scene four or so—where it all comes down. This is the moment that this narrative has been building up to all along. I can envision it now as a sequence of shots. Give it a visual treatment that befits its narratological importance: Try a slow-motion sequence—medium shot, me turning to write on the board as Raymond and Andrea turn to face each other—extreme close-up of the chalk in my hand approaching the chalkboard—close up of Raymond's and Andrea's angry faces in profile as he mouths the profanities—chalk breaking against the board intercut with Andrea's slap winging towards its target—tracking shot of the fragment of chalk falling—medium shot of Andrea wheeling out of her seat towards the door—reverse shots of me turning, astonished, confused, as Bill and his allies rise and exit—chalk hits the floor and disintegrates as door slams behind the dissenters. Then a longer medium shot of me, standing alone, flatfooted, in front of the class.

And the funny thing is I can remember it that way if I try; in fact, I've imagined it that way often enough as I have constructed this text that it's tempting to go ahead and tell it that way. But that's the very moment where my memory is poised to do the tidying up I was so skeptical about when this essay began. The fact is, though, that's just not the way it happened; the fact is that I can't clearly envision even an approximation of exactly how this moment looked. I can summon up enough particulars—things like the quality of light, the arrangement of furniture, roughly where everybody sat, and so on—that I could do an effective dramatization of this scene, one that even captures some of the themes I want to underscore here. The montage I can imagine suggests, for example, that this, the most important moment in the course, happened (figuratively, anyway) when my back was turned; that it happened simultaneously with, but also juxtaposed against, the teaching I was trying to do; that my work as teacher (captured in the writing on the board) and this intensely political, border-smashing social interaction (the closeup of Raymond and Andrea's faces as they argue) are interrelated but are also contrasts to each other. But to be honest, when it all went down, well, it just happened so fast, as the witnesses to auto accidents always say. The fact is that I can honestly say only that this incident happened, not exactly how it happened.

4

I was blind-sided, left holding the bag. Democratic classroom or not, all eyes were suddenly on me to see how I was going to handle this mess. What had happened to our critical democracy? How were we to respond to secession?

With no clear solution at hand and no time to think about what to do, I ad-libbed, scrapping what was left of my plans for the day—I can't even remember now what those plans were—to try to get the class to patch things together as best it could. I spent the rest of the period talking with the class members who remained about the meaning of the incident, trying to defend Andrea's reaction without unconditionally defending her actions, trying to argue that, in a male-dominated environment, a "SHUT THE FUCK UP" from a man to a woman was as violent, maybe more so, as a slap in the face. I tried to turn the disruption into an opportunity to shed a little light on the culture clashes that intersected there. But to do it I had to take control of the room in a way I had wanted to avoid. I realized at one point that I was standing behind the podium—a position I resolutely had stayed away from all term.

Raymond especially held out against me—maybe he could sense that his masculine authority among the students hinged somewhat on his ability to exercise spin control. He could come out looking totally disrespected or as if he had driven the opponent from the field. For the first time, I found myself openly and emphatically disagreeing with one of these students, not facilitating but just arguing, saying, "No, You Are Wrong." Was I trying to counter his masculine authority by cranking up my own—my ace in the hole all along, whether I realized it or not? Or was I trying to defend the right of all students to participate in my class without threat of violence, rhetorical or otherwise? Okay, I want the students to have agency about what we discuss, and how we discuss it, but don't I have an obligation to control situations like this, to thwart student-centeredness when it results in slapping and storming out? Don't I owe it to the University, at least from a risk-management point of view? I had found the very point where authority and authoritarianism (to invoke a Freirean distinction) blurred into one another, and I wasn't being given any time to do any research or theorizing. Instead I found myself—with some justification?—shouting students down. But what would have happened if I hadn't?

Later, I tracked down the white male students who walked out. By this time I had had some time to reflect on the incident in the classroom itself. Though I had (perhaps?) lost my grasp of my democratic methods in talking back to Raymond and his allies, I tried to recoup it a little bit here by not speaking for—or over—Raymond and company in this situation. Instead, I framed the incident for them specifically as a problem of a democratic classroom, as the inevitable, eventual side effect of a risky pedagogy. I believe this was important, because despite the way I had conducted my class up to this point, trying to shift agency and responsibility for the success of the class to the students, this incident—and Bill and company's response to it—implied criticism not only of Raymond but also of me. I had sensed as much at the time, and any doubts I had were dispelled when I talked to Bill and his cadre. I tried to convince them that I wasn't incompetent, that there was a reason I had refused to take a more authoritarian role, even if things had gotten out of hand. And as I reflect on it now, I believe that though undramatic, this important moment opened up in a very explicit way the theory underlying the operation of the class: a moment where I was not only teaching writing, but also teaching about the teaching of writing, demystifying not just the material but the class itself.

I encountered more difficulty when I tried to hint at the racial nature of the split they had enacted, without sounding accusatory. I'm not sure now how well that went, and I still have deeply mixed feelings about what Bill and Co. did. On the one hand, I admired their willingness to stand up for their beliefs in the face of disapproval, not only from their classmates but from me as well. In a way, it was a sign of their faith in the democratic nature of our classroom that they could engage in civil disobedience.

As a Southerner, though, I am very sensitive to any situation in which white men police the conduct of black men, especially when women are involved. I believe an element of an Anglo European, patriarchal gallantry entered their reaction, the white men defending the woman—even the mixed-race woman—against the depredations of black masculinity. (Perhaps, too, I saw this theme foreshadowed in the class's reaction to the O. J. Simpson verdict.)

Andrea turned up at the next class meeting quite on her own and told me she didn't want any apologies from anybody. I apologized anyway for failing in my duty to maintain a safe environment in which she could speak without intimidation, and I assured her she was right to walk out (if not to hit) in any such situation. Certainly, I think she should not have resorted to violence, and I rue her decision to move from words to blows even though, given the situation, I understand that decision. Still, to this day I admire her unwillingness to fold in a situation where her gender was not just in the minority but a miniscule minority, to say nothing of the fact that she was the only woman of color. If anyone's status in the class rose across the board coming out of this incident, it was Andrea's, and I am glad.

The class reunited under an uneasy truce that lasted out the term, though the shadow of the incident was cast over the rest of our time together. Everyone in the class had seen the limits of civility in their community; they had a sense of the risks of the writing process, the point at which discourse could come to blows.

I know that I certainly could have been better prepared for these students and this class; I hope I have gained some finesse in the exercise of authority without lapsing into authoritarianism. Still, I'm not sure that, all things being equal, I would do anything differently in that particular situation. I feel, on reflection, that this might have been a valuable episode, for me as well as my students, in and of itself. Perhaps the momentary breakdown had invested their work with a greater sense of urgency, with an awareness of what the unpleasant options were when intellectual inquiry failed (see Fox 1990; Pratt 1992; Lu and Horner 1999, 30–55). At the very least they had all witnessed that the cultural conflicts I was always assigning them to write about were a part of, not apart from, their university education. Instead of some lame, spectatorial "teaching the conflicts," a tourist trip around American injustice, we had occasion to engage those conflicts on the terrain of—not "the classroom" (see Graff 1992, Giroux 1993)—but *our* classroom, there on the first floor of Ryder Hall, Northeastern University, a literal stone's throw from Roxbury and Mission Hill and a short walk from affluent Brookline, in Boston, Massachusetts. (And there must not have been too many hard feelings—Andrea chose my section of composition the next quarter.)

Another valuable aspect of this class and its conflicts for me and for my professional practice are the important questions with which I was starkly confronted. But these are scary questions, to be sure: How can/should conflict stop at some point before the slapping begins? Whose job is it to define the limits of conflict? It is presumably the instructor's, but how are those limits enforceable without reverting to a traditional, authoritarian role? Much writing about critical pedagogy seems to endorse playing out cultural clashes in the classroom, but perhaps these discussions don't reflect enough on the potential for real violence, both physical and discursive. Nothing I had read prepared me for the situations I encountered on the ground.

5

I guess what I am trying to do here—perhaps what this volume as a whole is trying to do—is put something in circulation that people might turn to in similar situations. I hope this narrative might be useful in ways that mass-culture narratives of the cultural politics of teaching often are not: in resisting tidy conclusions, by inquiring into the larger significances and ongoing histories of struggle that intersect in specific places. Perhaps this reflection can recuperate, to some extent, the loss that occurred when my basic writing class lost its balance and its cool. But the use of blunder narratives is not unproblematic, not the simple application of a tool to a task. The deployment of these counternarratives requires, I assert, as much reflection and critical inquiry as the events that inspire the narrative.

Two years later I was teaching first-year writing at an upscale state university in a small college town in the Midwest, in an almost lily-white classroom of well-prepared, if somewhat complacent, students. Trying to find ways to disrupt their complacency, I found myself one day telling the story of my urban basic writing classroom, offering it as an example of a time when I felt like there was really something on the line, when things really went up for grabs. I hoped they would see that the classroom can be a place where teachers and students struggle to create and change knowledge, willing to risk failure and strife to do so. My nine o'clock class was nonplused: "Yeah, I had classes like that in high school," said one woman, "where it was so rowdy nobody learned anything." Unsettled by what I took for a deviant reading of what I thought was a tale of risk and rewards, I retold the story in my next class, and got a somewhat different reaction, if equally unsettling: These students cast me in the role of hero, saving their underprepared, urban counterparts from themselves. "That sounds just like *Dangerous Minds,*" one student remarked.

I went 0-for-2 with blunder narratives that Wednesday morning, as far as I was concerned. Not only had the story not had its desired effect, to illustrate the potential for engagement that exists in the writing classroom and the perils that ensue, but in fact, the very thing I was trying to thwart had taken place. The students had transformed my efforts at complicating our course into tidy, predictable narratives; my effort at subversion had, it seemed, met with almost effortless cooptation and accommodation.

In this affluent white university, it's really easy at moments like this one to ascribe failures of politicized pedagogy to the intractable inertia of the homogenous, privileged, culturally conservative student body, to shrug and say, "Whaddaya gonna do with these kids?" (see Mahoney 1995). What's more, my colleagues and I have a propensity for blaming problems on the landscape, making the possibilities (or lack thereof) for critical teaching an accident of geography. "This region is irony-impaired," one of my fellow teachers likes to declare. In this version of this place, efforts to wake up the slumbering critical consciousness of students are just whistling past the cemetery.

This analysis, pessimistic as it is, has one all-too-convenient aspect: It lets the teacher, the tale-teller, off the hook, even as it disconnects critical teachers from the places where they work. Notice that this critique can only come from someone who's "not from around here," an analysis facilitated by all those place-obscuring aspects of disciplinary and institutional academic practice I mentioned in the opening of this essay. Like soldiers in a Roman outpost on some bleak edge of the empire, the best we critical teachers can hope to do is hold the line and resist going native ourselves (and look forward to a visit to the metropole for the next Great Big Meeting). After a morning like I had the day I tried to put the blunder narrative to work in my classroom, that attitude is a strong temptation, even a guilty pleasure—but what would have happened if I had taken the place where I told my stories as seriously as the place where the story occurred?

In this instance I could have taken the whiteness and the class status of my audience into account, given careful scrutiny to what only appears to be the absence of race, the absence of political and cultural conflict, in this Midwestern setting. Conflict and struggle, and opportunities for engaging them, are not absent in these places but different; they don't take the forms Americans—teachers and students included—are taught to recognize using hermeneutics acquired from media culture, lenses that make strife visible only in particular kinds of places like the urban classroom.

Perhaps if I had taken the local conditions better into account before I tried to deploy my blunder narratives, I would have given some thought to the fact that narratives of conflict and struggle in urban classrooms—like *Dangerous Minds* or news media coverage of urban schools in crisis—are on the whole addressed to a white, middle-class demographic reflected in my Midwestern classroom (see Giroux 1997b, 297–304). These students weren't failing to respond to my pedagogical use of narrative, but responding to it in ways they have been powerfully trained in from early education, using interpretive strategies that are particular to their social location. Fitting my story in with the genre-conventions was neither difficult nor inappropriate for them: Their strategies protect their own position from criticism by suggesting either that white middle-class values can redeem classrooms or that conflicted, multicultural urban classrooms—spaces where white, middle-class values come under powerful critique—are failures.

My students' transformation of my narrative was facilitated not only by the interpretive framework they have, but also the framework they lack. My urban basic writing classroom just isn't the kind of struggle that these students have experienced or, likely, are going to experience. They aren't going to share the same investments in the narrative that underprepared urban African American students will. Moreover, even if a group of urban African Americans reacted to the story ostensibly the same way—fitting it into genres of heroic or incompetent teaching—that interpretive act would have a different meaning. Disorderly classrooms have different pathologies in the suburbs and the inner city or the country—where disorder might be more symptomatic of systematic underdevelopment than of simply inadequate classroom management skills on the part of the teacher. Heroic teachers have different mythologies in different situations, too—the relationship of a marginalized, underprepared student to a movie like *Dangerous Minds* might center more on use of the text to generate the powerful affective investments in education that are necessary to overcome the material and cultural barriers to education thrown up by politics and economics. When my basic writer Nick compared our classroom to a cross between *Welcome Back Kotter* and *Dangerous Minds,* it meant something different than when my Midwestern student made a similar comparison—Nick signified engagement where the later student signaled accommodation.

In the end, maybe the biggest problem of all was the way that I told the story, pulling it out of my pocket and attempting to apply it, like some kind of unguent, to another classroom, a different place with different problems and priorities. I acted in a solitary, monologic, banking model way. I'm sure blunder narratives can assist the practice of critical pedagogy, but they are not little machines that can manufacture democratic classrooms, as my experience in the Midwest shows. What could I have done, instead, to keep from bungling the blunder narrative? The possibilities are theoretically endless, but here are some alternatives that spring to mind:

Perhaps I could have demystified the act of telling the story by prefacing it (or following it) with consideration of the genre-trappings and race-and-class coding of this kind of narrative. Reflecting on the specific landscape in which I was working, I should at the least have, as I argue above, taken these factors into account. What might have happened if my students and I had gone further and taken these codes and conventions head on in writing and in discussion, creating a context in which both the story's potential fit with and critique of the genre-conventions of teaching narratives could be more visible?

Even more significantly, I could have found ways for students to participate in the narrative. This interactive approach to storytelling could be as simple as presenting the tale not as a legend originating from the podium, but instead in the form of questions. Since, given most of my Midwestern students' lack of experience in urban settings for underprepared students, the story is really a kind of hypothetical situation for them anyway; their relationship to the narrative is essentially imaginary. Perhaps, then, that's how I should have presented the story to the class, as a series of discussion questions centering on a hypothetical situation, questions that encourage them to envision the situation from a variety of perspectives, including, but not limited to mine or their own—the only ones my traditional, storyteller approach made available.

In any event I certainly should have students make their own histories more explicit so that I know better what the local conditions are, can understand what specific network of experiences makes up that classroom. I needed—I need—to work on understanding the political conflicts going on in the local area. Despite appearances, this Midwestern campus is not immune from conflict, but rather conflicts take particular forms that require particular approaches to seeing and responding to them. Last year, for example, our supposedly tranquil campus was the site of protests by African American students centering on a complicated racist incident. It's a story for another time, but it's a narrative filled with potentially different blunders of its own—so maybe what I should have done was used my own blunder not as a narrative in itself, but as an experience that helps me understand, in a comparative context, how to deal with the blunders I encounter in this different setting.

As that possibility suggests, there were in this situation potent alternatives to using the blunder narrative in the classroom at all. Instead of overlaying other places' conflicts on this particular room, maybe I should use the blunder narrative as a lesson in constructing syllabi and curricula that take risks in the name of addressing higher education to the challenge of establishing a truly democratic culture, and maybe, just maybe, reap some rewards (an appropriately agricultural metaphor for life here in the heartland). Perhaps the best thing I could do with this experience is to put it out here so you readers have the opportunity to use it in ways both similar and different as you all adapt this tale to your own local circumstances. Maybe the contributors to this volume can help create a body of lore that can be inflected with the specific conditions of all the material places of academic life—a body of lore that says that these liminal spaces of higher education present opportunities and obstacles unique to them, and need to be taken seriously in each and every unique place.

Acknowledgments

I give my thanks to the students of English 1013, section 20, Northeastern University, Fall 1994, who are truly co-authors of this story; I am also deeply indebted to the students of English 111, sections CE and EI, Miami University-Oxford, Fall 1997, who taught me much about how and why to tell this story. Pegeen Reichert Powell has profoundly shaped this manuscript and my pedagogies. John Tassoni and Bill Thelin have provided thorough and invaluable critique of this manuscript and have been remarkably patient with its author.

2

When Class Equals Crass

A Working-Class Student's Ways with Anger

Laura Micciche

English 243, a sophomore-level English course, originally met on the third floor
of an old building on campus, recently reopened after several years of renovation. I arrived early the first day of class to find the room incredibly hot that late
August afternoon. In addition to the lack of air conditioning, the windows would
not budge. As the students began to shuffle in, I realized that the room would not
be large enough for the thirty-five or so people enrolled. Those not lucky enough
to secure a desk sat on the floor while others leaned against the walls, book-bags
in tow. I was excited that so many students were interested in the course, titled
"Literature of the Women's Movement," but felt anxious about the small room
and uncomfortable heat. By the third class session, we had been moved to a basement room in a building across campus. While large enough to accommodate
all thirty-five students, this room, too, had its problems. The temperature, for
instance, was never quite right: always too cold, the students tucked sweaters
in their backpacks, anticipating the chilly seventy-five minutes ahead.

On the first day, I introduced myself as a graduate teaching assistant in the
English department. I was excited about the class, had not taught it before, and
told the students that I hoped we could work together to assess the readings, the
workload, and classroom discussions. Hoping we could incorporate reflective
and collaborative components into the class from the outset, I invited commentary on the shape and progress of the course itself. I then asked students to introduce themselves and explain their reasons for enrolling in English 243.

Most of the enrolled students were Arts and Science majors. The majority
were white, middle-class, heterosexual women in their early-twenties. Also
present were two male students, one Japanese American woman, and a Hispanic
woman. As expected, a number of students admitted that they simply needed
another English requirement and this class fit into their schedules. Others enrolled because they had previously taken women's literature courses and wanted

to explore the offerings further. Still, other students completely identified as feminists, were Women's Studies majors, and wanted an opportunity to study the literature of second wave feminism. In this group, one student identified as lesbian. Another, an older student, narrated her experiences in the 1960s by telling us that she had been "your typical woman": a married, middle-class housewife. When the women's movement emerged, something inside her awakened, compelling her to change her life. Now, she told us, she is Newt Gingrich's worst nightmare: a queer social activist determined to fight gender oppression wherever she finds it. Her forthrightness surprised many of the students and, in some ways, set the tone for the entire course. This would be a class where students, for the most part, unabashedly stated their opinions and, above all else, made the personal political.

This was never more obvious than with "Christina," a self-identified working-class student who frequently shared her unsolicited personal history with the class. Her stories recounted the abuse she suffered at her father's hand, her treatment in the mental health system, and her relationships with men, middle-class white women, and "so-called" feminists. Her fury at the various systems that constrained her potential often functioned as the basis for long, articulate monologues on the class bias of social institutions. For example, she argued that educational institutions have no idea what to do with lower class and minority students. Teachers generally come from middle-class backgrounds and, according to her, are unprepared to deal with the diverse students in their classrooms. Christina said that her experiences in the education system involved being ignored, feared, and despised by teachers, and that as a result, she had been tracked into low-skill classes despite her intelligence, silenced for speaking too loudly and too often, and told to focus on "practical" skills, such as typing and filing.

As noted above, this was a class where students spoke their minds about personal and political matters. Yet when Christina spoke, the students' facial expressions and body language indicated that she was perhaps too honest: She was perceived as being crass. In hindsight, I believe that Christina's failure to exercise "appropriate" emotions and modesty transformed the social relations of the classroom by subverting what I call the "good student script." That is, she did not abide by the middle-class value system that, according to bell hooks (1994), is not directly stated, but "taught by example and reinforced by a system of rewards." Speaking of her experiences as a working-class college student, hooks writes,

> As silence and obedience to authority were most rewarded, students learned that this was the appropriate demeanor in the classroom. Loudness, anger, emotional outbursts, and even something as seemingly innocent as unrestrained laughter were deemed unacceptable, vulgar disruptions of classroom social order. These traits were also associated with being a member of the lower classes. (178)

Janet Zandy (1995) reinforces this point in her introduction to *Liberating Memory* where she argues that working-class identities are "perceived as too rough, too loud, too dirty, too direct, too 'uneducated'" (2).

In this chapter, I seek to recount what happened when class issues collided with emotions in English 243. Among other things, this narrative shows my inadequate preparation to address the emotional responses that my "emancipatory" teaching inspired. Schooled in critical and feminist pedagogies, I had become practiced at helping my students question cultural values but was not prepared for the strong emotional responses that this form of questioning elicited. More interesting and suggestive than my lack of preparation, however, is that my blunder presents an opportunity to reflect on my classroom practices and their social significance. This purpose is, of course, different than using the occasion of the blunder to purge guilt for being a "bad" teacher—thus redeeming myself—or to heroicize my efforts to unmask self-identified (self-fabricated?) failure. My reflection begins by contextualizing English 243 so that the escalation of student emotion may be seen in connection with the very structure and development of the course. Thus, Section 1 describes the course objectives, requirements, and recollections of classroom discussions and student responses. In Section 2, I contend that teachers must learn to recognize how their own emotionality informs classroom practices. I develop this claim by examining how my own emotional responses to students, especially Christina, were often shaped by an underlying guilt. Guilt, I argue, is a fairly common product of pedagogies that place a high value on *difference* as a key concept for a pedagogy of empowerment. The final section, then, develops an understanding of anger as an integral, though often neglected, component of emancipatory pedagogies.

1. English 243

Course Description: This course offers a survey of the most important texts of second wave feminism spanning the 1960s through the early 1980s. The gains made by feminists have made possible the opportunities and choices available to women today, many of which are often taken for granted. In order to make visible the feminist achievements that have changed the quality of life for women and men, we will attempt to understand the development and context of feminist thought by focusing on the characteristic claims and questions motivating second wave feminists. Our specific objective will be to focus on the key terms and concepts offered by feminists in their efforts to identify, theorize, and struggle against conditions that oppress women.

Required reading for the course included Alice Echols' (1989) *Daring to Be Bad: Radical Feminism in America, 1967–1975;* Betty Friedan's (1963) *Feminine Mystique;* Cherríe Moraga and Gloria Anzaldúa's (1981) *This Bridge Called My Back: Writings by Radical Women of Color;* Robin Morgan's (1970)

Sisterhood Is Powerful: An Anthology of Writings from the Women's Liberation Movement; and a course packet including selections by Shulamith Firestone and Kate Millett, among others. Students were required to maintain a reading folder during the semester. Totaling 60 percent of final grades, this folder was turned in twice during the semester, once at midterm and again near the end of the semester. Folders included two parts: a definitions section, where students developed a glossary of key terms and concepts to be added onto throughout the semester, and a section of one-page, typed reflections on the course content. In addition, students wrote two (three- to four-page) papers, developed from the definitions section of their folders that explained how feminists defined and redefined, complicated and expanded, one key term or concept. Further, they were to evaluate the significance of this redefining process.

The course readings were divided into five sections: Historical Context; Kicking off the Movement; Historicizing the Movement; Dimensions of Women's Oppression; and Feminism's Self-Critique. The readings on women's oppression were further subdivided into Psychological and Sexual Oppression; Family, Marriage, and Motherhood; Heterosexism; and Sexism and Racism. While class issues did not constitute an explicit section of the readings, a good majority dealt with class divisions among women and feminists. Still, the lack of a special focus on class came to be symptomatic of the way class issues lingered over, but were never adequately addressed in, English 243.

One short writing assignment and the responses it evoked provide good examples of the ways in which class tensions surfaced during the semester. After reading Friedan's *Feminine Mystique,* which includes an analysis of women's magazines, I asked the students to analyze a current women's magazine in order to evaluate representations of women in the 1990s and compare these to Friedan's findings in the 1960s. During our discussion of Friedan, a number of students critiqued her singular focus on middle-class women to the exclusion of minority and lower-class women. Furthermore, they argued that by studying popular women's magazines, Friedan reinforced her concern for women with money who had too much time on their hands. My assignment, which asked students to examine popular women's magazines in the 1990s, created some of the same problems—but only Christina said as much. She did not complete the assignment, she said, because she refused to spend her money on "those crappy magazines." Rather, she turned in an analysis of the assignment in which she argued that a more "critical" assignment would have asked students to comment on how women's magazines are really *middle*-class women's magazines and, for this reason, they do not create an accurate or useful picture of the majority of women's lives.

Christina's analysis was articulate and well written, points that I remarked upon in my comments. I found myself agreeing with most of what she had to say, though I did not necessarily agree with her assessment of the assignment. I asked students to examine representations of women, guidelines that certainly gave students the option to focus on the class bias of women's magazines. What I came to see later, however, was that by asking students to replicate, albeit on a small scale, Friedan's method of analysis, I was perceived by Christina (and several other students who indicated as much in their reading folders) to be replicating Friedan's class bias. This perception gained force during the second month of the semester when students and I established ground rules for discussion.

During class discussions, student factions began to surface. Those who resisted and even resented feminism constituted a group of about five students who always sat together. When others critiqued the values they embraced (e.g., motherhood, marriage, heterosexuality), the "resisters," as I shall call them, responded as a group. In most cases, they argued that feminism takes everything—liberation, sexuality, economic fairness—to unreasonable extremes, villifying those women who choose to live more "traditional" lives. The self-identified feminist students, and especially those who came out as lesbian, had very little tolerance for feminist resisters. This was expressed through body language—rolling eyes, seat-shifting, heads down in frustration—as well as through verbal confrontations. During one discussion, for example, the resisters suggested that most of the feminists we had been reading seemed to be lesbians. This struck a nerve with feminists in the class, who argued that this accusation merely demonstrated the degree to which women are taught to stereotype and disparage one another's differences, especially sexual ones. They contended that women are accustomed to viewing one another as threats and, by presuming that all feminists are lesbians, the resisters were attempting to reduce the more widespread effects that feminism might have on everyone's lives. From a political perspective, I agreed with the feminist students and often found myself growing impatient with students who were clearly uncomfortable with challenging cultural norms and conventions. At the same time, I did not want to further delegitimize and alienate those students who resisted feminist ideology. While I tried to respond critically to all students, I have no doubt that my body language, tone of voice, and facial expressions betrayed my position.

From a pedagogical perspective, this classroom discussion was productive on many levels. For example, students seemed to be talking openly and honestly about what feminism means in American culture. Also, they were critical of one another and unwilling to passively occupy desks in a room. Yet, the productive aspects could not mask the very real pain and anger generated by classroom discussion. I could see the inflamed emotions on my students' faces and read about them in their reflection papers, which detailed students' feelings of being attacked, feared, and generally disrespected.

During the conflict between the feminists and the resisters, I watched and listened as students grew more impassioned. At several points, I tried to turn the discussion down a notch by repeating back what I heard them saying, but the period ended before I could adequately respond to or ask students to comment on the discussion. I decided that in the next class session, I would make it a priority to talk about the ways in which we had treated one another and the ways we would like to be treated. The discussion that followed was among the most memorable that semester. Some students spoke about how they were made to feel naïve or foolish when they expressed any resistance to feminism, how others treated them as if they had not yet "seen the light" and were, therefore, unsophisticated in their thinking. They complained that feminists in the classroom affected a superior tone and attitude when responding to their classmates. By contrast, the feminists argued that other students responded defensively to them and did not really hear what they had to say. They also maintained that argument and conflict are good and necessary parts of any discussion about feminism. Others disagreed, explaining that they did not want their entire value systems challenged every time they came to class. Some ideas, these students argued, were better left unsaid.

After listening to the points raised by the students, I was of two minds. Impassioned discussion critiquing those value systems that we take to be "natural" is an essential component of any feminist classroom. I wanted multiple viewpoints to be heard, to be seriously considered as different ways of seeing and living in the world. Yet, I did not want students to feel attacked while in my class. In an effort to acknowledge the need for a space where we could voice our opinions both honestly and respectfully, I decided that as a group we should develop ground rules to which we would all be held responsible. When a rule was "violated," students had the right to remind one another of the collectively agreed-upon terms. Together, we came up with the following:

1. Respect the views of others.

2. Agree to disagree; agree to have conflict.

3. No name-calling, insults, accusations of "false consciousness," or visible disgust of others' views.

4. Take responsibility for discussion by asking questions and asking for clarification when confused.

5. Arrange ourselves in a circle during class discussion.

6. When in small groups, introduce yourselves to one another.

As I was told later, many students found talking about how they felt during class discussion and constructing ground rules to be cathartic. Some told me that it is unusual for class tensions and feelings to ever be addressed openly; for this reason, they appreciated my efforts to make class interactions the subject of class discussion.

In the next class session, we began a discussion of the day's assigned reading. Midway through class, Christina walked into the room. She approached me and apologized for her lateness, which, she explained, was due to her work at a local women's shelter. She settled into a chair and almost immediately raised her hand. When I called on her she began a long critique of the ground rules established during our prior meeting. Christina felt that the rules reflected a class elitism by defining good classroom behavior as that which is passive, quiet, cordial, and collaborative. She questioned the idea that classmates could "respect the views of others" when the education system itself teaches us to disrespect and disregard the views of all nondominant others. In addition, Christina took offense at the idea that students should police their own and others' behavior, including facial expressions that might reveal "disgust." The phony courtesy that the rules created makes middle-class people happy, she argued, because they shield us from messy emotions and unapologetic differences of opinion. She grew more and more angry while her classmates listened, eyes fastened on her. When she finished speaking, I affirmed some of the points she made and proceeded to explain why the ground rules were productive in a number of ways. Rather than engaging Christina's critique of the class politics of English 243 and its significance in the context of feminist political work, I found myself reaffirming my decision to create ground rules and then shifting the discussion back to the readings as if nothing had happened. Also, though, I believe that my own liberal guilt about silencing a minority student informed my decision to allow Christina to "hijack" class discussion and pull us away from the readings in the first place.

My failure to really deal with Christina's comments make me now realize the limitations of my pedagogical strategies, many of which were based on leftist, feminist philosophies of education. Blundering can be an uncomfortable and unsatisfying trope for teaching practices, for it throws teacher authority and credibility into question and also has the potential to disturb "tried and true" assignments or approaches to reading material, and classroom discussion. Yet, it also presents an opportunity to develop rhetorical teaching by highlighting the consequences of our actions and decisions that might, at least in some cases, effect change in practices and in scholarly representations of these practices. My blunder has led me to think about the frequently neglected role of teacher identity in an emancipatory classroom—neglected both in radical pedagogy discourse and in my own appropriation of it. That is, I have found that oppositional pedagogies usually focus so much on facilitating student transformation that they often neglect teacher responsibilities in classrooms where student differences erupt. In addition, such pedagogies often do not consider that any number of factors can form teacher identities, including professional allegiances, institutional imperatives, and class status. Based on my blunder narrative, I explore in the next section the rather insidious concept of guilt as it relates to liberatory teaching. This discussion of guilt shows how teacher responses can be emotionally complicated, creating contradictions between teacher behavior and the goal to facilitate transformative learning.

2. Teacher Guilt and Emancipatory Pedagogy

[A]ll too often, guilt is just another name for impotence, for defensiveness destructive of communication; it becomes a device to protect ignorance and the continuation of things the way they are, the ultimate protection for changelessness.—Audre Lorde (1984, 133)

Having more experience and more time to reflect on English 243, I think of how Christina's anger might have enriched our study of feminism. Christina's interruptive narratives of the "good student script" were an important means by which she foregrounded concepts of difference in the classroom. Refusing to behave obediently and politely—both highly valued middle-class virtues—Christina used what Nedra Reynolds (1998) conceives as an important political tool for women rhetors. "Agency is not simply about finding one's own voice," Reynolds points out, "but also about intervening in discourses of the everyday and cultivating rhetorical tactics that make interruption and resistance an important part of any conversation" (59). Christina challenged me to ask myself how my lived experience gave me the authority to teach a class on the struggle for women's basic rights. And only later did I begin to wonder what version of struggle I privileged through my reading selections, classroom structure, and responses to students. How did I "represent others," especially classed others, to my students? Further, did I silently reward "well-behaved" students while undervaluing Christina's anger?

In the end, I was unprepared to engage Christina's anger at a professional level (it was my third year of graduate student teaching) as well as at a personal level, by which I mean that my conception of how people should behave in a university classroom was, and remains, very much a product of my own middle-class training. While I wanted my students to personally connect with the reading material, I later realized that I wanted them to do so quietly and politely. I have also come to see that my failure to engage Christina in further discussion was related to my guilt about being complicit in the valorization of middle-class values, a point that I develop below.

Modern composition studies encourage students and teachers to hone their questioning, reasoning, and critical thinking skills. The expression of "strong" emotions such as anger, rage, and sorrow are generally considered unacceptable in the classroom and are viewed as deviant—loud, crass, irrational, messy, and unproductive. "Good" students do not voice anger in the classroom, nor do they let on that they feel it. Psychiatrist and author of *Shame and Pride,* Donald Nathanson (1992) says that, for many of us, emotion interferes with thinking (23). He claims, "We demean arguments by calling them emotional, discredit people who seem emotionally involved in whatever bothers them, trust feelings less than cognition" (23). He goes on to say that how and what we think is shaped by our emotional experiences, our affective relation to the world. Likewise, empowering learning is not simply an intellectual process. It is also an emotional one, whether affective or disaffective, which carries with it the potential to change students' views of the world and their place in it. Thus, critical and radical teachers who have a stake in politically transformative education need to develop pedagogical theories and practices that address the emotional dimensions of teaching and learning.

Perhaps one way to begin this project is for teachers to describe the shape and content of their own emotional investment in emancipatory teaching. I believe that we blunder in the classroom when we ignore the emotionality of the pedagogical situation, when we make no effort to create a language for conceptualizing how education has the potential to make personal, political, and

emotional transformations. In *A Life in School,* Jane Tompkins (1996) comments on the emotional, personally relevant interventions that education can
make. She advocates an approach to teaching that "would never fail to take into
account that students and teachers have bodies that are mortal, hearts that can
be broken, spirits that need to be fed" (xiii). A holistic approach to education,
Tompkins continues, "would recognize that a person must learn how to be with
other people, how to love, how to take criticism, how to grieve, how to have fun,
as well as how to add and subtract, multiply and divide" (xvi). Just as education
happens to the whole student, not only to the mind of the student, teaching is
also more than an intellectual undertaking.

Whereas I experienced a range of emotions while teaching English 243, I
focus on guilt here because it helps illuminate my relation to Christina. Theories of emotion regularly link guilt and shame as forms of experience (see Piers
and Singer 1953; Lynd 1958; Lewis 1971). Nathanson explains the link as follows: "Included in the experience of guilt is a moment of discovery or exposure. In some cases the exposure is actual, while in other cases it is fantasized.
But since shame follows the exposure of what one would wish hidden, we may
be sure that shame is involved in guilt" (144). Elsewhere he writes, "Whereas
shame is about the quality of our person or self, guilt is the painful emotion
triggered when we become aware that we have acted in a way to bring harm to
another person or to violate some important code" (19). Guilt is an internalized
process that carries with it moral connotations. That is, the experience of guilt
emerges from a sense that one has violated or transgressed, as John Demos
(1986) says, a "'code' of values that individuals carry around inside them—and
that serves to regulate their actual deeds" (70).

As a feminist I am committed to the possibility of improved social relations based on the idea that cultural differences are strengths not weaknesses.
This code of values clashed with Christina's identification of my class bias. My
response, informed by guilt, was to allow Christina to interrupt class discussion,
deflect attention from my practices, smooth conflicts away, and quickly move
on. Instead, I might have interrogated my teaching practices for what I could
learn about my unwillingness to question or engage seriously with Christina's
ideas. In short, at the time it seemed to me that Christina interpreted my teaching practices as violations of a feminist "code," in the language of psychology,
and this made me uncomfortable and uncertain about how to deal with her.
What is perhaps most interesting about all of this is the reformulation of what
it means to be an empowering teacher. Prevailing conceptions of such teachers
do not seem to take into account that an empowering teaching situation is complicated not only by the diverse students who populate our classrooms, but also
by the teacher's cultural location and his/her willingness and ability to see beyond it.

Radical teachers and critical educators need to produce pedagogical theories that acknowledge the way our classroom agendas invite students to see
their worlds differently—a change that transforms both intellectual and emo-

tional conceptions of reality (see Worsham 1993; Worsham 1998). In addition, such theories should acknowledge that emancipatory teaching, perhaps more explicitly than other kinds, has an important emotional content for teachers as well as students. Because the expression of emotion is very much an expression schooled by one's location in the social hierarchy, radical aims to restructure social relations might be understood as aims to restructure our emotional worlds.

Conclusion: The Importance of Being Angry

I'd like to shift gears here by returning to the title—actually, the subtitle—of this chapter. "A Working-Class Student's Ways With Anger" intends to both acknowledge and affirm the value of Christina's anger in English 243. As recent school violence proves, not all forms of classroom anger are productive or valuable pedagogical tools. Indeed, there is a world of difference between anger as a force behind destructive, violent behavior like that at Columbine High School and anger as the motor that drives political change. Peter Lyman (1981) explains the latter form in "The Politics of Anger": "[A]nger begins to become political when it is a specific response to what one feels is an unjustified violation of one's self and that which one cares for. Anger can be seen as the pathos of subordination, the emotional response we feel in being dominated, whether as a victim of insolence or contempt, or through ongoing social subordination" (61). I understand Christina's anger to be an expression of her refusal to abide by classroom conditions that offend her sense of self and her experiences as a working-class woman. Yet, because of her insistence on the corrupt nature of social institutions, I also believe that her anger was not just about herself. It was spoken in the name of a principle of justice, which, as Lyman argues, "is the fundamental reason why one can define anger as the essential political emotion" (61). Teachers of political theory and proponents of emancipatory teaching must learn to see how anger can transform the classroom in productive, though not always comfortable or pleasant, ways. It is my hope that these concluding remarks will persuade English teachers to see how anger can be an important rhetorical and political instrument, especially in classrooms where teachers seek to enact emancipatory pedagogies.

Notions of appropriate and inappropriate anger are not simply differentiated by situations, but, as my narrative suggests, also by one's class location. In "Anger and Insubordination," Elizabeth Spelman (1989) notes that "while members of subordinate groups are expected to be emotional, indeed to have their emotions run their lives, their anger will not be tolerated . . . " (264). The anger of the underprivileged poses a threat to dominant culture because the angry person assumes that it is her right to be angry and that she is in a position to establish grounds for her anger. Spelman explains:

> If [the object of the subordinate's anger] is in other ways regarded as my superior, when I get angry at him I at least on that occasion am regarding him as no

more and no less than my equal. So my anger is in such a case an act of insubordination: I am acting as if I have as much right to judge him as he assumes he has to judge me. So I not only am taking his actions seriously but by doing so I am taking myself seriously, as a judge of the goodness or badness of his actions (266).

Spelman goes on to say that emotion, and anger specifically, has a politics: "the systematic denial of anger can be seen as a mechanism of subordination, and the existence and expression of anger as an act of insubordination" (270).

Outright suppression of, or benign refusal to acknowledge, the anger of the oppressed is especially politicized when we consider that anger is a necessary response to inequity, a response that, historically, has functioned as a catalyst for collectively organized social movements. The second wave of feminism gained a collective voice shortly after the publication of Friedan's *Feminine Mystique,* a book that catalogued the numerous ways in which 1950s American culture constructed women as sex objects and baby-machines. Women's anger about their situation and growing awareness of the predominance of sexism motivated them to form consciousness-raising groups and to organize collectively for change. Writing in 1971, Susi Kaplow explained, "Controlled, directed, but nonetheless passionate, anger moves from the personal to the political and becomes a force for shaping our new destiny" (41).

Audre Lorde further extols the purposes of anger in her 1981 speech "The Uses of Anger: Women Responding to Racism." She argues that anger is an appropriate and necessary response to racism. "Anger is a grief of distortions between peers," she writes, "and its object is change" (129). For Lorde, anger is useful because it seeks to unmask the distortions of racism and internalized effects of those distortions. Her understanding of every woman's "arsenal of anger" is enlightening not only in relation to racism, but in the general context of political struggle against oppression.

Christina's arsenal of anger and her naming of the many sources that triggered it—schools, the government, men, family, the health care system, feminists, etc.—often produced a numbing effect on her classmates. It was Christina's insistence, I believe, her strong desire to be heard, that made her especially crass and tiresome to her classmates and sometimes to me. The story of English 243, at least this version, can teach us something about emotionality in the classroom. When our students confront new conceptions of reality, they get angry, feel shame, express guilt, joy, pain, disgust, envy, rage, and disappointment. When radical educators seek to deconstruct and challenge those normalizing forces that silence and degrade people, these kinds of emotional responses are inevitable; though, given the culture of the academy, they are likely to remain unvoiced, or at least under-voiced, in our classrooms. This muffled expression might strike us as appropriate, schooled as many of us are in the virtues of discretion, politeness, and reverence for the teacher—even the "empowering" teacher whose stated goal is to subvert traditional, teacher-centered models of education. I want to suggest, however, that empowering teachers must learn how to recognize and name the numerous ways in which cultural and political knowledge may disrupt our daily lives intellectually and emotionally.

Even more specifically, because anger has the potential to create change, educators must pay attention to the ways in which "empowering" pedagogies produce different kinds of anger. While Christina's anger was, among other things, an expression of her profound disappointment in feminism, other students, who felt empowered by the course readings, expressed anger at the persistence of sexist discrimination: at other women who, in their view, perpetuated sexism; at their families who taught them to hate their bodies; and so forth. When we consider the very different ways of being angry, questions arise concerning how teachers can acknowledge and address the emotional content of progressive pedagogies for both themselves and their students. Teachers should begin to reflect on our own class positions and socialized responses to strong emotions such as anger. We should also begin to ask what the relation is between anger and guilt in the pedagogical situation. How do middle-class teachers work with students whose affective lives are structured by anger and disappointment? How can teachers responsibly negotiate this terrain?

As I reflect on English 243 and my narrative of it, I realize how my lessons learned have influenced my choice to highlight Christina's presence in the classroom—a choice that surely reflects my own discomfort with, and troubled relation to, class identity. For, I might have told you about the class meetings when I lectured and students dutifully took notes, or the boredom on students' faces during class discussions, or my disappointment when they failed to do the readings, or a number of other familiar scenarios that characterize the daily reality of teaching politically charged material. My presentation of a teaching blunder, that is, reveals my willful desire to politicize classroom relations and to envision teaching as, at least in part, political and cultural work. To me, this suggests that rather than demystifying authority and decentering classrooms, liberatory teachers are probably more in control than we would like to think. Perhaps this is already painfully obvious; nevertheless, it is an important point that should encourage teacher-scholars to qualify too-lofty pedagogical goals and too-reductive scholarly accounts of liberatory teaching. Critically examining classroom blunders and the ideological content of our decision to see them as "blunders" might serve as a way to reflect further on the actual difference between emancipatory and traditional teaching. Moreover, it might also encourage teachers to analyze their own participation in, and facilitation of, classroom blunders.

Acknowledgments

I wish to thank Amy DeJarlais for her thoughtful and intelligent responses to early drafts of this chapter. As usual, she made time to read and comment when there simply *was no time*. I would also like to acknowledge the timely and incisive feedback offered by the editors of this volume. Their comments were instrumental in my recovery of the narrative aspects of the chapter. Gary Weissman provided insightful comments at all stages of this draft. His frank feedback helped me to re-see my own investment in writing about English 243. Gary also offered invaluable moral and emotional support through the endless writing and rewriting of this chapter.

3

Blundering the O. J. Simpson Verdict

Black Female Subjectivity, Pedagogy, and the Personal

Riché Richardson

> But the grammar of the meta-narrative has been forcibly limited to the question, Did he? The answer is available to some, certainly to Mr. Simpson, but any other answer is a hunch—educated or uninformed, but still a hunch. So the substitute question is, Do you think he did it? As a stripped-down, litmus test question it gets an answer: Yes, I do. No, I don't. (Morrison 1997, xxiv)

> In classes on African American literature one must remain attentive to the tensions and failures arising before and even around one; one must even create some tensions and failures oneself. (Barrett 1994, 230)

1

"I thought he was guilty, and I thought he should have been prosecuted to the fullest extent." These words I spoke in reference to O. J. Simpson in the aftermath of what Patricia Williams (1997) aptly termed "The Bomb of the Verdict" that cleared him of the charge of murdering his ex-wife Nicole Brown Simpson and her friend Ronald Goldman (273). At the time I uttered them, I was a graduate student teaching assistant for an upper-division course in African American women's autobiography at a prestigious university English department.

O. J. verdict vigils had likely kept the vast majority of a by and large committed, respectful, and engaged class of students away on that particular day. Notwithstanding my own enthusiasm and excitement about the assigned reading for the session, even the handful of students who came to class couldn't focus on the introductory comments that I was making about Zora Neale Hurston's (1942) *Dust Tracks on a Road*. One, a black female, seemed to be glaring at me and finally interrupted me, pleading for me to take the class to a nearby dormitory lounge to hear the verdict, an idea that other students eagerly chimed in to support. Inwardly, I wrestled with whether I should go by the book and keep them in class, which seemed, under the circumstances, like punishing those few for being responsible enough to come. In addition, I was thinking about what might be at stake in deviating from the teaching itinerary on Hurston that the course instructor expected me to carry out that day. However, I certainly didn't want to risk a walkout, which I feared was imminent given their eagerness to hear the verdict. I finally agreed on two conditions: first that we be away for a maximum of fifteen minutes, and second, that all students would promptly come back to class.

The lounge was already packed. My students found sitting or standing spots around the television in the middle of the floor among other students, housekeeping staff, and other workers on campus who had also gravitated to the room in anticipation of the verdict. As the verdict was announced, all eyes were on the television screen with the exception of a white male student's from my class. I noticed out of the corner of my eye that he was watching me. It made me uncomfortable. I ignored him as best I could, wondering what he was looking for in me that had made him so willing to miss the big moment on television for which all the rest of the world seemed to be waiting.

The clerk stumbled when pronouncing "Orenthal." Some in the room laughed and mockingly repeated her mispronunciation, exclaiming, "They can't even say his name right!" or they talked back to the screen, urging the clerk to "Get it right!" Once she finished, cheering erupted in the room over O. J.'s victory. I was intrigued that O. J. had become so much the victim in the minds of some people in the room that the clerk, even after she had completely finished reading a verdict in his favor, had been coded as one of his prosecutors, an encoding evidenced by the continued mocking of her mistake. The mocking spirit extended to Kim Goldman. Some laughed at her when the camera highlighted the look of devastation on her face as she sought comfort in her father's arms, and they called out, "That's right. You lost!" This was particularly cruel and disturbing to me. The room began to feel suffocating, and I didn't want to witness the moment of O. J.'s vindication any longer. I think that perhaps to trivialize it, to escape from it, or to dismiss it, I walked out after making—what must have been barely audible given the celebration in the room—the announcement that my students should come back to our classroom building.

I took up Hurston again as students began to trickle in and take their seats, stiffly continuing as more and more came in. I didn't want to let any of what was going on in the world back into what was going on in our classroom. In retrospect, I've also realized that my serious tone was likely a deliberate way of setting up a stark contrast between the festive lounge and our classroom. I believe this was my way of "dissing" O. J., a way of snuffing out, raining on, and protesting against the parade of his victory. The students seemed to be looking at me somewhat blankly, perhaps in sheer disbelief that I could be so focused on talking about Hurston after what had just happened. Recourse to a lecture allowed me to avoid talking *with* them and to keep at bay all of my own complex emotions—including my disappointment and anger—regarding the verdict. I very well may have come across as talking *at* them. This was a gross misuse of my pedagogy. This episode poignantly hints at the levels on which the personal can be asserted in the teaching process and underscores that there is nothing "objective" about how we teach. But the specific thing that I wish to ponder under the blundering paradigm happened toward the end of class and has to do with the difficulties that I encountered with opening up class discussion on a racialized public discourse.[1]

I didn't want to seem dismissive of what had just taken place. Therefore, in the last minutes of class, I asked the (mostly black and few white) students if they had any comments about the verdict. The aforementioned white male student immediately turned the question back on me and asked me what I thought. This struck me as part and parcel of his consistent style of questioning in the seminar, which was sometimes overbearing and disruptive. I ignored what I suspected were the politics lurking behind his question and glibly answered him: "I thought he was guilty, and I thought he should have been prosecuted to the fullest extent."

"Don't you think he was prosecuted?" he asked.

The early moments of the case, in which O. J. had been swiftly removed from the threat of the death penalty and Al Cowlings had been acquitted of the charges for accompanying him on his slow chase down the freeway, flashed through my mind, along with the more recent failings of the prosecution. "No" was the brief and unqualified response that I gave because I wanted to open the floor back up to the class, and because I didn't want to allow this student's usual Socratic style of questioning to take over as it so often did in class discussions. I asked if there were other responses to the verdict. No one said anything. They were silent and still; nevertheless, I could sense a kind of energy in them that was bursting to explode. I had the feeling they had a lot to say about the case; they just weren't particularly interested in talking about it in our classroom. The silence was uncomfortable for them and me. Our time was up, so I dismissed class.

Regrettably, my negotiation of that class session allowed me little time to open up a nuanced discussion of the case, and certainly little space for anything close to my own reading. Like many other people in the United States, and along with a popular and news media that perhaps had not been as fascinated with or as enthusiastic about headlining a mysterious crime since "Who Shot J. R.?" in 1980, I had followed the case for months. During that time, the O. J. case was a topic that I discussed frequently with my peers in graduate school. Furthermore, with my close black women friends outside of the academy, I ran my long distance bill up night after night talking about the trial and swapping information that we'd gleaned here and there about the major players. While black female subjectivity had been virtually illegible in mainstream conversations, Marguerite Simpson Thomas, O. J.'s black ex-wife, provided one of the most viable subtexts of the case for us. For us, Marguerite was the woman in the attic á là Bertha Mason. When considering allegations that he had been unfaithful and abusive when he was married to her, we marveled over her unconditional support of O. J., even to the point of fighting the prosecution's subpoena. We joked constantly among ourselves about how glad O. J. should be that he hadn't been married to one of us and rehearsed the frank and incriminating things that we would have said about him on the witness stand and to tabloid reporters if we had been in Marguerite's position.

Particularly curious and disturbing to us was Marguerite's assertion on a national news show that O. J. had never hit her and that if he had tried, she would have hit him back with a frying pan. While Marguerite had once rebuked the press for endowing O. J. with superhuman qualities, it is interesting and ironic that she fantasized herself as being invincible enough to, with no sweat, knock out a 200-pound, muscular football player. This comment to us reflected her seeming internalization of the defeminizing strong black woman myth. In addition, it also pointed to how the codes of domestic violence and the possibilities for self-defense in the face of it are given a specificity by some black women. This is a factor that might have complicated mainstream feminist arguments in the aftermath of the verdict that merely made the predominately black female jury and black women more generally out to be clueless or insensitive regarding the issue of domestic violence.

Faith Ringgold's painting *The Flag is Bleeding* (1967), which features behind an American flag a white woman standing between and linking arms with a (knife-toting!) black man and a white man, encapsulates the disembodiment that the media discourse on O. J. seemed to attach overwhelmingly to black women. For with the exception of the condescending critiques of the jury, black female subjectivity was by and large implied by the media to be so marginal and irrelevant to the case that even to point out when and where it entered seemed to almost require the kind of boldness that one needs to claim to "see things" and "hear voices." This factor also underscores the difficulty of framing the case as the black feminist issue that I felt it was to some extent.

My own experience on the day of the O. J. Simpson verdict highlights for me the sheer complexity of dealing with racialized public discourses in a multicultural classroom and also of the issue of authority in the classroom as it relates to teaching assistants. In addition, while it was a public issue, the O. J. case became very personal for me and some of the black women I knew because it was the site that we were drawing on regularly to discuss, in light of our own private lives, the complexities of black male-female marriages and relationships and various kinds of interracial relationships and interactions. We were also using the case to ponder differences among black women in and beyond feminism, particularly in terms of generation. Therefore, because this case got so wrapped up in the fabric of my life and many others, I find it a particularly useful site to draw on for pondering issues relating to using the personal in pedagogy. Finally, this discussion accords with work by scholars such as bell hooks (1994) and Valerie Smith (1998) that indicates the usefulness of black feminist perspectives in critical pedagogy.

2

My problems in class regarding the O. J. verdict began with the complexity of negotiating the issue of authority in the classroom in relation to students from my standpoint as a teaching assistant. Henry Giroux (1992), who suggests the use of "oppositional forms of authority," reminds us that authority is always already attached to professors in university settings owing to their historical status as sites of power (157-158). It should go without saying that this necessary authority is attached to some extent to graduate student teaching assistants as well. This is a point that is well suggested in the politics of my pedagogy after the verdict. On the other hand, the vulnerability in the classroom that I felt when students pressured me to allow the verdict viewing confronted me with the limits of my authority as a teaching assistant. Because of a betwixt and between positioning as both student and teacher, the authority of a teaching assistant is necessarily in the balance. While they are often perceived by their students to be more empathetic than course professors, even to the point of being perceived as interlocutors and intercessors, teaching assistants are also vulnerable to having their authority challenged. Indeed, a sense of "double consciousness" relating to the dialectics of negotiating responsibilities as a student and teacher seems to be embedded in the teaching assistant's experience.[2]

I suggest that more discussion of the teaching assistant category would enhance the conversations in critical pedagogy relating to "power" and "authority." Interestingly, the discourse of critical pedagogy seems to be organized so much around a professor/student binarism that it often loses sight of the space in between that graduate student teaching assistants frequently occupy. In general, the discourse of critical pedagogy needs to become much more responsive to the specificity of graduate student teaching experiences and also to issues relating to graduate education. More legibility for the teaching assistant category in critical pedagogy may also improve the possibilities for the field to impact significantly teaching philosophies that are often crystallizing in crucial ways during the years of graduate study.

The issue of teaching assistant authority also relates to broader negotiations of teaching assistants in contemporary academia. The talk in the profession about teaching assistants as apprentices and the importance of maintaining collegiality between them and the professors for whom they teach—talk that is frequently deployed, for instance, to offset union formation and the claiming of employee status of graduate students—seems especially disingenuous when considering that the recent job crisis has made the *pièce de résistance,* or, that is to say, teaching jobs on which all those valuable skills can be put into practice, elusive for many. As some have noted, the rhetoric of collegiality obscures the power relations that obtain between teaching assistants and professors (see Bérubé 1997, 153–178). At any rate, this fantasy of collegiality has not precluded what might well be a problem of crisis proportions in graduate student teacher training in the contemporary academy. For the realities are that most professors do not have much self-conscious involvement in the teacher training of graduate students and that gaining teaching experience as a graduate student through close mentoring conversations is not the norm in this profession. While resources that support graduate student teacher training vary from institution to institution, these sites wherever they are available could, in many instances, use much more support from faculty. There should be more conversations about the possibilities for the widespread implementation of a collaborative model of teaching assistant/professor interaction that integrates more mentoring and team-teaching techniques. This model might well complement the forms of support that are frequently offered by teaching groups and centers at colleges and universities. In addition, a more interactive teaching assistant/professor model might be a viable alternative to the isolating *laissez faire* form of teacher training for graduate students that sometimes puts them in the classroom with little or no experience.

Black female subjectivity further complicates issues of authority for a teaching assistant; perhaps a black woman's authority as a teaching assistant becomes even more volatile. And black women professors often face very similar kinds of problems with establishing authority as well. What did it mean, for instance, that the same white male student who asked me what I thought about the verdict regularly interrupted the professor during lectures, once even asking her her age in class? As the assistant professor that I am now, I've wondered how much and in what specific ways black woman status makes a difference whenever students have made remarks to me in and beyond the classroom that I'm almost certain they would be more reluctant to make to a male professor who was fifty years old and white. Along with other black female professors with whom I am in frequent conversation, I have noticed that some students assume that black women in teaching positions lack doctorates. These students are more likely to challenge or critique black women professors openly in the classroom, and they assume that the university will be on their side rather than a black woman professor's if they choose to make recourse against her in any way therein. One of my close friends who is also a black woman professor recalls how a fraternity guy who had interrupted her class to give something to a friend slowly looked her up and down and asked, "So *you're* the professor." I am constantly reminded of the connection between issues of authority and age as well as race whenever lost students in my building who come to my open door seeking information take the time to ask me first if the office that they see me sitting in is indeed mine. So much for my voracious reading about image management and my investment in a neutral wardrobe of wool gabardine and wool crepe suits and silk charmeuse blouses to look "professional" (see McKay 1995).

As relates to the O. J. verdict, the most intense moment of powerlessness and voicelessness as a teaching assistant occurred as I observed the professor, because some students told her what I had said, claim a moment as she led the next session to assert her belief in O. J.'s innocence. She invoked statistics that the vast majority of domestic violence cases do not escalate to the husband's murder of the wife. It seemed to be an effort to use her status as the professor to, in a manner of speaking, "'spute my word." I got a taste of my own medicine in the sense that her "word" on the case had made me feel silenced as I sat in the back of the class and looked on in a way that was perhaps very similar to the ways my own statement about the verdict had silenced students in the previous session. This was a very clear manifestation of how power underpins professor–teaching assistant relations. In the end, I felt as if my authority in the classroom had been undermined not only by the students, but also by the professor. And months later, I was fully outdone when I realized, from a joke that the professor made in her office to a student who had been in the class, that word had gotten back to her that *I* had been the one "leading the line to see O. J."! My efforts to respect students' wishes by allowing the verdict viewing had blown up in my face. What happened in class that day and on the day of the verdict viewing were things that I didn't feel comfortable bringing up to the course instructor and that she never mentioned directly to me.

3

Many questions have come up for me since then. What specific violence may my remark have done in the classroom to stifle conversation? Was it a diminished level of trust in me that accounted for their reluctance to speak? Were they angry with me because I'd urged them to return to class? What were the conditions of possibility that day for a conversation relating to the O. J. verdict in a multicultural classroom? Given my own identity as a black woman, to what degree did my acknowledgment of a belief in O. J.'s guilt give students who also believed in his guilt a rationale for ignoring the deeper racial politics of the case? Did African American students who supported O. J. feel a sense of betrayal because of my belief in his guilt? Was this feeling of betrayal compounded because I proclaimed this belief in response to a question that a white male student in the class had asked, turning me into, in their minds, the proverbial black woman who colludes with white men to bring the black man down? What motivated this student to ask me the question in the first place given that he must have seen my face fall in the lounge?

I will turn at this point to a consideration of how I might have enhanced the possibilities for blundering toward a more liberatory pedagogy as I drew on public discourse in the classroom on that day. I will also address some of the general uses to which public discourse might be put in teaching. A discussion of the O. J. verdict is probably what should have happened that day immediately when we returned to the room. It was a mistake for me to defer it. In a course that was fully mine, I might have felt freer to devote the remaining class time to discussion of the case. At any rate, my marginalizing negotiation of it proved insufficient. Public discourse cannot be dealt with in that way. My initial reluctance to let the world into the classroom negated "the inseparability of representational and pedagogical practices from the culture in the which we live," to borrow Valerie Smith's (1998) words (138). The principles of critical pedagogy that affirm the potential of education to shape the relation of students to political and social spheres would suggest that such public discourse as that relating to the O. J. trial and verdict is ideal for engagement in a classroom setting. It is important, however, to be vigilant in the search for strategies to make these kinds of moments more palatable for the classroom. In retrospect, I wish I had done more beforehand to anticipate what Kimberlé Williams Crenshaw (1997) well summed up as the "polarizing discourse on the verdict" (98). This discourse, which was manifested in the media in the aftermath of the verdict, for instance, tended, in the essentializing way so characteristic of binary logic, to associate blacks with the belief in O. J.'s innocence and whites with the belief in his guilt. On that particular day in class, I think it might have been most useful to focus conversation on anticipating some of the possible reactions in the nation to the verdict, and also, on brainstorming about some strategies that might be used to promote productive conversations on the subject of race in its aftermath.

While it is crucial not to deal with public discourses in a marginalizing way in the classroom, I also think that drawing on public discourses in teaching is best done very selectively. Because the class time for engaging them is usually limited, it is generally best to stick to the more salient narratives, for these are the ones that students will have the most literacy about. Since O. J., I have found public discourses to be particularly useful in instances where I have desired to highlight how readings in class might be drawn on in day-to-day conversations. For instance, in the fall of 1998 for a course in African American literature, I found it very useful, as a way of introducing William Wells Brown's ([1853] 1989) novel *Clotel,* to draw on the Thomas Jefferson/Sally Hemings rumor and the Monica Lewinsky/Bill Clinton discourse. My purpose was to promote a deconstruction of ideological media terms that have been widely circulated in recent times, like *truth* and *morality.* I wanted to open up for critique the curious media narrativization of this nation and the "American presidency" as sites that were pure until Bill Clinton emerged in the contemporary period and defiled them. I made use of Annette Gordon-Reed's (1997) book entitled *Thomas Jefferson and Sally Hemings: An American Controversy,* a volume that is provocative in arguing that history as a discipline misappropriates terms from legal discourses such as *evidence, burden of proof,* and *proof.* Our discussions on these topics proved the most excited of the semester, indicating the kind of engagement public discourses can inspire in students. These sessions, in other words, highlight the extent of the silence my utterance about the verdict had produced in the earlier course.

Still brimming with emotions that I had hoped lecturing would suppress and hide, I was shocked and surprised by the frankness with which I had spoken regarding the O. J. verdict. My actual utterance would have been better left unsaid, but I believe, especially in light of classes I've taught since, that the verdict was something the students and I needed to address—only in not so cursory a fashion. The complexity of the case and the complexity of my feelings and the students' feelings about the case demanded as much: I blundered in my attempt to drive public discourse to the margins.

My utterance might have been cleaned up a bit on the spot in a number of ways. It would have been most important to articulate a version of Toni Morrison's words that frame this essay, which underscore that thoughts about O. J.'s innocence or guilt are purely speculative. I should have clarified my position on O. J. as one that did not advocate the death penalty for him or disavow in any way the reality of police abuse in black communities, including the more seldom remarked upon abuse of black women by police. In light of the rash of police brutality in this nation in recent times in cities such as New York, Riverside, Los Angeles, and Chicago, I would respond "VERY!" to the question that Susan Bordo (1997) later raised about how persuasive the notion is that "O. J. was in the eyes of the police despicable and dispensable slime by virtue of his race" (97). I should have clarified my position as one that was well informed by the problems relating to how black men are disproportionately swelling prison rolls.

My statement reflected my frustrations with the prosecution. I should have acknowledged that I was aware of what could be read as the prosecution's failings. At the same time, I could have emphasized that those issues and even the verdict itself did not translate for me into an actual belief in O. J.'s innocence.

I should have also pointed out that I wasn't drawn into the rhetoric of O. J.'s innocence by the more minor conspiracy theories on the grapevine beyond those relating to Mark Furhman and the L.A. Police Department frameup. Why had the Colombian mobsters who had allegedly murdered Nicole Brown Simpson and Ron Goldman singled *them* out? Shouldn't these mobsters, with the volume of celebrities using drugs, have made L.A. a literal bloodbath by now? That O. J. knew who did it and just wasn't telling, another theory best depicted in the video for "Natural Born Killer" by the rappers Ice Cube and Dr. Dre on their *Murder Was the Case* soundtrack, wasn't satisfactory to me. O. J.'s history of domestic violence and his obsession with Nicole over the years, to the point of stalking her, actually had me thinking that he *had* to do it himself in the sense that he would have been jealous of anyone who would have done it instead of him. It would have been important for him to see her standing before him in fear before he took her life and to let her know that *he* was the one who was taking it. Another conspiracy theory was vindicating O. J. on the basis of the rationale that he couldn't have killed two people at the same time. My own response was always, "Who says he did?" It was indeed possible that there was more than one murderer, as the autopsy reports confirmed. But it was also possible that Ron

Goldman came on the scene immediately after Nicole's murder and was taken unaware as he was investigating the gruesome sight of Nicole's body and gearing up to go for help.

I might have explained my own belief in O. J.'s guilt further by pointing to how little weight the declarations that O. J. wouldn't have ever done such a thing by his character witnesses in the media like Dionne Warwick had carried for me. I know that I wouldn't have ever thought that one of the guys with whom I attended school (and Catholic school no less) would have shot to death another one of our former classmates and some other man one night early in the previous year. I couldn't have ever imagined that he could shoot someone five times like he shot that other guy, and two of those times point blank in the head. And this shooter, owing in part to black bourgeoisie politics, was vindicated for both murders in my hometown, Montgomery, Alabama. Given that the sharing of my opinion had already to some degree been an assertion of the personal, perhaps I should have gone deeper to indicate how the experience of losing a family member to violence early in my life, and witnessing the trace that that loss had left on my great aunt (she had already lost her other son at age eleven when he was accidentally killed by a little girl while playing), had made the mocking of Kim Goldman in the lounge particularly disturbing to me. In short, "I thought he was guilty, and I thought he should have been prosecuted to the fullest extent" fell far short of generating the kind of inspired, relevant dialogue the event deserved.

In my own case, I was a teaching assistant who had the privilege of being at an institution that offered teaching support through a variety of sites. I had the rare privilege of serving as a teaching assistant for a course that fell within my field of interest, and I could also plan my sessions on the writers with autonomy on my scheduled teaching days. My failed attempt to open up discussion on the verdict had made the case something of a Pandora's Box for me, and I didn't mention O. J. in class after that, even though my own reading of the case, as outlined above, made it relevant to issues relating to black women's autobiography. It's now clear to me that discussion flows best when the engagement of public discourse that carries the weight that the O. J. discourse carried is sustained, and when such discourse is tracked periodically in the classroom.[3]

During one of my sessions, I might have—among other approaches—identified the case as one that exemplified the historical politics of a marginalizing black female subject negotiation in this nation. I could have added force to this argument by drawing intertextually on the materials of the course. Texts such as Maya Angelou's (1971) *I Know Why the Caged Bird Sings,* Marian Anderson's (1956) *My Lord, What a Morning,* Gwendolyn Brooks' (1953) *Maud Martha* and bell hooks' (1998) short and important piece from *Talking Back* entitled "Writing Autobiography" all speak to the problem of black female subjectivity and the difficulty of coming to voice, and of the relation of voicelessness to trauma. It might have been useful to point out how Lorene Cary's (1991) "Ain't I a Woman?" becomes so assertive toward the end of *Black Ice* to underscore that this is just as relevant a question for black women in the contemporary period as it was for Sojourner Truth in 1851 in Akron, Ohio. For, as Patricia Williams (1997) notes, black women continue to be subjected to a "de-aesthetizing masculinization" in the cultural imagination (285).

I've regretted that I didn't actualize this itinerary back then. Doing so would have been more conceivable had I made more attempts to draw on in my teaching the kinds of critical readings of the O. J. case that were going on in my circle of friends and the personal significance that we were attaching to it. It is very ironic that articulating the connections that the case had to black female subjectivity was difficult for me even as I supported the teaching and learning objectives of a course in black women's autobiography. But at the time, it seemed so difficult to highlight in a public setting the deeper implications for black female subjectivity that we were considering in relation to the case because, as I've already suggested, such issues were so invisible in the broader culture. This problem also points to how challenging it can be in general to translate the very personal subtexts that sometimes feed into black feminist epistemologies. And certainly, this missed opportunity suggests how useful knowledge can get effaced when the personal and the pedagogical fail to come together.

4

In recent years, with the increasing publication of memoirs and other autobiographical writings by scholars (Frank Lentricchia [1996], Alice Kaplan [1994], Patricia Williams [1997], Jane Gallop [1997], and bell hooks [1996] among them), there has been substantial critical reflection on the status of the personal in the writing of academics. A 1996 issue of *PMLA* included a guest column entitled "Four Views on the Place of the Personal in Scholarship" featuring essays by Michael Bérubé, Sylvia Molloy, Cathy N. Davidson, and David Palumbo-Liu, as well as a letter forum that addressed the uses of the personal in scholarship.[4] H. Aram Veeser's volume entitled *Confessions of the Critics,* also published in 1996, featured a broad range of scholarly perspectives on autobiographical criticism. However, critical reflection on the status of the personal in teaching, which has primarily taken place in writings on feminism and critical pedagogy, has been less visible.

There are certainly potential problems that can result when the personal and pedagogy intersect. Diana Fuss (1989) shares her reservations about the personal in the classroom in *Essentially Speaking: Feminism, Nature, and Difference:*

> Nowhere are the related issues of essence, identity, and experience so highly charged and so deeply politicized as they are in the classroom. Personal consciousness, individual oppressions, lived experience—in short, identity politics—operate in the classroom both to authorize and to de-authorize speech. "Experience" emerges as the essential truth of the individual subject, and

> personal "identity" metamorphoses into knowledge. Who we are becomes
> what we know; ontology shades into epistemology. (113)

In spite of the risks involved in using the personal in pedagogy, however, this
practice should not simply be dismissed. There is a need for a more careful
critical contemplation of the possibilities for using the personal in pedagogy. It
is significant that the personal/anecdotal has so richly fed the field of critical
pedagogy—for most of us draw to some extent on our experiences in the classroom when we discuss our teaching with colleagues. At the same time, because
anything that goes wrong in teaching, or for that matter, too right, can be held
against teachers in decisions on promotion and tenure, sharing teaching narratives, including those of the blundering variety, falls not only easily within the
discourse on the personal, but also can carry the weight and anxieties of the con-
fessional. Perhaps my not being able to transcend entirely what Eve Kosofsky
Sedgwick (1997) regards as a domineering paradigm of suspicion in contemporary criticism made me wonder more than once to what extent the narrativization of my blunder might be apprehended as a bungle in the profession. I've
wondered if an economy of blundering narratives would be met in the profession with the kinds of attitudes that one might get, from some in African American culture, for airing dirty laundry? These questions are particularly important
for junior faculty members.

Uses of the personal by black women and other women of color have oc-
casioned major critical and theoretical paradigm shifts in and beyond feminist
discourses in recent years. Paradoxically, black women and other women of
color, perhaps owing to the salience of the testimony genre that developed in
the work of feminist critics like Gloria Anzaldúa and Audre Lorde, are routinely
perceived as those who substitute narratives relating to experiences for the
meat of scholarship. They are often judged to be less "theoretical" than black
male scholars and other male scholars of color and stereotyped as being more
nurturing, accessible, and "personal." In her essay entitled "Black Women Intellectuals," bell hooks (1991) links this problem to the ways in which the historical stereotype of mammy informs perceptions of black women in and beyond the academy in the United States:

> Running counter to representations of Black females as sexual savages, sluts,
> and/or prostitutes is the "mammy" stereotype. Again, this image inscribes
> Black female presence as signified by the body, in this case the construction
> of woman as mother, as "breast," nurturing and sustaining the life of others.
> Significantly, the proverbial "mammy" cares for all the needs of others, par-
> ticularly those most powerful. Her work is characterized by selfless service.
> Despite the fact that most households in the United States do not have Black
> maids or nannies working in them, racist and sexist assumptions that Black
> women are somehow "innately" more capable of caring for others continues
> to permeate cultural thinking about Black female roles. As a consequence,
> Black women in all walks of life, from corporate professionals and university

professors to service workers, complain that colleagues, co-workers, supervisors, etc. ask them to assume multi-purpose caretaker roles, be their guidance counselors, nannies, therapists, priests; i.e., to be that all nurturing "breast"— to be the mammy (154).

It is crucial that a climate emerges wherein the ways in which black women and other women of color deploy the personal in their intellectual work will not be devalued. In addition, it is crucial to get beyond the stereotype of black women as "hyperpersonal" that hooks so eloquently elaborates.

My response to the O. J. verdict was very much inflected by the very personal aspects of my status as a black female subject. Race and gender were thus the salient sites through which the personal inscribed my pedagogical process. I've found black feminism to be a useful site to draw on in thinking through strategies for negotiating this subject positioning. In general, black feminism has some important implications for critical pedagogy in the sense that this discourse is one that's very useful for mediating a liberatory pedagogy in the field.

As I stressed toward the beginning of this essay, "objectivity" is a dubious concept when it comes to the setting of teaching agendas. Teaching is intimately informed by our range of subject positionings, and sometimes even by the more personal aspects of our lives. While the personal can be a very valuable pedagogical tool, we have to be also ever cognizant of its potential misuses, which can dictate our teaching methodologies and ultimately narrow the possibilities for achieving a more visionary pedagogy.

5

Do I still think that O. J. is guilty? I submit an admittedly speculative "Yes, I do." And yet, a "yes" or a "no" in matters like this must of necessity be complicated in a racially charged public sphere. My "yes" does not align itself with the "yeses" to the question of O. J.'s guilt that were shaped by the racist, criminalizing view of black masculinity, for instance, that seems to be so pervasive in the cultural imagination. All through his criminal trial, I felt, for the most part, that O. J.'s coding as a victim was a gross exaggeration. But even as I have maintained my belief in O. J.'s guilt, I have actually found myself sympathizing with him in a couple of moments since then. This first happened for me in the aftermath of his civil trial because the hateful public glee over his loss was making me just plain sick, in spite of how happy I was for the Brown and Goldman families. I had a similar feeling when Bob Enyart, a talk show host in Denver, Colorado, set sixteen-thousand dollars' worth of O. J. memorabilia on fire in front of the Los Angeles courthouse in February of 1999. This struck me as a symbolic lynching. Neither set of issues makes me regret any less that the bungles in his criminal trial ultimately failed to result in a conviction. But inevitably, my critical thought processes about them have brought me into conflict with those who also believe in his guilt. These incidents highlight how complex a racialized public sphere makes thought processes relating to public discourses, even when one does have a few strong opinions about them. That the negotiation of public discourses with race at their very core can function somewhat like navigating an obstacle course indicates all the more for me how imperative it is, from a pedagogical standpoint, to promote critical thinking about them in all their complexity. A simple "yes," or a simple "no," as Morrison suggests, just won't do.

Notes

1. I use the term "public discourse" to refer to the issues that become salient in the cultural imagination through extensive coverage in popular and news media, sometimes to the point of becoming spectacle. These issues are frequently controversial and tend to generate a lot of public opinion. Recent examples of the racialized variety include the Anita Hill/Clarence Thomas hearings, the Rodney King trials, and Mike Tyson's alleged rape of Desireé Washington.

2. The inspiration for this phrasing comes from a frequently quoted passage in W. E. B. DuBois' *The Souls of Black Folk,* which is most ostensibly concerned with the subject positioning of blacks in the United States at the beginning of the twentieth century:

> It is a peculiar sensation, this double-consciousness, this sense of always
> looking at one's self through the eyes of others, of measuring one's soul
> by the tape of a world that looks on in amused contempt and pity. One ever
> feels his two-ness, an American, a Negro; two souls, two thoughts, two
> unreconciled strivings; two warring ideals in one dark body, whose dogged
> strength alone keeps it from being torn asunder.

3. I owe this point to Susan Bordo.

4. See *PMLA* 111 (1996) 1063–1079; 1146–1169.

4

What Happened in English 101?

Scott Hendrix, Sarah Hoskinson,
Erika Jacobson, Saira Sufi

The experience of studenthood is the experience of being just so
far over one's head that it is both realistic and essential to work at
surviving.

—Mina P. Shaughnessy

Introduction

Anonymous student comment on semester-end evaluations: "Don't answer questions with questions as much."

Saira, Erika, Sarah, and Scott: This narrative began as a seemingly routine
story of a writing course, two teachers, twenty students, and a crowded classroom, and of something that seemed to go wrong once upon a time a long time
ago just a few semesters ago. In short, it was supposed to be a simple educational
narrative—teachers graded, students struggled. Life went on. But that isn't what
happens when critical pedagogy is at stake.

As the four of us look back over two years now, the story has gained many
layers of complexity. While still about the teaching in one particular class, the
story has also become a story we four share together, separate from the other
101 students. In fact, this blunder narrative has produced pedagogical lessons
concerning the tensions involved in the teaching of writing that far outstrip the
teaching/learning work we accomplished in that fateful English 101 class those
years ago. As long as we four work on this writing, we move forward, enriching
and complicating our perspectives, forcing ourselves to ask more questions that
can be only answered with questions. This paper, therefore, has two facets: One,
it details what happened in our particular class, and two, it scrutinizes the diverse

theoretical influences—we might also call these reasons or excuses—that we grapple with to explain events from the time of the blunder to our sometimes different current perspectives on that particular teaching and learning semester.

Background

Saira, Erika, Sarah, and Scott: The instructors' plan for a flexible and democratic English 101 class, with a challenging exploration of language, writing, and equity in these United States, seemed—from the instructors' perspectives, anyway—for a time to be going along smoothly. Without the instructors' knowledge, however, this class turned into a student revolt, with several of the students at one point marching (*en masse*) to the Writing Program Administrator (WPA). What happened along the way to this revolt? And how do we four writers understand the aftermath of the revolution? These are just some of the questions that we attempt to answer with the full understanding that these types of questions do not always have answers. By revisiting some of the tensions in this course, first from a contemporary viewpoint and then retrospectively, we can perhaps carve a sense of practical knowledge—and answers to the above questions—from the experience of teaching and learning. In this paper we play back voices of English 101 participants, bounce these voices at one another, and piece together the semblance of a collective understanding, although multi-voiced and retrospective.

Erika and Scott are the two appointed teachers on this particular stage. As co-teachers for English 101, they shared classroom teaching duties on a daily basis—both in the classroom at the same time, with sometimes one teacher leading, sometimes the other—and occasionally, true co-teaching. Saira and Sarah are two students from the course who will read, write, and critique the teacherly scripting of the drama. Our collective hope is that this writing and collaboration will function as a kind of post-course "After-Class Group" that helps us gain greater insight and respect for one another's perspectives, knowledges, and life desires (see Shor 1996).

Erika: I feel like I am looking for some reasons for the student rebellion so that I can avoid these problems in the future; but I also want to reaffirm that what I thought would work and didn't is not necessarily ideologically flawed, or even circumstantially flawed, indeed, perhaps not flawed at all. This, in fact, is the nature of critical pedagogy. When teachers encourage students to challenge an ideology, they just might challenge our ideology and what we represent. In this case the students fulfilled their role in critical pedagogy and challenged us in a way that, for a time, made me think I had failed as the educator.

Scott: Erika and I co-taught an English 101 class, where we tried to read, write, and enact some of the pedagogical and life lessons in Mike Rose's (1990) *Lives on the Boundary* and Victor Villanueva's (1993) *Bootstraps* (along with bell hooks, Ira Shor, and Sapphire)—with one another and with our students.

We were both graduate teaching assistants (GTAs) in the writing division of a large Midwest English department, at a Research One university that considers itself the flagship of the state regents system.We planned what we hoped would be a flexible and challenging class, interrogating language, writing, and educational equity.

To further explain the classroom situation, I was an experienced GTA; Erika was a GTA new to the writing program. The system our WPA developed paired new GTAs with experienced GTAs or part-time adjuncts for their first semester of teaching in the department. Before the class began we agreed on the term "co-teachers" as the best way to describe the relationship we wanted to have with one another and that we desired our students to see, as well as (ideally) the role we hoped students would claim for themselves in the class.

Erika: Scott planned and led the first few sections of the class, although he would run these plans by me via e-mail or conversation before the class met. He encouraged me to jump in at any point, but I was a little insecure. I planned and executed several sessions, but I'm sure everyone knew what was really going on: We just weren't addressing it in the classroom. I was far from achieving co-teacher status, and I think Scott began to overcompensate for our unequal power arrangement. He seemed to work hard at trying to relinquish his power to me and to students by responding to our questions with questions.

Sarah: When I think back to the classroom set-up, what I recall most is the entire class gathered together as a large group. I remember what I guess would be termed as "lectures," yet they seemed to be more of an introduction to Scott's theories on education rather than writing. I do not remember the class being about writing. I remember the class being about class division and the injustice of the educational system. You could say that was what Scott's lectures were about. Small groups stand out in my memory as well, but I assume that is because I disliked being involved in them.

Note from WPA (on Scott's memo requesting books not on the approved list of readers for English 101):   "Ok, you're welcome to try. I suspect that *Bootstraps* will be less accessible than *Lives,* so do be careful to keep the class focused on writing. . . . Let me know how the course goes."

Saira (post-course comment):   First, I think the books that we had to read were quite boring and not very interesting—so it was hard to write about them. Next, it was very difficult to know what the two teachers expected from us. Also, it seemed as if there was a patronizing tone—especially about "weeding us out." Lastly, I didn't think the comments on our papers were helpful enough to let us know how to improve.

Erika and Scott: As one attempt to clarify the course goals for students, three quotes appeared on the syllabus, just beneath the list of required course texts. An astute observer can certainly imagine that such front-loaded teacher proclamations were destined to backfire, or explode. Just as Paulo Freire cautioned that we North Americans and other educators could not apply his ideas, but must reinvent them, so too one cannot directly apply Ira Shor's urban and working-class pedagogy to a first-year writing class in Lawrence, Kansas.

Nonetheless, we included these three quotes on the syllabus to introduce keywords that we later, and perhaps recklessly, used to challenge and confuse our English 101 students:

> Let us imagine what it would be like if the history and culture of working-class people were at the center of educational practices. What would students learn? (Zandy 1995, 3)

> The current great interest in literacy coincides with the economy's shift from industry to service, which also coincides with economic crisis. Those in truly dominant positions need a larger middle-class work force. They need more mental laborers. So hegemony fosters the commonsensical notion that mental work is not labor (Villanueva 1993, 136).

> What I thought the students would want to learn was in fact astonishingly different from what they decided they wanted to learn. . . . I was astounded by the difference between what I had anticipated the areas of study would be and what the students themselves decided they needed to know (Reid 1992, 103).

Some readers will recognize the theft from Shor's (1996) *When Students Have Power* and the attempt to leap the hegemonic gap between our freshman and the academic folks who know words like *hegemony* and actually talk about such matters in hallways and at meals as casually as they talk about what's on the TV. Since students would be reading Victor Villanueva later in the semester, there seemed some sense in their knowing his work up front from the beginning. Looking back, these quotes are curiously ambiguous and could be interpreted in many ways. For instance, students coming to college with the hopes of escaping their working-class identities in favor of elititist aims, and expecting that teachers expect the same, could find these quotes demeaning. Working-class students could understandably hear Zandy saying that they would learn nothing if teachers focused on where they, the students, came from; they could hear Villanueva telling people in dominant positions what they need to do to prosper; and they could hear Reid expressing shock over the stupidity of her working-class pupils. This reminds us briefly of the importance of contextualization: far from starting our course from the level at which students perceived reality (see Freire 1970, 52), we had already constructed an understanding for them; we had assumed their engagement with education issues without asking them what the nature of their engagement might be.

Scott: We asked students to write their first reaction paper—an ungraded sample essay written during class—based on one of the three quotes on the syllabus. All but three students selected the third quote by JoAnne Reid, about asking students what they want to learn. Were these responses red flags we failed to see? No one selected the Victor Villanueva quote concerning hegemony. In retrospect, this outcome is not surprising. Villanueva's comment on hegemony skated right past a class of first-semester college students and novice writers. This kind of language is specialized and arcane—understandable to these students certainly, but very unlikely to make any sense that early in a semester. They let it buzz on past.

Two of the students who wrote about working-class culture interpreted Zandy's phrase to mean "middle-class," at least based on the jobs they discussed. In part, we in the U.S. suffer from a general and popular denial of class as a valid category. The pervasive myth is that we are all middle class, with a few elites, most of whom have somehow earned their elevated status (e.g., Bill Gates, the Kennedys, Bruce Willis). Education that focused on the history and culture of the working class would, at least one student's response suggested, be detrimental to students. The student proposed that the working class's lack of knowledge would keep them from seeing the perspective of the elite: He believed that the working class developed a strong work ethic precisely because they learned about and tried to emulate the rich. In seeming contrast to this student, Sarah—who had worked in a local plastics factory and a telecommunications center for three years—asserted in her paper that education based on working-class culture would produce an educational process "based around techniques of mental survival as opposed to fragile idealisms." The reason for this is that "people engaged in a working-class world must be flat out mental survivalists. It is a day in and day out struggle with meaninglessness. [T]his is how you will make a living: sweating, sleepless, shouldering humility and disdain—to no apparent end. What a wonderful world, indeed." Indeed! This was an exciting paper to read at the beginning of the semester. However, while on the surface I find Sarah's response preferable to the first student's—not only in terms of its incisive observations and sharp rhetorical focus, but also because it is more in line with my own beliefs—in its end the basic point is fatalistic: We must resign ourselves to the status quo.

One goal of the writing course, on the other hand, was to promote, incite, or at least wave the dream of expanded access to literacies of power, economic, and life chances, and hope for more equitable social relations for all people living under the burden of working classdom. Too bold of an agenda?

Erika and Scott: We wanted to set up and work with the theme of education throughout the semester. For the first "big" writing assignment, we asked students to "determine for yourself—and then detail in your writing and for your audience—the key element of education in the short story 'Push,' by Sapphire [1996]." We assigned them to "pick a single key educational element in the story and build your own paper around this idea."

We hoped students would either relate to or critically situate themselves in relation to Sapphire's story of Clarice Precious Jones, an African American teen living in Harlem, who manages—with the help of a teacher—to "push" herself to a new literate life. Our goal for the assignment was for students to reach a level of critical thinking, linking personal experience—one way or another—to a piece of writing. We discovered, however, that while many students were able to either re-tell the plot of the story or make some generalization regarding the story, few were able to accomplish this writing assignment in the way we had hoped.

The second paper incorporated similar ideas and readings. This assignment was more complex and challenging, however. We asked students to "Read Rose [*Lives on the Boundary*] in light of Ede [the required course rhetoric], Sapphire, and your own schooling experiences—to put together the pieces of the texts and stories we've read so far in this course—and to determine how and why Rose complicates and/or extends Ede's discussion of writing as 'process.'" In conjunction, the students wrote two shorter response papers—which broke down these complex ideas—to help them prepare for this longer paper. Overall, however, we did not perceive understanding or excitement being generated by the ideas we were asking class members to read about, investigate, and interrogate for this writing assignment. Similar to our responses to their first writings, we thought these papers lacked critical thinking: They did not seem to want to make any connections between their readings and their experience, nor to complicate their views, nor to grapple with the educational myths that the texts challenged.

Student comments:
"The assignments oftentimes needed to be clarified for the students."
"Some of the assignments seemed confusing, but they are nice teachers, who always made time to help us."
"[Writing] Prompts were vague and unreadable. Word choice was also unreadable."

Assigning Writing, Not Blame

Erika: As I read *Lives on the Boundary* and *Bootstraps* before the semester started, the themes of education and literacy seemed to be intimately connected with the goals of a first-year composition course. After Scott and I first met, I learned that I would be teaching the section with *Bootstraps* as the reading text. Although I felt intimidated by Villanueva's cross-genre, multiple-voice text, which interweaves more theory than I had ever tried to tackle, I attempted to design a challenging and interesting lesson plan for the class. I wanted students to take their understanding of the educational system and vent what I assumed would be their frustrations with it. To push students toward this goal, I asked them to incorporate their own experience in education with the experiences and educational critiques of the texts we had been discussing in class:

PURPOSE: To read Villanueva recalling our other class readings and your own experiences and to write a letter to an educational authority figure and challenge his/her contribution to an ideology of education.

A series of questions followed this "PURPOSE." I designed these questions to spark student interest and avoid the surface skimming I had perceived in the first two assignments:

Does this person [the authority figure] make overall decisions about educational systems?
Does he/she consider the students in this ideology? What is your educational ideology?
How does Rose's attitude toward education contribute to Villanueva's attitude of education and the hegemony surrounding it? Consider also Ede, hooks, Shor, and Sapphire—would their experiences support an overall change in education?

Looking back at this assignment and thinking about my own experience as a first-year college student, I see how I, the knowing teacher, was asking the students to attack, armed with rhetoric, a community of which they were striving to become a part. Students come to a university expecting teachers to help them to enter into the "academic discourse community"; my assignment was implicitly asking them to challenge this same community. Although I did ask students to articulate their own educational ideologies, the deck was obviously stacked, regardless of what students chose to say. Of course Rose, Ede, hooks, Shor, Sapphire, and Villanueva's experiences support changes in education: Obviously, I had already formed what Knoblauch and Brannon (1984) would call an "ideal text" inside my head for students to ascertain (120), and this text left little, if any, room for students to establish their own interests and concerns.

As students read Villanueva, our classroom work centered around this letter writing assignment. Despite many class periods with discussion surrounding the term *ideology* and the ideologies of the writers we were reading, the students hesitated to use the word. In fact, one of the major complaints taken to the WPA was that they were being asked to write about *ideology*—"whatever that meant." It is clear now that although that term is part of my language, I did not acquire it in one sitting and start using it soon after. Students asked for definitions of *ideology* and Scott and I offered the definitions we knew and even tossed in Raymond Williams' (1976), but this explanation seems to have gotten lost in transmission. We watched as students either inaccurately used or avoided using *ideology* and *hegemony* in their own writing, despite their recurrence in discussion, the syllabus, Rose, and Villanueva. For this assignment one student used *ideology* six times in her four-sentence introduction, but did not mention it throughout the rest of the paper.

Yet another factor that plays into this classroom circumstance was my own inexperience as a teacher. At this point in my teaching career I was unfamiliar with the work of Paulo Freire, and I still believed that as the teacher I was obligated to be the knower and be able to answer all questions about a given text. I confess that *Bootstraps* intimidated me, and it oftentimes scared me that I didn't have answers any more than the students had. I was honestly answering questions with questions because I certainly did not have any answers. As a rookie, I was struggling with my role and with my power (of which I was very aware and scared).

Sarah: The most prevalent memory I have of the atmosphere after the first few weeks was that of palpable tension in the classroom. This tension seemed to ebb in the last couple weeks when we, the students, created our own assignments. I believe that this release was due to the fact that after having instilled in us a firm sense of powerlessness over our futures (in the class and in life), we suddenly had the chance to exercise some control.

Educational Ideology: Words and Actions

Scott and Erika: Two students took this ideology assignment as a chance to write letters directly to us. One student addressed the letter only to Scott, the other to both teachers. Both students critiqued the class and framed their concerns to us in concrete terms tied to their reading of *Bootstraps*. These letters only hinted at what would later become the primary complaint against us, which was that we didn't care about the students. This view of us as uncaring teachers might have developed from the aforementioned method of answering questions with questions, but we could also have been giving mixed messages regarding the subject matter, particularly regarding a series of discussions on what students came to call "weed out classes."

Many students, in both the meeting with the WPA and in semester-end evaluations, reminded Scott and me of our discussion about the idea of "weeding out" students, introduced in our class by Mike Rose's *Lives*. Rose discusses the VocEd program as a euphemism for bottom level. According to Rose, this element of our educational system attempts to explain why some people will be selected for college and professional careers and some will not. With the implementation of universal schooling and increase of access to public education, responsibility for "weeding students out" has been shifted to the colleges and universities. Discussing this visible and yet rarely talked about subject, we intended to raise student awareness of the structural flaws in a university system. If students were to personalize this issue of "weeding out," the theme of educational ideology might seem more relevant to them.

Scott: The rebel group of students (led by Saira) met with and delivered a long letter of complaint to our WPA. The letter—signed by several other students who couldn't make the meeting—listed the weaknesses of the teachers, detailed student attempts at intervention, and outlined their continued frustration with the teachers and the class. Grades were on the list the students brought to our WPA, but grades were not at the top. The fact that we teachers didn't seem to care was at the top: Didn't care about their grades, didn't care about them as people, didn't take their words seriously, belittled them in class, and called them names. According to our WPA, we would have been "proud" of the students, as they expressed themselves eloquently, directly, in a clear and concise manner. This is not particularly surprising when we see the investment that students had in this piece of writing. The rebellious students continued with the class—they had to get through the writing requirement, after all—though they hammered us in semester-end evaluations.

I still don't know how to read some of these final comments. One student claims that I ridiculed student questions; another asserts that I called students "stupid" during class discussions; another complains about my use of the term "Aaargh!" as a response comment on student papers (which I intended as humorous). While I can recall one classroom incident when I asked a student if she were "stupid"—in response to an ironical observation she had made about Rose's *Lives on the Boundary*—I said this in a joking context and tone. At least I thought and intended my remark to be joking. It's certainly possible that she did not catch the irony in her statement about Rose. It's even more likely that I didn't unwrap and lay out the irony for other students in the class to see plainly—so that they might catch the dueling of irony and satire and joke. Frankly, I don't remember this incident much. For me it was not important—just another impromptu commentary.

Saira: As far as what the students felt in the beginning, I am only able to explain what I, along with the friends I made in English 101, was thinking. I already knew one person; we had gone to high school together. When class started in the fall, everything seemed fine. We thought the teachers were fine and we would be able to get along with them. They seemed pretty laid-back. As we started to discuss the literature in the syllabus, however, there was an obvious change in attitude. I was able to detect the humor in many of Scott's jokes, but my friend from high school found his comments offensive and assumed they were degrading to her. There were mentions of the fact that we, as students, just accepted that English 101 was a "weed out" class. It seemed as if he were saying we were not intelligent enough to do anything about it. As I began to converse with the students around me, I realized some of them were having the same concerns as my friend.

I think the actual start of the revolt came when we got our first papers back. I received a lower grade than I was used to getting. I did not understand why, and Scott's comments did not help much. A number of students were in the same position as I was, and that is when we first thought we should talk to someone about how we felt. I tried to get an explanation from Scott, but his responses were basically the same as what he had written in the paper.

My friend had told me that she talked to the WPA about the situation and that it might benefit us to do the same. That is when I talked to the students who sat around me, and we discussed what should be done. We decided to make a list of what we thought was wrong with the class. Almost everyone agreed that we had no idea what Scott was trying to achieve or what he expected from us. We also included on the list that Scott insulted us and that his comments about "weeding out" indicated that he did not want us to succeed.

We gave this list to the WPA, and after they discussed it with Scott and Erika (at a separate meeting), I truly believe Scott and Erika did what they felt was necessary to make the class run more smoothly. They began asking us what we felt was necessary to make us have a better learning environment. They listened to our concerns, Scott cut down on the offensive comments, and our writing assignments were easier to understand. Erika and Scott went into more detail and conveyed exactly what their comments meant. It was easier to ask them what they were getting at without getting an ambiguous response.

I realize that everyone was not included in this little revolt, including Sarah. I guess it was sort of the clique a few students had formed during the course of the class. I think we mentioned the revolt in class at least once and anyone was welcome, but I assume the people who knew one another felt more comfortable with such a project. I still do not know if the way we went about solving the problem was the correct way, yet I do feel it helped better the environment in Scott and Erika's English 101 class.

Erika: In this period of recovery after the revolt, we had students design the final two assignments and then determine how the classes would be run. These final two assignments didn't have the same demand for complexity as the earlier assignments. The first one was a movie critique and the second was an apocalyptic narrative about the last twenty-four hours of the world. The students seemed comfortable writing in these areas and the overall tension was dramatically reduced.

Post-Course Reflection

Erika: As a teacher and an idealist, my summer planning had given me a vision for the students and for my new role as a teacher. Although Scott and I never sat down and shared our philosophy of teaching, from the beginning we shared a belief in the abilities of the students and our desire to academically challenge them. But as is often the case, teacher goals and student goals don't always work together. An example of the miscommunication that comes out of incongruous student/teacher goals was our on-going class discussion of "weeding out."

The students seem to have understood the "weed out" discussion as a threat or even a scare tactic. Despite our intent, our teacherly act of imparting the "truth" of the educational system was manipulative. We wanted students to recognize the danger of an educational system that is concerned not with education, but with determining who gets the stamp of approval to move on. But our presentation of this reality contradicted the critical pedagogy from which we were working. From a Freirean perspective, we reenacted the traditional banking model of education that, in its worst form, is destructive to the blossoming of critical consciousness.

Although I feel I can justify how a student might have misinterpreted our presentation of the term "weeding out," I cannot excuse my response to their fears. Throughout the semester different students would bring the discussion back to "weeding out" and I never listened long enough to hear the personal frustration and anger. Only much later did I realize what I wasn't hearing. Students were continually asking Scott and me for more explanation of terms like *hegemony* and *ideology*. Their questions were surely a form of protesting our heavy-handed use of politically volatile academic jargon—teacherly jargon that seemed designed to keep students at an arm's length from their goals of success at the university. Concerns for grades were certainly important, but as first-semester students at a large university, they didn't want to be "weeded out" because that would undermine their identity and who they hoped to become, personally and professionally. Drowning in talk of *hegemony* and *ideology,* students may have already felt negated: weeded out.

As Saira has astutely pointed out to me since this class, "Hey, we were just freshmen and you acted like we should've known all this stuff [words like *hegemony, ideology*]." Our expectations of these first-year college writers were perhaps too loaded for us to instigate anything but a revolt. In the epigraph to this chapter, Shaugnessy suggests that there is value in challenge, but students saw our "challenges" as being so far over their heads that it seemed unreasonable for them to even try. As a consequence, the class developed an aura of intense frustration and futility. Their frustration magnified our frustration and probably elevated our standards, which increased classroom tension. This is what led to the student praxis of going to the WPA.

I was scared for my job, my future as an academic, my ability as a teacher, and my value as a kind person. The students appropriately challenged us with the same power with which we had challenged them. This blunder, upon analysis, sounds much more productive and valuable than it did at the time. In the beginning I had hoped they would personalize the issue; now, looking back, I recognize that some students did intimately personalize the issue.

Sarah: Scott's prophecies regarded our future destinations despite diplomas and degrees in a somewhat pessimistic light. It was made clear that some (or all) of us were simply fated to fail regardless of how hard we worked, what we learned, or what we planned to do. The system, in other words, had labeled, packaged, and processed us with little regard to our individual needs and identities. In this way, we resembled the characters we read about in *Lives on the Boundary* and *Bootstraps.* Yet, at the same time, we were not like them. As

Scott pointed out, none of us came from harsh, inner city backgrounds. We, for the most part, were middle-class kids from decent schools. This is where I personally lost track of Scott's intended point. Did he mean that among the other white privileged students at the university, we were the bottom of the barrel and so were related to the downtrodden we read about? Did he mean that we should recognize the reality of "No one is free when others are oppressed?" Was it, perhaps, that he sought to establish a sense of powerlessness among students in the controlled environment of the classroom so that we could have a small taste of what some individuals spend their entire life experiencing? Was it all of these things? I didn't know then, and I don't know now.

Scott: I know that I was trying to *add rigor* to my writing classes, while still keeping some of the openness that had characterized past courses. The previous semester—according to their end-of-semester evaluations—several of my English 101 students had complained that some of the writing assignments and research requirements they themselves had designed turned out to be "stupid," "not really worthwhile," even though "somewhat fun" and "personally valuable." I decided that I would take more charge of crafting assignments and course readings. I wanted to add academic rigor and teacherly control over curricula, but also leave openings for students to develop their own ideas—within the frameworks that I had determined. Now I have to wonder: Were these frameworks too rigid? Too narrow? The wrong categories or goals?

Outside of the classroom, dead-end Sprint jobs haunted me as the semester began. A new Kelly/Sprint calling center had just blossomed downtown in Lawrence and heavily recruited university students to take these jobs: $7.50 an hour, the company of other students, flexible work hours. Yes, it might sound like a good job for students. But it frustrated me that for too many of my students (and others not my students), this would be their best job offer even after they've completed their degree, in our downsizing, de-skilling economy, flooded with growing temporary positions and fewer and fewer living wage, benefit-bearing, worker-respecting jobs. While numerous studies and texts argue these recent trends, I had been reading John Schwarz's (1997) *Illusions of Opportunity: The American Dream in Question* and know that this text was a theoretical influence as I prepped for this particular semester of teaching. Schwarz seemed dead on with his description of narrowing options for many in the U.S.—and especially accurate in his analysis of reduced options for young people, even for mainstream college graduates, in the coming years.

Anonymous Student Evaluation Comment: "The subject matter of this course seemed to revolve around the instructor's personal interests and politics—wasn't necessarily of interest to the students."

Erika: Students resented the political slant and disliked the withholding of information that we were expected to have regarding issues of education, even if we didn't have this information. But this wasn't the case for all of the students. Sarah clearly saw a tension between critical pedagogy and subjectivity.

Sarah (post-course comment):   My point here is that this class was done in an experimental fashion, and I can appreciate that. The complaint I ALWAYS had, and always will have is a more general one. There's always this assumption on the part of students that teachers, because they are THE TEACHERS, have the answers. I would dread being an English instructor, because how do you go about judging a paper?

Interpretation of poetry, fiction, etc. is an abstract art. The greatest English class I ever had was my senior year in high school. The instructor was this aging hippie guy, very laid back. Very amusing. The thing is, he always made a point of not interjecting his opinion of the literature we studied. You know how it goes—everybody would come up with their theories on what was being said and then look to him for the final word, like, "Which one of us is right?" and he would give this why-do-you-think-I-would-know kind of response. When he did interject an opinion, it was always tempered with the reminder that his ideas were no more valid than ours. Even so, there is an ingrained pattern of thinking among students that the approval of the teacher equals success. Likewise, there is a trait among teachers of asking questions with obvious endings. They know the answer they want, and they keep at it until they can get that answer. Why?

Erika: At a baseball game recently, my friends noted that baseball is the only sport/activity that measures errors and that a batter is doing well if he or she is 30 percent successful. I disagreed, noting that teaching meets both of these requirements too. This whole collection on blundering is really about that. We are stopping to look at the errors and the failure rate. This examination will not remedy these failures but might force us to see what skills we need to readjust our pedagogical form. Like any good baseball team, teachers of writing will inevitably look to the success stories (a record number of home runs, an award-winning student writer) to keep us going. We should remember, however, that we teachers are not supposed to be the designated heroes here. In fact, we need to recognize that the failure is an essential element of learning for both teachers and students—difficult as this recognition may be to hold onto sometimes.

So we will continue this learning process, constantly examining our theories, our actions, and our process so that we might clearly understand how our experiences have formed our respective educational ideologies.

Denouement

Erika's story: As a privileged white woman from the suburbs, I recognized educational injustice as a child, but because I benefited from it, I wasn't going to challenge it. In elementary school I remember wondering about the difference between my "gifted" classes and the "regular" classes. While I always felt like somewhat of an outcast for being in "gifted" or Honors classes, I liked them and I enjoyed my classwork; I enjoyed thinking because I was continually told that I was good at it. Consequently, I grew up on the Honors track. In Rose's terms, I was certainly pre-selected to succeed. Because of this background, Scott's class plan was particularly attractive to me—a chance to redeem myself.

After my first year of undergraduate work at a small, private, midwestern university (funded by grants, loans, and my parents), I knew I loved the academic environment and wanted to incorporate it into my career plans. Graduate school would continue my education and also provide the opportunity to "try out" teaching in an academic environment. I never imagined the difficulty of combining graduate studies and teaching. Additionally, I certainly had not thought about my own writing and how I came to learn it. I was not self-reflective or even aware of my own process of writing.

I never took English 101 so I had little, if any, understanding of the concept of a composition class when I was assigned to teach English 101 in fall of 1997. My uncertainty regarding a class titled "Composition" was furthered by the fact that I had spent my first year of graduate school being told by "distinguished" professors that I "couldn't write" and that they "couldn't teach me at this point." Essentially, I feared writing and was not sure how to do it—and certainly not sure how to teach writing.

I am not a hero in my classroom because I do not have all the answers. Although I am not afraid to admit this to my writing students now, three years ago I was still too uncertain to be willing to admit it. Knowing that I don't have the answers has helped me to learn and work with my mistakes, like the one documented here. A benefit of working with Sarah and Saira on this paper is that now we have seen how the miscommunication and difficulty, at that time, ended up working out—at least for the four of us. Without anyone offering a definite answer, I think we all learned something valuable. The semester was not a lost cause.

After this semester I became more familiar with composition theory. I learned about Paulo Freire and David Bartholomae and the theory behind what Scott and I (and Rose and Villanueva) were doing. A frustrating element of this training is that knowing the theory still does not necessarily help one make any sense of the practical teaching experiences. Rather, a practical sense comes from trial and error experience and the sharing of ideas with other teachers and with students. This understanding is only possible in a classroom that moves away from the banking model of education (see Freire 1970, 58).

Teaching English 101 has made me a more critical reader, a more purposeful writer, and I think, a more interesting person. I have improved as a teacher, as well. I am clearer, funnier; I try to explain to students why I answer questions with questions, and most of all, I know that my responsibility is not necessarily to impart knowledge; instead, I am teaching students to grapple with complex ideas about writing and their world. Idealistic? Absolutely. As Mina Shaughnessy suggests, grappling with complexity is the "experience of studenthood" and of teacherhood as well.

Saira's story: As I look back, I can remember walking into Scott and Erika's class and understanding that I was in a completely different environment than I was used to, an environment without a syllabus, books, or people that I knew. Once I came to college, there was a sudden realization that all teachers do not have the same expectations. While I was in high school, I was under the impression that there was a specific way to write. Scott quickly made me realize that I was mistaken. I now have the knowledge to figure out what type of writing a particular teacher enjoys and try to adapt to it. Scott and Erika helped me utilize my creativity and change the writing style that I was accustomed to. English 101 also pushed me to go beyond basic ideas and see where authors were coming from. I constantly heard that other classes were writing about controversial topics, such as the death penalty and birth control. At first I was upset that we were not taking that route; however, now I realize that what we discussed, particularly education, has given me more ways to examine situations in which I find myself.

Even though English 101 helped me in certain ways, I had concerns with how the class was organized and run. I noticed that a lot of students were not comfortable with the smart aleck comments that Scott made. I was under the assumption that they felt he was patronizing them. Furthermore, I suppose that Scott expected a lot from us in the beginning and used vocabulary in discussions and writing assignments that was foreign to a lot of students. Lastly, I never felt as if I had a clear idea of what the teachers expected from me. I was also not very comfortable talking to the teachers about my concerns; I thought the only way to get anything solved was going to a higher authority. I did gain a lot from Scott and Erika's class, but some issues hampered it being the best educational experience.

Scott's story: Rhetoric? Changer of the world? In fact, Carolyn Marvin (1995) reminds us, high literacy, persuasive rhetoric, is often on the side of the big guns—after all, to make a "killing" on the stock market is all the rage and the goal of every good boy in the U.S.A. Clearly, I deployed rhetoric, speaking and writing, as a weapon aimed to change a world. But in doing so, did I primarily reinscribe on our students the violence of high (or academic?) literacy, make a killing in the market of everyday life? I'm still not sure how to answer this question, but I agree with Erika that the blunder we committed was not necessarily wrong, or without value—to our students or ourselves.

This is a hopeful assertion—one that drives my optimism and helps get me out of bed. Some mornings when I am exhausted from this teaching life that I've chosen and from the hectic academic hurly-burly that is most often invisible to my students (committee work, the bitter rite of grades, etc.), I fight hard to remember and then reject fatalistic thoughts, such as Sarah expressed about working-class life: "[T]his is how you will make a living: sweating, sleepless, shouldering humility and disdain—to no apparent end." I think my teaching work is important, and does have ends—ends I claim as decent, individually and socially relevant, nearly always striving toward equity, even when I am tired and dragging at the end of a week or semester, even when burdened by the failure of pedagogy or by mistakes that seem too big and fast to ever outrun. So I guess I try to face them—own and embrace my blunders—in order to keep my optimism and hope alive for another day.

Victor Villanueva has the following to say in *Bootstraps,* and I mostly agree with him, so I'll end here with this hopeful, even "utopian" claim—also with the full knowledge that there are no guarantees of the outcomes of my work teaching and living in language:

> Change is possible, I believe. Language used consciously, a matter of rheto-ric, is a principal means—perhaps the means—by which change can begin to take place. The rhetorical includes writing, a means of learning, of discov-ery; it includes literature, the discoveries of others. Rhetoric, after all, is how ideologies are carried, how hegemonies are maintained. Rhetoric, then, would be the means by which hegemonies could be countered. And the classroom is an ideal site in which to affect change. (1993, 21)

Scott and Erika (teacherly conclusion):   We continue to make distinctions to explain our blunder: Success or failure? An experimental class or another "traditional" English 101 class taught at the university? Academic exercise or the "real world" issue? What do these designations mean? If we tried some-thing that was pedagogically unique and blundered trying it, then what?

Two years after the beginning of this fateful semester, the four of us con-tinue trying to retrospectively and collectively examine this experience. The letter of complaint was destroyed and so all we have is our recollections. In the meantime, life has gone on for us all. Scott completed his Ph.D. and has taken a position at a four-year liberal arts college in Michigan. Erika continues to teach English 101, while preparing to teach a course on "literacy narratives" and finishing up her master's in English. Sarah and Saira are both very suc-cessful students beginning their third year towards bachelor's degrees. Both women have plans for advanced degrees once they finish their current program.

The bottom line in this whole story is that students in this kind of educa-tional setting will succeed and students will fail, either in their terms or in the teacher's terms. We teachers need to maintain a commitment, not just to those students who succeed, but to those who fail or struggle as well. The luxury we, Scott and Erika, have with this collaborative writing experience is to see two students who have fared very well. In a large university we seldom get this op-portunity to see what, if anything, students take from any particular class that we have taught.

Sarah's story: My attitude upon entering Erika and Scott's English 101 class was less than enthusiastic. It was my first foray into a college class-room after being out of high school for over a year and a half. I had decided to attend the university, not out of desire for a degree, but because I found the day-to-day reality of full-time work at a meaningless job to be tedious, degrading, and dangerous to my idealism. I was working at a teleservice center, answering phones and setting appointments for a company that consistently screwed over its customers and then required us to cover for its actions. The job was highly repetitive, not unlike the work I had done previously in a plastics factory—I just used my voice instead of my hands. It was a completely mindless, soulless enterprise. I wanted to recapture the sense of challenge and discovery I had encountered in my prior academic endeavors. English 101, however, was not the place I expected to find that. Instead, it was, along with Algebra 101, a means to an end—a class I was told I had to take regardless of who I was, why I was there, and what my ultimate intentions were.

It was with resentment, then, that I walked into Erika and Scott's pedagogical experiment. If they played the role of experimenters, then we as students were the uninformed, unsuspecting subjects. English 101 being the first class most of us took at the university, we sorely lacked the background necessary to appreciate the complicated concepts our teachers were asking us to immediately comprehend.

I do not believe this is empirical evidence of our underpreparedness for university level academics. After all, the ideas Erika and Scott proposed were in opposition to the overall status quo. The high schools we came from were part of this traditional structure. Why would we have prior exposure to the concept of the university as a machine, a business, an institution infiltrated by social and political inequalities?

Scott's assertion that some people, such as honor students, were "preselected to succeed" while many of us were designated to fail was what really hit a nerve in the classroom. Although his intention may have been to create awareness, I believe many students took this as a personal attack on their right to self-determination. At this point, a controversial yet highly plausible concept became a tool of disempowerment wielded by a seemingly aloof authority figure. The result was the aforementioned "student rebellion."

I was not a part of this revolt, nor was I invited to be by my fellow students. In truth, I do not think I would have taken part, although I did share many of their frustrations. I simply did not feel threatened by the notion of predestined success or failure. Success, after all, is a highly subjective idea. In this context, it seemed to be used in the sense that those who are preselected to succeed would get the degrees, the status, the high-paying jobs, the political clout, and all parts of the alleged American dream. None of those things were on my agenda while I sat in Erika and Scott's writing course. I counted success then, and now, in the opportunity to be around intelligent people, doing meaningful work, in a progressive environment.

By that definition, my time in English 101 was a success, although not immediately apparent. I took away from the course a better understanding of academia as a business, as well as a renewed conviction in my own ability to influence and interpret every nuance of that business in my own way. I was lucky to have wound up in a classroom environment that was more awake than automatic right upon entering college. For me, it presented a glimpse of the possibility existent within all the classes to follow.

5

The Shadow Side of Teaching

The Instructor as Outsider

Darrell g.h. Schramm

1

She became my Lilith, my Lamia, *sans merci.* I began to feel enervated, as though she were sucking my blood. Even after I'd resolved a major blunder with my composition students, I dreaded going to class. She was not a shadow behind, before, or to one side of me; she was an all-enveloping, all-consuming shadow, looming over all I said and did in the classroom. Sometimes I would initiate a good class discussion that would soon fizzle to a whimper. Her shadow, I would learn through later interviews, loomed over some of the other students as well, her Gorgonian stare intimidating them, turning their participation to stone. I ended that semester feeling, in the transit of my teaching career, like so much damaged goods.

Teachers can be hurt, damaged, by the shadow, something that blocks the light of understanding or insight. They can be hurt and even perpetrate hurt themselves precisely because teachers serve a moral function in the lives of their students. The classroom, writes Leroy Searle (1996), is "always a scene of moral suasion" (19, 21). We touch lives and touching is a moral act. But touch can hurt, touch can repulse, touch can anger, touch can repress. That teaching is personal and often intimate does not guarantee appreciation or affirmation of our pedagogy. We must look beyond ourselves, beyond self-congratulation. We must be prepared to see our students not as abstractions but as specific individuals. In short, we must acknowledge the inner lives of students, both the lives that long to be touched and the lives that recoil from touch.

We must raise our own critical consciousness to realize that the gift of our pedagogy to students remains inadequate when we espouse the great generalities of justice, compassion, and unity in diversity, yet overlook the immediate detail of our lives and theirs. And while we may never learn the motivation that

68

generates the shadow in the classroom, we must make every attempt to interweave personal selves with public selves. I am convinced that to use Gerald Graff's (1992) injunction is to discover a more adequate and negotiable form of discourse in our classrooms: We must "teach the conflicts themselves" (12 and *passim*).

2

I had taught twice the course I discuss in this essay, a second semester, first-year college writing course that I'd entitled "Multicultural Perspectives in Class, Gender, Race, and Sexuality," before I became aware of certain shadows in the classroom. The population of both classes had been diverse in ethnicity, race, and sexual orientation, and had had fairly equal numbers of men and women. Fervent, exciting, vocal, class participation had flowed. Encouraging them to see culture as conversation, as a way of knowing, I had told those students that I was eager to hear their views, to understand their perceptions of the world. I'd wanted them to see that what mattered was not that we all agreed with each other but that we could negotiate our perceptions and understandings of the world in order to arrive at thicker interpretations, deeper insights. I'd wanted them to realize that finally "what matters is our loyalty to other human beings clinging together against the dark, not the hope of getting things right" (Rorty 1982, 166). The stimulating dialogue of those two classes, the essays therefrom, the evaluations at the end, and the bonding with so many of the students affirmed my pedagogy and my person.

Validated, enthusiastic, and happily aware that students in these classes had become allies, I altered the name of my course slightly for my third occasion of teaching it: "Multicultural Perspectives" became "Multicultural Alliances." But this new class differed immediately from the previous two: It contained twenty women only. Never before had I taught a course of all women. Our first reading was Hanan al-Shaykh's (1992) *Women of Sand and Myrrh,* a novel concerned primarily with gender issues; I wondered how it would go. The students had written several responses through the course of the novel, so I know that they did have something to say. But during class discussions only one woman contributed often and zealously; two or three others would make an unfervid remark now and then. A shadow had descended on my teaching.

It was not to be the only shadow, nor the darkest. According to colleagues and random readings, the shadow of nonparticipation in the literature or writing classroom is not uncommon. Psychologically speaking, I see it characterized by repression. Two other shadows also would soon make their appearance: the shadow of alienation and the shadow of false consciousness (to be explained later). Like the first, these two shadows were animated and motivated by the forces of language. Long before the semester ended, I would be reeling, become dispirited, even filled with dread. The shadow side of teaching embraces that which is debilitating, destructive. It can kill the spirit.

However, initially I was only mildly concerned about the lack of student participation. I had been teaching for twenty-five years and had encountered reluctant classes before; I knew something about initiating classroom discussion, keeping the conversation going, and preventing the silence of those who had something to say but were hesitant to do so. And almost invariably I had effected a change in the reluctant, the hesitant, the silent. Unless they were late or I was involved in conversation, I greeted my students when they entered the classroom. I tried to avoid judgmental statements and questions that expect convergent thinking, that is, answers that are either wrong or right. I made room for a variety of acceptable responses, often not commenting beyond a nod until I had heard several students speak. When a student's comment seemed merely to skate on the surface of the topic, I tended to ask, "Can you say more about that?" But this time nothing worked. This time my students seemed phantoms, entities who hadn't realized themselves. All I knew and had practiced before could not draw them into an exchange of ideas. The one zealous student, understandably, dropped the class.

Was this reluctance to speak in class an issue of religious ideology, given the fact that I taught in a Catholic university? I think not, for most semesters I take a poll of my classes that generally reveals that slightly fewer than half are Catholic, and not even half of those are practicing Catholics. Was it, then, a race or caste issue? Eleven of these women came from marginalized groups, perhaps accustomed to being unheard or ignored; were they unwilling to trust yet another white male instructor? Was this reluctance to speak in class a gender issue, my body representing white male privilege and patriarchy? Was the disinclination to ask questions, to answer them, to comment, to agree or disagree, to challenge, the result of social construction, a demonstration by these nineteen women of deference to my very presence as expert or authority? Had I first read Graff's *Beyond the Culture Wars,* I would have asked these very questions then; determined to understand, I decided—belatedly—to chart the internal workings of the class. Near the end of the semester, I interviewed ten of the students. All denied that this shadow, the repressive shadow of noninvolvement, suggested a gender issue.

One student, Diantha, said there was "definitely an undercurrent of tension in the class. I don't know where it came from. I felt none personally, but there was some. You could cut through it with a knife. People were afraid they'd offend somebody. Their negative attitude made the semester drag on for me." Fear of offense. This fear that they might offend someone in the class was echoed by most of the students I interviewed. Afraid to offend, they repressed what they had to say aloud. Two or three women would voice opinions more boldly in written responses, but often censored themselves when I asked them to tell me more during class time. True, people do not wish to be accused of sexism, racism, or of other bigotry even when it applies. But by repressing their attitudes, beliefs, or ideas, by remaining silent, they can maintain the myth of mainstream U.S.A. that, in community and classroom, life is serene and safe and correct.

Unfortunately, this self-repression not only distorts the real situation, but also allows oppression and injustice to continue. In such silence and lack of participation, democracy falters, falls apart.

The shadow of repression is further complicated when students fear offending the instructor. Not surprisingly, a number of students perceived me as a homosexual man. A course's content, and especially that of this one, "does not," as Mary Elliott (1996) writes, "in itself, insulate the teacher from scrutiny" (705). "I didn't want to offend you," Tanya declared. When I had asked her earlier in the semester how she might offend me, she was reluctant to explain. Indeed, she broke all four scheduled appointments with me during the semester. During her interview the last week of classes, she spoke at length of her initial embarrassment and reluctance to hold a dialogue with me. "People are so far from understanding homosexuality," she said. "It's a cultural thing. You're never taught how to be around gay people. You have no real ideas if you're not raised around it."

This edge of the repressive shadow raises the question of teacher self-disclosure. While I am always prepared to disclose myself as a gay man, and have done so in the classroom or my office, spontaneously or when questioned, I have been disinclined to force the moment. Even had I come out to these nineteen women at the start of the semester, what assurance might I have had that students such as Tanya would feel any less discomfort discussing homosexuality? Engaging students in such conflictive issues as homosexuality, remarks Graff (1996), may "deepen fear, tension, and anger. But once these feelings are already present in a college's atmosphere"—and in mine they definitely are— "they will probably only get worse if the conflicts are *not* engaged" (148). While I had engaged my students in the issues, I did not engage them in the actual conflict. I had kept it abstract by discussing homosexuality in the writings of James Baldwin, Mab Segrest, Tom Spanbauer, and others. Is this an example of what Hephzibah Roskelly (1995) would call, "the loss and damage that occur when personal experience and intellectual inquiry get divorced" (718)?

Yet, had I entered my own sexuality into our nominal discourse, might I not have been perceived as an authority once again, a representative and a representation of all homosexual persons? I am not and refuse to be a representative of my race, my nationality, my gender, my sexuality. And so I did nothing: Let sleeping dogs lie. Clearly, then, just as my students cast the repressive shadow of noninvolvement, I, too, cast a shadow, that of nondisclosure. We were the shadow sides of each other. My solution might have been to present the teacher self "as an individual rather than an 'agenda'" (Elliott 1996, 706). That is what I thought I had done, but I had gone only so far: I had stopped short of complete revelation, and that, in this case, was a blunder.

On the other hand, a heterosexist view would claim my blunder was to have allowed (my) sexual orientation a place in my curriculum to begin with, but this ignores the fact that heterosexuality has always been a given, always assumed the bias of exclusive place in canon and curricula. No, my blunder was to have ignored the usual clues and cues that give me leave to be forthright with my students: the occasional exchange of glances between two students and those smiling whispers that I had learned to read over the years to mean "Do you think he's gay?" I should have stepped into the breach, acknowledged my own sexuality in a course that, among other issues, addressed sexuality and the self. Why didn't I? Not because I feared for my teaching job—I had, as I've stated, come out to other students, other classes, and certainly been open with my own colleagues. No, I think my reticence occurred because I felt shy and uncertain before an all-female audience. Nineteen women and me: It was all too new, too different. Though aware of my audience, I had little sense so early in the semester of who each member really was, what they expected, how they might react. And did my homosexuality even matter to them? Obviously, as I learned, it did.

Like bell hooks (1994), I have brought to my classes pedagogical strategies that acknowledge and respect the presence of racially and ethnically diverse students and have encouraged them to participate in classroom discourse (84). And as a gay person, I have felt—like bell hooks—"how easy it is to feel shut out or closed down" so that I am especially earnest about engaging all the voices in my classroom (86). Much of what I say and ask and how I say and ask it is informed by my own past experiences of being a student excluded as both poor working class and homosexual, an outsider who has learned to survive by viewing my world with a divided perspective. Like those students who code-switch from their dialect to academic English, I learned to be in two places at once (Qualley 1994, 32–35). Consequently, I was surprised, then frustrated and finally discouraged, to find dialogue at a minimum: the instructor as outsider.

3

Still, another edge to this shadow of repression: The interviews revealed that many students felt self-conscious. They did not wish to appear foolish or uninformed. "Not everyone is used to talking about homosexuality," said one woman. "It was a tension of not knowing enough, afraid we'll be wrong." Apparently, two other students in the classroom provoked this self-consciousness. "Our class was uncomfortable at times," Noelle told me. "We got bad attitude from other women in the class, especially on the race issue. They'd look at us in certain ways because we spoke up. Made us feel uncomfortable." She mentioned two women in particular—one of them Hazel (of whom more later)—who would glare or roll their eyes, curtailing, even silencing a self-conscious participator. After all, "the stare," we are told, "conveys dislike or disapproval" (DeBruyn 1996). During the semester, I had not been aware of this peer attempt at censorship. Regardless of the source, the shadow of repression denies the self.

Jungians tell us that the shadow, generally destructive, contains the repressed, the unfavorable, the hidden. The indifferent and foreshortened student contribution to our classroom conversation was contradicted, however, by three students who irrepressibly engaged in whispering sessions for several consecutive class periods early in the semester, thereby unwittingly shaping the shadow characterized by the hidden. Why, I wondered, if they had so much to say, did they not engage in a dialogue with the rest of the class? One September morning I lost my patience: "Will the girls in the corner please stop behaving like girls and participate in class discussion?"

Immediately I regretted my words. We had been reading and writing about gender issues. What hidden shadow in me had blundered (again) and no doubt alienated at least one of them? And I knew I had alienated some of these women, when the next two sessions were even less productive, less discursive than before. It seemed now more than ever I taught in Averno, the Gateway to Hell, calling to shades, students without substance.

A week later I found an anonymous letter sandwiched between student essays:

> Although I am still unclear of the definition you have on gender, I am definitely aware that I was appalled and disgusted by the hypocritical, crass, hurtful, demeaning, chauvinistic, and unnecessary name calling that was used to merely quiet a corner discussion. As much as you perceive their actions to be immature and disrespectful of other's [sic] time, it was doubly disrespectful to patronize those women by contradicting your own lecture and minimizing their personalities as "girls." What exactly did you mean by saying, "Will the *girls* in the corner please stop acting like *girls* and participate in the class discussion?" I'm sure the entire class of women did not appreciate that snide remark. As a woman I was terribly offended. If we were making light of the issue of gender, perhaps I would not feel compelled to make this complaint. However, being in a female dominated class I feel we all take this matter very seriously. That statement embodies all the oppression you spoke of, and to actually say it out loud questions the authority and morals you have as a college professor.

Though, as I have mentioned, I had not yet read Graff, I knew of only one thing to do. At the next class meeting I intuitively began teaching the conflict itself: I confronted the shadow of the hidden. I told the class that, as I'd said the first day, I wanted our classroom to be a safe place and that I was still a growing human being, still learning my way through life. The classroom was more than just a place for the head, for bodiless discourse; our feelings had a place in it also. And so I wondered how many of them had ever said something in frustration or anger that they later regretted. All nineteen students raised a hand. I stated that I had done the same and mentioned my recent admonishment to the three women in the corner. Revealing that I had received an anonymous note regarding the incident, I read them the letter.

Finished, I paused, then said I could perhaps excuse myself by saying my mother still referred to herself as "one of the girls" or that a forty-one-year-old friend had recently sent me a change-of-address card referring to herself as "that same crazy girl." But those would be mere excuses. The truth was that my words had been the result of a gradually increasing annoyance over the distraction and disrespect of the constant whispering. Nevertheless, that did not excuse my demeaning or hurting anyone. I then apologized to the three women and to anyone else I might have offended. But, I added, I had indeed thought of the rest of the class as women in contrast to the three. What I had meant by the term *girls* was children; they had been behaving like children. Again I offered my apology then asked if anyone wished to say anything on the matter.

One woman remarked that it was more my tone than the words that had distressed her, that I had never sounded authoritarian before, that she had been taken aback and felt pained by my "voice of authority."

I replied that I too was a product of my culture, that the authoritarian stance had been activated by my frustration and anger, and that obviously I still had more work to do on myself.

The words "product of my culture" triggered a shift in the incipient discussion. It moved from the letter to the topical content of the course, and I moved with it. Perhaps I'd learn why this class was so unresponsive or resistive.

Several students confessed their difficulties understanding writing about sexual issues and gender. I reminded them that they were to supplement their reading in order to understand and converse more knowledgeably and that I had given them a bibliography for that purpose, but I also reminded them that the oral exchange of ideas was necessary for understanding and clarification. It was then that Tanya said she had shied from speaking for fear of offending me. I assured her I was not easily offended, felt rather objective, had worked as an editor, had granted As on student papers with whose arguments or main point I'd disagreed. I also urged those students who were still hesitant to voice their concerns to speak to me in my office; three or four students made appointments to do so.

When they next met with me, many of these nineteen women were almost loquacious. Emancipation. Transformation. About half the class asked questions, voiced opinions, even politely disagreed with one another, a pattern that continued through most of the semester. I had blundered into change. Lewis Hyde (1983) reminds us in *The Gift* that one can interact with the shadow by avoiding or ignoring it, by attacking it, by identifying with and joining it, or by addressing it to "see what it wants. Such a dialogue requires that the ego position be suspended for a moment so that the shadow may actually speak" (255). Had I avoided or ignored it, the shadow would have eaten me alive. Had I attacked it, I would have hated myself for acceding to that patriarchy against which I had been struggling for years and years. Had I colluded with it, perhaps by giving only worksheets, tests, and other written work, content with no real interaction, I would have taught only in the greatest of misery. Because I addressed it, I "made everyone think," as Brigid put it later at her interview. "That note sparked our dialogue."

Tanya concluded, "Before the note incident, a lot of us had a negative attitude. We were afraid we might offend. You opened a door."

"I started to take the course more seriously," Noelle added, "started look-ing inside myself more."

In addressing the shadow of alienation that I had introduced to the class by my outburst, I had also addressed the shadow of repression. And while the writer of the note remained hidden in anonymity, I had exposed to myself (and the class) vestiges of dominating authority hidden in me. When we confront the shadow, acknowledge a blunder, we can initiate change. Indeed, I formed a bond with several of these young women, especially with those who seemed to res-onate with me on issues of class, sexuality (androgyny, bisexuality, homosex-uality), and other issues contending with mainstream, privileged, white Ameri-can culture. Eventually finding ourselves in a similar community of affect and effect, we participated in a dialogue of identification, self-disclosure, and in-vestigation. Of course there is a limit to what we can learn about our students "within the sociological confines of the academic composition classroom" (Cushman 1996, 19), but the point is not so much learning about our students as to stimulate their thinking, encourage their exploration of ideas, and listen to their narratives, thereby refusing exclusion and initiating inclusion for social change. What matters is an honest and concerned dialogue to establish a praxis of truth and solidarity. This matter of honesty was to direct my approach in re-lating to my students and classes hereafter. Henceforth, determined not to di-vorce intellectual inquiry from the personal life, I would, in a lesson or a lec-ture on social diversity, reveal my sexuality as one among other attributes of the genetically and socially constructed self. In the semesters that have followed, I have had no adverse repercussions.

4

But despite the elimination of these two shadows in my classroom, all was not well. The most damaging shadow still stretched across my classroom, prevent-ing the complete turn-around of what might have been, finally, a dynamic class.

This shadow, in the form of a twenty-four-year-old student whom I shall call Hazelelponi—Hazel for short—made its presence felt at the end of our second class meeting in which I had introduced the theory of gender as a social construction. Walking up to me after class, Hazel said, "I've been going to school a long time now, and I've never heard of any such things as you've said today about gender." Her voice was arrogant, metallic, cold.

"Perhaps," I suggested, "you haven't taken any courses yet that would ad-dress gender issues."

"I'm a nursing major, and it's made up mostly of women. All my instruc-tors are women. They've never brought up anything about gender being socially constructed, whatever that means."

After giving her another example by way of explanation, I recommended some readings, and she left. I gave the exchange no further thought.

However, as time went on, my encounters with Hazel became more frequent. Querulous, defensive, demanding, self-indulgent, she found fault with what I said, with what I required for the course, with specific assignments, with my comments on her paper, with the very texts we read. She wanted extensions on her papers; she wanted exceptions to my rule regarding late work. Demanding, defiant, hostile, she left messages on my answering machine, spoke to me just before class, immediately after class, and in my office between classes, but rarely—except in small groups of three or four—did she speak in general class discussion itself. Because her shadow fell on us all, the turn-around of the class was not complete. By mid-term, despite the progress I had made, I longed for the semester to end.

After we had begun reading and discussing the final novel of the course—Tom Spanbauer's (1991) *The Man Who Fell in Love with the Moon,* a text that through its issues of race, class, gender, and sexuality articulates, in the words of Earl Jackson, Jr. (1995), "a mode of cultural agency and resistance" (142)—Hazel's shadow fell again on my office door. She could not, she would not go on reading the book. It was offensive. It dealt with things she didn't want to read about, things she had a personal problem with.

What do we do when a student announces she rejects a required reading? Simply fail her? "Willed not-learning," according to Herbert Kohl (1991), is most often evidenced in "withdrawal and defiance" (41), sometimes in sullen silence. Hazel had exhibited at different times all three reactions. This time it was openly proclaimed withdrawal. She believed she shouldn't have to explain her aversion to the text, yet she did not wish to lose any credit for refusing to read what was assigned. My internal radar signaled to me: Thinking of the incestuous rape scene in the novel, I considered that we teachers do have a moral obligation to our students, that even as we defend civil liberties and respect diversity, we must also defend and respect the right to privacy. Telling her I could respect her reluctance to read further, I asked what she might suggest as an alternative for her. Perhaps, she offered, I could give her something else to read and report on. For a mad moment, feeling by now harassed and dismayed, I wanted to say, "Read Proust's *Remembrance of Things Past.*" Brushing madness aside, I considered that, although it had seemed my professional duty to empower her life by overcoming her resistance, her reluctance to engage in the course, to make her "generate knowledge by 'dealing with' [her] beliefs" (Bruffee 1986, 777), to make her wrestle with what seemed anathema to her, perhaps I had been mistaken. Did she feel her integrity was at stake? Her sense of safety? Had she come to me this time because she wished to keep at bay her fear of a world she could not control?

Conducively, I assigned her two articles, one from the most recent issue of *Harvard Educational Review.* Over the weekend, she left a message on my machine stating that she had been unable to locate the latter article, that our university library did not subscribe to the journal. When after our next class session I informed her that our library did indeed carry it, that I had often read it there, including the current issue, she snapped, "Do you think I'm lying?"

I wanted to snap back at her, wanted to let go of my politeness and rationality, but I had been too long and too snugly imbued in professionalism. "Perhaps," I said calmly, "you didn't look in the right place, or you didn't recall the name of the journal correctly. I suggest you check again." I checked the periodical room myself that afternoon and found the review instantly. I felt drained.

Surely now, I reasoned, I could relax from the coldness of Hazel's shadow as she pursued her individual and separate assignments. And, indeed, she did inform me later that she had felt enlightened by both assigned articles.

In the meantime, however, I learned that she had gone first to her advisor, then to the head of my department, to claim that I was teaching pornography. The Spanbauer book, she maintained, was pornographic. I was stunned. How could this—why did this—happen *after* I had allowed her to discontinue reading the novel? I saw her as a Lilith, a night-phantom gliding about where I could not see her, an enemy not to newborn children, but to new ideas, undermining my course, my students, me. What was it that motivated her? I realized then that without unflinching introspection or reformation of her own behavior and life, she would continue with business as usual. The coldness and hardness, the negativity and animosity would continue regardless of my words or action. Jung's famous disciple Marie-Louise von Franz (1964) claims that some people are "too lazy to consider how the unconscious affects them" (176). I was inclined to believe, however, it was not laziness, but fear and perhaps anger. To continue one's life by displacing and projecting one's emotions onto others is easier than dealing with those emotions—to that degree she may have been lazy. Obscuring her own perspective and thereby obstructing her understanding and her passage to growth, Hazel, I suspect, displaced onto me her fear of or hostility toward something, someone. This displacement became also an obstruction to any genuine human relations between us (172). "It is up to the ego," asserts Marie-Louise von Franz, "to give up its pride and priggishness and to live out something that seems dark" (175).

What pained me most was Hazel's clandestine attempt to undermine me, her secret attempt at censorship. Hegel would have termed her action the result of "bad insight," that which agrees to political oppression. I term it the shadow of false consciousness. This is that ill-formed consciousness that essays to disseminate the illusion that all will be well if only the appearance of things fits a narrowly prescribed definition or agenda, if all words and behavior and material reality are reckoned to a common denominator of unswerving pattern, of unchanging nature. It is a reductive enterprise. And the problem is two-fold. First, obviously all nature, whether human or otherwise, not only suffers change but cannot exist without change. One may presumably freeze a word, halt a behavior, preserve a material object for a time, but of these is none "but doth suffer a sea-change." Second, they who cast the shadow of false consciousness are themselves victims of those who proclaim to know *the* truth, those absolutists who pursue their own narrow and fearful ends. Perhaps I should not have been surprised since "the principle threat to academic freedom these days comes . . . from the dominant ideologies among students and faculty" (Johnson 1995, 19). Censorship is the result of a conformity determined to constrain ideas, if not life; it is a dangerous outgrowth of false consciousness, which presumes its own essential enlightenment. How, finally, can one gainsay a moral dogmatism that, in order to remain justified and safe, avoids dialogue and refuses to be tested?

By now, into the last four weeks of the semester, I felt utterly demoralized. I dreaded going to this class. Even though the administration perused the novel, supported me, and informed Hazel that the book was not calculated to arouse its readers sexually, that it was literature and not pornography, I had lost all enthusiasm for teaching this course. What would Hazel find next to complain or accuse me of? I found myself either avoiding discussion of any sexual issues or passing over them quickly, dismissively—a retreat from possible blunder, no doubt a kind of blunder itself. And Hazel continued on her own relentless, adamantine way.

For the final paper I had assigned the students to explore the social construction of their own selves: How had they been shaped by class, gender, race, sexuality, religion, or another facet of culture? A week before the paper was due, Hazel, accompanied by her two cohorts (not the same students as the three whisperers early in the semester), approached me after class. "I don't think it's fair that we have to reveal in our papers what's so personal to us."

"Hazel," I said, "I haven't asked that you reveal your darkest self nor your most personal secrets."

"But the thing that's shaped me most is the most personal."

"It's still not the only thing."

"Who else will see the essay?"

"No one. Only I."

Her final paper was competent but careful and remote. Hazelelponi had retained to the end all the attitudes reflecting the shadow: the repressed, the hidden, the ultimately destructive.

Had she been a victim of rape? Though I may never know, I believe so; it is the only answer that makes sense to me. What I have is nothing scientific—only shadows. And so it is circumstantial evidence that informs me Hazel had been a casualty of sexual abuse. She had, after all, stopped reading the Spanbauer novel when she had come to the rape scene. And though she rarely spoke in class, the most significant statement she made was her last, in response to another student, on the final day of class: "Sex isn't the only reason men rape. It can also be the need to show power." Shortly before the semester ended, a female colleague revealed to me that she had been raped at fifteen and again at seventeen. Years later when reading a Jerzy Kozinski novel, she found herself reading a rape scene that so sickened and repelled her that she first tore out the pages then burned the entire book. "And I love literature," she said. "I'm a reader, not a book burner. But I simply couldn't deal with it." Hazel could not deal with the Spanbauer novel. As the only male in the class, was I perhaps to pay for what another male had done? Had I became the representation of all rapists, or even of all men, for her anger and resistance?

Two other possibilities suggest themselves in an essay by Joseph Litvak (1995): Hazel may have presumed that, because I am a homosexual man, I don't like women, in which case she might have resented me. Or she may have been a closeted lesbian herself and feared I might "blow her cover" (29). Yet surely she saw my friendly but professional relations with the other students. Furthermore, she did write one essay on nursing gay AIDS patients and another on homophobia in the medical profession. Those papers would lead me to discount her resentment or dislike of me for my sexuality. At the same time, during the interviews, one student informed me that "there were about five students who thought if they talked about homosexuality, they'd get a good grade. So they'd discuss homophobia." And Kristin stated flatly, "They say one thing but act different. That's how girls are." (When I pointed out to her that she had used the term *girls,* Kristin replied, "That's what we call ourselves"! A suspicion began to nag at me: To what extent had my initial blunder been shaped by an identity politics and a political correctness not my own?) Had Hazel been one of those students, writing what she assumed would please the instructor? As to her sexuality, I perceived nothing. "They just didn't like sex, period," said Tanya of Hazel and one of her cohorts. If, then, Hazel had been raped, was there anything that I could have done, anything anyone could have done, to dispel her hostility, to overshadow her shadow?

Whatever the cause may have been for her response to me and the course, she remains the shadow that was the most damaging. Cold and discontented, she reflected for me the "poisonous judgments and negative thoughts" of the shadow (von Franz 1964, 173). I have tried to see Hazel's life not as a snapshot, not as an utterly disparate moment in my course, but as a story, a narrative with its own *telos,* its own meaning. And I have tried to ferret out my blunder within that story. But I am left with no beginning and no end: hints, suggestions, circumstantial evidence, but not facts. I have entertained only a dialogue with myself, a monologue. There are shadows to which a curriculum may have no reply.

5

Addressing or confronting a shadow does not guarantee a successful outcome. Von Franz confirms that efforts to integrate the shadow through honesty or insight do not always succeed. The shadow may be so intensely driven that no efforts can dissuade or assimilate it (173). And while it appears I did reasonably succeed in integrating the shadow of repression cast by my students in general and the shadow of alienation cast by myself, Hazel's shadow of false consciousness still haunts me. Rarely, I believe, can one penetrate and change a dogmatic and complacent epistemology.

The blunders I've made, the unanswered questions I hold, have confirmed in me my theory that any pedagogical approach must be born and reborn out of our relation to each individual classroom of students we teach; each semester in each classroom we must examine and re-examine the intentions and objectives we have set for the course. Invariably, however, I must, we all must—if we wish truly to be insiders of the classroom—be prepared and willing to teach the conflicts that arise. But we must also move a step farther into the sun: We must anticipate and address the conflicts inherent within the conflicts. Though it may not make the shadows disappear, we must address and teach the conflicts within the classroom, and the conflicts within ourselves. Presenting composition through the lens of diversity and civil and human rights means we have to respect the voice of the student who casts a shadow, means we may have to live with the shadow, means there may be no final and soothing answer to the conflicts we teach.

6

On Blundering as WPA

(And Making a Half-Way Decent Job of It)

Brad Peters

1. Shooting Elephants

Jean-François Lyotard (1984) says, "Narration is the quintessential form of customary knowledge" (19). But sometimes the story we need to tell silences us instead, because we don't yet know what we know. Or maybe we can't tell the story without asking other people to help us get it right. Being in a position of public or institutional scrutiny can put another kind of slant on what we need to say. Teachers deal with this problem frequently, and writing program administrators struggle with it even more so. For instance, a WPA may not get an icicle's chance in August to tell his story, because others, oddly enough, insist on telling it for him. My most difficult times as a WPA have occurred when I couldn't tell a story because no one wanted to listen. Lacking the safe haven of a friendly human ear, a story can wander off and get lost, unless the teller is smart enough to tell her cat or turn it into a prayer that finds God in a hearing mood. There are also times when a story *itself* won't let a person tell it. That's the kind of story that won't abide the dishonesty that comes from the teller's intermittent moods of pettiness, anger, or terror. Customary knowledge, as it turns out, isn't so easy to get at.

Right now, I'm wrestling with a story about some blunders I've made, and whether or not I've learned anything useful that other people might want to know.

Let me start out with the two-cent version of my story. Once upon a time, during a spell of controversy about public education, I accepted a position as director of composition at a large California State campus. With me, I brought a deep but somewhat ingenuous commitment to critical pedagogy. I encouraged some incoming teaching associates to help me rewrite our program's first-year composition curriculum along those pedagogical lines. I also went along with

81

the university's pressures to get the TAs to use technology in their classes. Unfortunately, the university didn't follow through with the technological support we needed. Bad things happened—a *lot* of bad things. The TAs began to question (and resent) everything they'd learned, as we all struggled to find a way to get on with our work. I did not know quite what to do. We did not live happily ever after. But most of us, I think, emerged the wiser, despite (or perhaps because of) the blunders I made.

Put like this, my story doesn't *seem* so difficult to tell. When I stretch it out to make room for the details, though, I keep having to trim back the urge to justify or defend myself. I don't want to end up looking like a fool. Nevertheless, I may well have been one.

Out of just such an instinct for self-preservation, I've said—to anyone who'll listen—that an administrator can make no right decisions. Whatever a WPA does will be perceived as a bungle by someone, especially if the WPA doesn't shy away from actions he or she deems necessary but not popular. I want to add, in justification and defense, that if a WPA's decision leads to a blunder, it will probably point to some obvious good intent forged in the hope of changes that will benefit people. Do I presume too much in claiming as much?

The way I see it, blunders often happen as a response to bungles. The kinds of bungles I'm talking about (and the people who commit them) promise changes as well—usually in the name of tough love, but never as an indication of good intent, and always in an effort to make others submit with unquestioning conformity. Unfortunately, bungles fog up the distinctions between good and bad, so that blunderers can even become bunglers in their efforts to make silk purses out of a sow's tail. For example, I might have some useful insights about places where I went wrong in this story, but in other places, I might leave gaping, unexamined holes that could identify me as a bungler as well. Such complex little twists tempt me to wonder if the mere fact of being a WPA inherently leaves a person in such a wobbly position between blunders and bungles that the question of intent becomes a fallacy. To avoid getting into a morass of these niceties, however, I'll provide another example of bungling that seems so spectacularly bad as not to be mistaken for anything else.

Shortly after I came to direct the writing program at my California State campus, the Chancellor and Trustees of the state system began to enforce a mandate to reduce *remediation* among *unprepared* first-year students by 90 percent by 2004. They wanted most of the unprepared students to be *disenrolled*—an interesting concept, given that 62 percent to 70 percent of freshmen needed remediation, yearly, on my campus. The Chancellor and Trustees panned evidence and teachers' testimony that *courses in remediation,* especially basic reading and writing, improved retention and got the academic performance of many young *remedials* up to college level. Most of the *remediated* students were bidialectical or spoke English as a second language, and they often came from overcrowded high schools with barely enough funds to keep the buildings standing. I suspect that employers in the service industry, in retailing, or in other corporate entities—who all wanted a large labor pool from which to hire these young people at substandard wages—cheered on the Chancellor and Trustees. As for the young people who managed to *remediate,* the Chancellor and Trustees were hard-selling technology—again, I suspect, to make education conform to the drill-and-kill, teach-to-tests mentality that renders the "transmission of knowledge" as a means "to supply the system with players capable of acceptably fulfilling [but not critically examining] their roles at the pragmatic posts required by its institutions" (Lyotard 48).

A bungle of this magnitude is hard to put into perspective. I had to think about it as an elephant in my living room. The summer I arrived at the campus, the upper administration assembled senior composition faculty and WPAs, telling us to come up with a response that demonstrated compliance to the mandate. We wrote a set of objectives and outcomes for the basic and first-year courses. General consensus was that the objectives/outcomes document would suggest to higher powers that everyone on campus taught writing the same way, doing their teacherly best to push unprepared students up through the system, fast. In a program that fluctuated ambiguously (on its good days) between the so-called current-traditional and expressivist models, I guessed these objectives and outcomes meant that all of us were in for a wild and wooly ride.

On the one hand, the objectives/outcomes document emphasized teaching writing to elicit coherent organization, competence with Edited American English, familiarity with genres, proper documentation of sources, and appropriate uses of technology—good things in their own right, but potentially capable of boxing teachers and students into a cult of unthinking correctness and technocentrism, given our context. On the other hand, the objectives/outcomes document included concern about multiple drafts, collaborative learning, reflection on multicultural texts and perspectives, ability to see fallacies or biases in language, and the discovery of democratic practices through writing—elements that could contribute strongly toward establishing a critical pedagogy in the program.

When I began designing the preservice seminar for incoming TAs, I fretted considerably about being the messenger who would deliver the objectives/outcomes document to them. I fretted even more about urging them to favor a critical pedagogy over the current-traditional one that the document also implied. It occurred to me at the outset that I might be setting myself up as a blunderer, and maybe from the TAs' perspective, a bungler. To introduce what I felt the TAs would need in the context of this programmatic shift, I prepared two additional tools. The first tool was a list of multiculturally themed composition anthologies and a complementary collection of non-fiction, book-length works. I gathered the titles from experienced teachers in the program who were interested in what I hoped to encourage, and I added a few titles from my own professional library. The second tool was a general syllabus that suggested a topical progression from home culture, to academic culture, to social and workplace culture—a developmental movement I felt our students needed. I pulled together descriptions of promising activities and assignments that I'd observed in the classes of teachers, and again added ones I'd tested myself. Then I shared both tools with experienced composition faculty, to elicit further suggestions. I intended to provide both the booklists and the general syllabus as likely interpretations of what the objectives/outcomes document proposed, which the TAs and I could then revise collaboratively.

We began the preservice seminar looking at various theories of composition because it seemed the best way to situate a critical pedagogy. The TAs would be going regularly into classrooms, working with students and experienced teachers. They would be examining student writing, learning techniques to help ESL students, finding out how to use the campus writing center, attending technology workshops, and writing up observation projects. They needed the theories to have ways of categorizing and appreciating what they saw. Moreover, I set up a listserv. From previous classes I'd taught, I knew that this was a friendly introduction to technology, and the anecdotal evidence in research had already convinced me that online discussion of all kinds—e-mail, listservs, bulletin boards, MOOs, and chatrooms—could facilitate a critical pedagogy (see Faigley 1992; Daniel 1999). I'd also found research matched my own tentative findings that asynchronous formats such as listservs encouraged online discussions more "richly embedded with information" than either in-class conversation or synchronous online chats (Bonk, et al. 1998, 302). The more information the TAs could share, the more readily they might critically reflect upon it.

Many of the TAs immediately noticed and got confused by the differences they saw in their introductory readings on theory in *The Writing Teacher's Sourcebook*. Janet, a former junior high school librarian, put the most useful spin on it when she wrote:

> I feel like Dorothy, with a cyclone of composition theories swirling about me into the heavens. I see Lazare go by, then Hairston, then Berlin on a broomstick . . . just as one seems to make sense, I see another that blows it away. . . .
> Is it a matter of coming up with a combination that suits us as individuals?

The readings also enabled the TAs to notice how variously the more experienced teachers were interpreting the new objectives/outcomes document in their lessons and assignments. The TAs were not yet ready to critique anything they saw. Still, they were beginning to sense not only differences in their readings, but contradictions between the readings and actual classroom practices as well. As Janet implied, their confusion indicated that they were alert and trying to negotiate among their own choice of theoretical approaches within the setting of our institutional context.

My confidence in the listserv discussions reinforced itself when we moved from our survey of different theories to Harriet Malinowitz's (1995) *Textual Orientations*. Malinowitz's study highlights critical pedagogy from the perspective of helping gay and lesbian students to develop an ethos in an academic setting that is not welcoming to them. I mentioned to the TAs at this point that our readings would take up the question of what the objectives/outcomes document meant by encouraging students to reflect on multicultural texts and perspectives, and I suggested the situation of gay and lesbian students represented that notion in *bas relief.* Janet, again, launched the listserv discussion by expressing the TAs' initial and general reaction: a need for clarification. In particular, she found Freire's (1970) process of critical reflection and "the knowledge that one has agency in the world which results from liberatory education" especially thought-provoking (95). She wondered: "So has this meant that in freshman composition where process writing and discovery of the self is taking place that Standard English is part of the patriarchal, 'banked' education to be avoided as the language of the oppressor?"

Landi, a former businesswoman, leapt right in, saying: "Correct, formal prose—oppressive and intimidating? Well, there are lots of jobs out there that don't require good writing skills. . . . But *appropriate* is the issue here. I don't see the point of educators openly encouraging sexual self-revelation in a class setting." She felt we had to establish an important distinction between teaching writing and teaching "personal culture."

In support, Carole, a self-declared Catholic, asserted: "If one is a Harriet M. teaching a class with the specific purpose of dealing with . . . sexual orientation, that's terrific. . . . But how else is it appropriate? . . . I will be regarding your writing, dear freshman, from the viewpoint of a woman who loves men only."

Stan, who thrived on critical theories, replied: "It should follow that culturally marginalized sexual orientations would be addressed in the context of teaching freshman composition. . . . I would imagine that alternative orientations would make up a significant part of our nontraditional student demographics."

Lori, a former lawyer, said: "The issue is not about sex, but about the fact that people read texts and life differently. . . . We've never really thought about how our orientation affects our point of view—at least, I didn't."

I was excited by how the listserv had given rise to such a discussion because of the way it apparently affirmed a critical pedagogy as the one toward which the majority of TAs were seriously considering and even gravitating. Such speculations make me sound embarrassingly naïve, however, as I surely suspect a critical pedagogy can take hold on a *semiotic* level, without revealing what's in the hearts, the guts, or the actions of people who talk the talk. I turn my skeptical words on myself, more than on the TAs—because one eventual follow-up to our work with *Textual Orientations* occurred some weeks later, when I brought in the booklist I'd compiled, accompanied by the books themselves. The TAs seemed subdued as they paged through various ones and started thinking about how these texts would substantively define their early professional lives. It came home to me with the force of a ball-peen hammer that they might be wondering why they weren't trusted to come up with their own intelligent choices for texts. When a WPA espouses a critical pedagogy yet is working under the constraints of several conflicting institutional expectations and forces, a moment such as this not only impinges on the dividing line between blundering and bungling; it beggars irony.

On the listserv, several pointed out how uneasy they felt about the texts. After some debate over whether they should also be allowed to teach the literary fiction and belletristic essays they knew the more experienced teachers in the program were using, Eulie—who was deeply influenced by Malinowitz—posted the following:

> I think the use of texts that explore issues of race, class, gender, sexual orientation are so important, because the structures of this society (government, justice system, educational system, media, etc.) are rooted in fundamentally racist, sexist, homophobic ideas. [H]ow does that connect to academic writing? [It] connects . . . to how we equip students to think and write about themselves, for themselves, and for others. . . . I am always discovering how my ideas can be so shaped by stereotypes, and even though I struggle to unveil them, they are there, deep inside of me. . . . I just imagine class discussions on these kinds of issues to be fiery sometimes . . . because we will be exposing ourselves.

Other TAs respected Eulie's point, but the debate led them to go out searching, with my blessing and encouragement, to find other nonfiction works and anthologies with which they might feel more comfortable exposing themselves. The nonfiction list grew from seven titles—such as Angelou's (1971) *I Know Why the Caged Bird Sings,* Crow Dog's (1990) *Lakota Woman,* and Rodriguez's (1982) *Hunger of Memory*—to eighteen titles, including Orenstein's (1994) *SchoolGirls,* McBride's (1996) *Color of Water,* and Jordan's (1994) *Technical Difficulties.* The anthology list of five titles—including Bizzell and Herzberg's (1996) *Negotiating Difference* and Massik and Solomon's (1994) *Signs of Life*—grew to a more modest list of eight, with the addition of Colombo, Cullen, and Lisle's (1992) *Rereading America,* Goshgarian's (1996) *Exploring Language,* and Clee and Radu-Clee's (1999) *American Dreams.* I had indeed hoped that this would be the TAs' response. Accordingly, the listserv seemed to coax them from reflection to reflective action.

But the consternation the texts had generated opened the way for further resistance that had to be resolved. A few weeks later—when I brought in the general syllabus and the TAs examined its topical structure, its suggested activities and assignments, and its relevance to the objectives/outcomes document—I felt my position as WPA once again type-casting me as a potential hybrid blunderer/bungler. And once more, Eulie assumed a lead, this time protesting: "Is it fixed? Are we fixed? I see flexibility in the syllabus, the possibility, but yet I was shocked . . . about the implicit explicitness of what we are to teach and how we are to teach it."

Janet chimed in on a similar note, saying: "As an example, as a template, it was fine [but] I was in the process of developing the syllabus I intended to use, was extremely excited about many of the ideas . . . and had to chuck them."

Landi, however, posed another view, saying: "Because this will be my first semester teaching freshman comp, I appreciate the guidelines. . . . I like the way students will be eased into the writing. . . . I can see the influence of many instructors in this syllabus."

Karen, who prided herself on her adaptability (after leading the movement to expand the booklist), saw the general syllabus as a starting point: "I can see areas of value such as the basic structure [shorter activities expanding/synthesizing into three major essays], and I can see areas that I will have to rework to fit my own style. . . . I look at the syllabus [and its suggested assignments] the same way I have been looking at our booklist . . . it's flexible within reason . . . open to negotiation."

Brenda, the group comedienne, quipped: "Interesting compositions about BIG BROTHER and syllabi. I am glad for a syllabus at all that I can extrapolate from, according to my persona/style. Frankly, at this point I don't feel like I could put together a decent syllabus without a prompt."

I wanted to think that this debate would preface another upsurge of reflective action, as had the listserv discussion of textbooks, but later on still—at the culmination of the semester—I discovered that it was not to be. Once the time came for the TAs to start designing a series of their own activities and assignments with which they might begin their first semester of teaching, Brenda balked:

> Looking at the syllabus again in combination with trying to write up an assignment, I realize HELP! I NEED SOMEONE to explain . . . the mechanics of how to do what we are expected to do in the fall. . . . Yes, everyone says, we can borrow assignments from other already established TAs . . . but I still would like to think I could design one on my own. . . . Sorry to vent so, but . . . . the truth is I am still feeling quite unprepared to teach next fall. I am not going to pretend anymore that I am.

Initially, this post looked like a premature attack of natural, preteaching jitters. But if Brenda's cry-for-help/venting is to lead me anywhere nearer to an understanding of blunders, I have to speculate again on the connections Lyotard makes between narration and knowledge. Brenda's post implies a significant revelation about my role in the TAs' community history. Lyotard says that in a community—such as this group of preservice writing teachers who wanted stories of what worked in the classroom—narrative knowledge "certifies itself in the pragmatics of its own transmission without having recourse to argumentation and proof" (27). Just so, no one thought to contest me when I first told the TAs about the objectives/outcomes document. I merely transmitted the story that "this is a guide we will use to help us teach," because the document was, after all, composed by experienced teachers among whom I was one. In like kind, it was entirely acceptable for me to suggest that there was a more effective and less effective way to interpret the document, because a community perceives that narrative knowledge—as Lyotard puts it—"makes someone capable of forming . . . 'good' prescriptive and 'good' evaluative utterances" (18).

Even more acceptable to the TAs was the eventual discussion of critical pedagogy, because embedded in it was what Lyotard identifies as "the narrative of emancipation," which invited the TAs to join in as equals with "knowing intellects and free wills," to work out a kind of consensus through dialogue (60).

Less acceptable was the introduction of the booklist, but because the listserv discussion led to the TAs' movement to expand the booklist themselves, they could "actualize the [emancipatory] narrative" in Lyotard's terms, "by putting themselves into 'play' in their institution" (23). At this point, though, the TAs also seemed to apprehend a change in my role, since there was a material shift away from the kind of text that was currently being used in the program. They must have wondered what I was up to, exactly. Then along came the general syllabus. Even though some of the TAs took this document in stride, several seriously questioned it, and me as the apparent author of it, notwithstanding the contribution of other experienced teachers to its compilation. My position as a knowledgeable narrator, if I interpret Lyotard correctly, became nearly invalid here because for some TAs, the consensus that came out of the listserv discussion of the syllabus might well have seemed, in retrospect, to be a concession to "the system . . . the object of administrative procedures . . . an instrument to be used toward achieving the real goal, which is what legitimates the system—power" (60–61). Accordingly, Brenda might have sensed a "loss of meaning," because, as Lyotard would say, she—as narratee—could no longer *recount herself* through the narrative I'd first presented to the preservice seminar; knowledge in the preservice seminar was, for her, "no longer principally narrative," but a function of a university system, of which I had shown myself to be an agent (23; 26). As a result, she felt too new at the game to write a series of activities and assignments that would pass muster.

Whether or not I'd blundered indeed by changing my role into an oppressive one, some of the TAs at least thought I had. That perception carried weight. And I wasn't sure how to remedy it. A final incident in the preservice seminar lends some unfortunate credibility to my suspicions that I'd blundered/bungled. I learned that the program's computer classroom, which had been destroyed in an earthquake, was going to be reconstructed by the fall term. Much earlier in the semester, I had already told the TAs that they would most likely be teaching one class a week in this facility. When some hedged at my confirmation, I explained it would be a requirement of their training and a part of their inservice seminar that fall. I assured them that they were well-versed enough in technology to have their students use listservs and e-mail, post drafts, and work with word processing. Workshops for more sophisticated techniques, such as Web page teaching, would be offered in the summer as well.

Before the fall semester began, we'd meet in the computer classroom several times, I told them. We'd also meet there weekly all semester to test out different techniques. I would be teaching in the computer classroom too, so we'd all be learning together.

Clark, a former tutor in the writing center, summed up everyone's leery response to my pitch. He recalled our first day of preservice together. I'd handed out a sample in-class assignment that I said the TAs might want to give their students the first week of class. I told them we were all going to write a response to it and then critique our responses in small workshop groups, just as we'd have our students do. Clark said: "I was, as I'm sure many of you, shocked to find Dr. Peters writing our in-class assignment along with us. What a great feeling to know that he was walking along with us down Dante's path. [But] I have yet to be convinced every other class in a computer lab is worth trying."

When I read Clark's post, I no longer felt that he or the others saw me in the same companionable light. Instead, I felt that I had become an elephant in the TAs' living room.

2. A Theater of the Oppressed

Bill Thelin and John Tassoni tell me there's a world of difference between blundering for change (which real, live, fallible people do, even in their best moments) and bungling (which institutions and bureaucracies do for no damned good reason at all, as I see it—just plenty of bad reasons). The problem that I want to reiterate is that the distinction between blundering and bungling gets all mixed up in a WPA's life. Sometimes a WPA is just a person relating to other people whatever he or she thinks is knowledge-worthy in the collective effort to teach young people to write. And sometimes, as Susan Miller (1991) points out, the WPA is an emblem

> endowed with quasi-mystical powers . . . , an authority over the "janitorial" and inconsequential activities required of large numbers of people who do not accept the status of their low-life services . . . , a filter through whom all that is "low," ad hoc, and transient moves, even as this filter represents the [university's] regulating gaze. (168, 172)

In lay terms, that means a WPA is often going to get pegged as a bungler, even if he or she's more of a blunderer. And there are times he might richly deserve it.

In August, three weeks before classes were due to begin, all the assurances that the computer classroom would be ready for training workshops went down the gutter. The classroom might be ready by the first day of class, but who knew? The furniture hadn't even arrived—it was being manufactured at a prison factory (a detail that points to what happens in a society that denies education and jobs to a certain segment of its population). The TAs were still scheduled to alternate class days between teaching in the computer classroom and a regular classroom. However, several full-time faculty wanted to use the facility, too. My own section of comp had not been scheduled in the computer classroom at all. Neither was the TA inservice. I protested to the person in charge of room assignments, who told me that if I wanted all TAs to teach in the computer classroom, I couldn't have the TA inservice or my own class booked there. I'd better choose. I backed off, wondering how the TAs would ever construe my decision as a "sacrifice" in the interest of their professional development. All they'd probably see in this little administrative tiff was an excuse for my own inconsistency and an attempt to justify why I wouldn't be teaching under the same unpredictable techno-conditions as they.

Was that a blunder or a bungle? Whatever it was, it signified effectively that I had left the TAs alone, wandering down Dante's cyberpath without me.

Not much later, I learned that the smart classroom we were expecting had suffered a drop in IQ. In addition to time constraints for installing equipment, administrators had changed their minds about the allotment of funding. No overhead and pull-down screen connected to the instructor's main computer would be available. No RoboTel system would be installed to provide instructors access to any other computer in the room or to flash any student's screen or an instructor's own on all the screens in the room. Instructors also would have no access to the local classroom network from any outside computer, so the TAs could not plant assignments or handouts on the system before coming to class. And no space would be set apart for round-table class discussions because the computers would be arranged in rows. I decided against passing along this information; it would be like flashing a sign that read, "Abandon hope, all ye who enter." Besides, how could I tell the TAs what equipment they *would* have to work with if the administration suddenly made further last-minute cutbacks?

Was that a blunder or a bungle? Again, whatever it was, by keeping silent I effectively kept the TAs from knowing that if they'd planned any activities based on what I'd promised them earlier about the equipment, they'd have to change their tacks. Instead, I knew they'd have to walk into the classroom physically, the first day, to find out what was waiting for them.

When we did meet for our first presemester workshop, I told the TAs about the construction delays and got them to work in groups on their syllabi. I'd asked all to put together a three-week "chunk"—no more—and four of the TAs had already constructed those chunks as Web pages. These TAs looked at me forlornly. Over the summer, they'd participated in a workshop called the "Web Course Project" and now couldn't demonstrate what they'd learned. I felt a gnawing fear in the pit of my stomach that they might not be able to demonstrate what they'd learned to their students, either, if they weren't able to rehearse it in the workshop. But I reasoned with them all (and with myself) that introducing students to the semester's activities did not require technology; it required friendly firmness in conveying the expectations the TAs had about their students' engagement in the course.

Then I broke the news that we'd probably not be able to have any of our inservice meetings in the computer classroom—but that we would concentrate a lot on the pragmatic issues that occur in *every* kind of classroom, regardless of whether technology was available or not. I added that we would be having extra Friday workshops in the computer classroom, as soon as I could develop a schedule.

Was that a blunder or a bungle? Regardless of what it was, the TAs effectively interpreted my spiel, our before-classes meeting, and the projected in-

service seminar as a recycling of what we'd already done—with no new help
for them in this brave new, yet-to-be installed or nailed down world. I could see
it in their facial expressions. I could hear it in their whispered questions to one
another. I could feel it in my own growing sense that I was inextricably complicit with the administration's betrayal of promised readiness and support.

Things worsened. In the opening weeks of the semester, we discovered that
the university computer center had Web server software that would not accommodate the surge in campus-wide activity—it kept shutting down—so neither
the students nor the TAs could get more than the most sporadic access to Web
pages, the Internet, the HyperNews program, e-mail, or listservs. Even when activity occasionally ebbed, we found that none of the TAs' offices contained computers that were ethernet linked, so the TAs could not work on their Web pages
or even read anything the students managed to post, unless they went to another
worksite. One day, a virus got into these computers and ate up WordPerfect and
anything else it found because no antivirus software had been installed. The
college's newly hired, desperately overworked tech assistant had only been able
to rig up a program at the twilight hour on the hard drives of the machines in
the computer classroom, so I couldn't schedule many of the extra Friday workshops I'd hoped to schedule. Instead, the tech assistant had to set aside this time
for the system's maintenance and redesign. The Friday workshops I *did* manage to schedule conflicted with over half of the TAs' extremely busy schedules.
Those workshops amounted to little more than playing with the evolving program on the system. What did I really know about technology, I wondered?
How were my own limitations revealing to me and to others the likelihood that
I'd merely given in to administrative pressures I hadn't fully and critically an-
alyzed or understood? The only thing I knew beyond doubt was that I'd found
myself floundering on the wrong side of what Cynthia Selfe (1998) has repeatedly called "the serious need for professional development and support for
teachers," set against the institutional race to invest itself in technology uncrit-
ically ("Technology and Literacy," *online version*).

At the same time, the quasi-mystical powers to which Susan Miller al-
ludes—powers that I certainly would have liked to locate and use—must have
got snarled up in the techno-maelstrom somewhere. For instance, when I
phoned to see why neither the TAs nor I were at least able to set up class listservs on the university system, no one would reply. When I e-mailed the technology center, the manager told me only faculty could have the privileges I re-
quested; I needed to contact my full-time faculty supervisor, he said. When I
e-mailed him back, saying that I *was* the supervisor—and sent copies of our
discussion to the department chair and the college dean—I got my own privileges to establish a listserv reinstated. But it took three more weeks of memos
to get approval for the TAs to have the same.

Moreover, no responses came back to me when I sent out messages about
the disabled/disabling university server. Although I eventually managed to get
someone on the telephone, my inept yammering didn't connect, very likely because I lacked the techno-language needed to make myself clear. I never told

the TAs of my failed attempts because, frankly, I was embarrassed. Somewhere along the way, I was not picking up the literacy in campus politics that was required to get things done. The one proactive measure I could take at this point was to ask an experienced teacher/staff member from the university writing center to join our listserv, so that she might lend her technological expertise and better understanding of university politics to our discussions. I let the TAs know that Sharon was online with us.

In the midst of all this blundering/bungling—and yes, I am still using the terms ambiguously—the TAs were beginning to form coalitions among themselves. Not only did they trade notes on what one another was doing, but I rarely visited the computer classroom to find one TA alone. At least one other was usually there, facilitating. Although I felt increasingly an outsider among them, I couldn't help but be pleased that these wonderful, smart new teachers were coming into their own and maybe even drawing on some of the knowledge they'd gained from our preservice seminar together. In fact, I was sure they were doing so—and secretly wished they'd realize as much.

The TAs had got past their desire to develop independently as teachers and had fully acknowledged their need for what Lyotard calls "a fabric of relations" where "[n]o one, not even the least privileged among us, is ever entirely powerless" because a teacher's ability to position herself more advantageously in an oppressively chaotic system "is even solicited by regulatory mechanisms, and in particular by the self-adjustments the system undertakes in order to improve its performance" (15). Given the way my blunders had made me a representative of the system to them—a representative who encouraged their collaboration as a survival technique, even while I seemed to exercise a regulatory gaze on that collaboration—I think the TAs felt power and authority being transferred to them: a power that could only constrain them if they transferred it back to me. If this isn't the stuff of satire, I can't think what is.

In the disheartening but darkly comedic situation I've outlined, the listserv took on an increasingly important role: It became the main instrument of reflective action whereby the TAs not only began to affirm and share their growing technological literacy, but started to reconfigure their positions within, and political relations to, the university. Augusto Boal's (1985) theoretical work on a "theater of the oppressed" sheds a clear beam of light on what I'm trying to explain.

The principles of a theater of the oppressed, harmonizing with Freirean teachings, blur the distinctions between performers and spectators. Liberating alternatives to oppressing situations are dramatically imagined, rehearsed, and critiqued as potential strategies. For the TAs, cyberspace turned out to be the best arena for enacting these principles, because it fostered a discourse that, according to Michael Spooner and Kathleen Yancey (1996), demonstrates "multivocality and at the same time create[s] enough coherence that a spectating conversationalist can enter the fray, [and] can discern what the fray is" (273). At the same time, this multivocality led to what Cynthia Selfe and Paul Meyer

(1991) might call ownership of an online discussion, through interpersonal and performative levels of dialogue, which enabled the TAs to participate in what Boal identifies as "simultaneous dramaturgy" (Boal 134; see Landow 1992, 179). That is, the TAs would confer among themselves and then post messages whose effect on others and on the situation "coincide[d] with its enunciation" (Lyotard 9).

Janet initiated the most eye-opening illustration I can give of such principles at work. She started one week by hitting the limits of her patience. She wrote:

> It is now Monday morning and I STILL haven't been able to access . . . the [university] server on the net. And I'm asking my students to access it to confirm reading assignments, post on HyperNews, etc.!!?? Was the Web Course Project designed as a joke? To get all of us to create interactive teaching tools in order to build skills our students need, and then to pull the rug out from under us by not having a system that can support them? I get more angry every day.

Some dialogue on the interpersonal level went back and forth among her and Brenda and Sharon about the possibility of transferring the TAs' Web pages to the server that belonged to the writing center. Sharon hesitated at first, but then persuaded the director of the center to let the TAs do so. Yet this assistance did not fully address the larger problem, as Landi pointed out:

> I've been watching the incoming e-mail messages . . . and it has become apparent that I should not wait for [further] evidence to file a complaint over the inept handling of the Computer Center server. This problem must be dealt with immediately. It's become too frustrating for everyone. . . . Therefore, on [our next inservice meeting date], I will bring a copy of the letter I intend to submit to the network administrator, cc to the [university] President and [the campus newspaper]. I'd like all of you to take a moment to look it over . . . and then . . . out the sucker will go. Any suggestions?

This example of dialogue on the performative level shows how a participant in a theater of the oppressed, in Boal's terms, "assumes the protagonic role, changes the dramatic action, tries out solutions, discusses plans for change— in short, trains [herself and others] for real action" (122). Landi's unfailing pluck got an immediate response from Sharon, who said, "Lodge a complaint with [the campus office of technology services] that the frequency and duration of these outages are interfering with your course work. The more voices, the more clout." I, too, entered the discussion, advising Landi that the first and most politic move would be to address her letter to the department chair, since he had supervised the reconstruction of the computer classroom and might not react well to her going public with the problem, prior to his having a say. I also suggested that it would be very effective if a number of others wrote to the chair. (And if this were another blunder, I thought to myself, at least I might be blundering in the right direction.)

How might the chair perceive the TAs' complaints? Would he think of the complaints as evidence of ineptitude on my part? I had no misgivings that he would. Yet, I suspected that he'd also be gratified by the TAs turning to him. As the person who had ultimately been "in charge" of the computer classroom getting constructed on time, he, I sensed, felt vulnerable to criticism, too, and would be anxious to intervene on behalf of the TAs. My blundering, therefore, could not help but marginalize me further when I referred everyone to the chair—but if he helped us get out of our predicament (if only, perhaps, to avert ground fire in his direction), I'd gladly send my ego out to sea.

The politics of blundering/bungling are astonishingly sticky. The politics of a theater of the oppressed are cleaner. The TAs divided up tasks. Brenda decided to take on the campus technology services. She assembled a group of e-mail messages that she'd received from students just that week. All of the students had told her they'd tried to do an online assignment over the weekend and found the server was down. Brenda sent copies of her e-mail to the director of technology services, his immediate supervisor, and the supervisor's dean. She politely explained the situation, said that faculty and students alike were becoming more concerned, and that it was unfortunate but chairs of departments, deans, and other administrators were growing increasingly aware of the students' and faculty's inability to do their jobs effectively. She wrote:

> As I understand it, there is no one staffed at [the campus tech assistance desk] after hours or weekends so that we can get information as to the status of the server. So whom do we call? . . . I will be forwarding the individual student e-mail complaint messages from my [English course] so you can understand the extent of the problem.

After a delay of a few days, the director of technology services wrote back, saying that his staff had designed a new program to temporarily address the problem with the inadequate server software. Meanwhile his superiors were investigating other kinds of software. He provided a phone number to call a tech operator who would reset the program manually whenever the problem recurred. He answered in doublespeak—no doubt about it—but despite the university's reluctance to invest properly in technological support, this small adjustment cut down the frequency of shut-downs.

Landi and Kurt (another TA who was becoming more vocal in these trying times) wrote pithy letters to the department chair, alerting him to the need for the right server software as well as the need to replace the dead computers in their offices. Sharon—who was rapidly assuming status as a guardian angel—also wrote a friendly and extremely timely note to the chair and me. News had just come to her that the writing center was receiving some extra high-powered, internet-capable equipment. Suddenly, there was a surplus of "20 486 DX computers which are ethernet ready, loaded with WP6.1, Netscape and a few other things. . . . The department or college would have to take care of pick up and installation—we would survey them out to you for record-keeping purposes."

How many did the chair want? The chair contacted the TAs and recruited a couple of them to collect one for every TAs' and part-timers' office. He also began pushing administrators to provide funds for proper server software instead of relying on stopgap remedies.

In such instances, Boal asserts that a theater of the oppressed can transform its participants, "to focus the action according to a single, predetermined perspective" (175). A WPA—even if he or she's perceived as belonging among the oppressors—might help participants realize that their own vision of reality is one that others share, and that through them and with them, "they can intervene in the action. The action ceases to be presented in a deterministic manner, as something inevitable, as Fate. . . . Everything is subject to criticism, to rectification. [T]hey must simply act it out, to give a live view of its consequences and drawbacks" (134, 139). At one of the inservice seminars, I emphasized as much, telling the TAs that their efforts were succeeding because they were educating everyone concerned, letting the administration know that they, as new teachers, only wanted what administrators themselves had promoted: an effective integration of technology and instruction.

At the same time, the listserv gave the TAs the critical narrative structure with which they could develop and know themselves as teachers. That is to say, the TAs used and indeed needed the listserv to "determine criteria of competence and/or illustrate how [the criteria were] to be applied" (Lyotard 1984, 23). Accordingly, the listserv helped them decide where theory, practice, planning, and critical reflection all converged.

One example of this convergence took place later in the semester, when the TAs' activism had born enough palpable results to let them concentrate on what was happening in their classes. Clark heated up the frying pan when he referred to one of the readings I'd assigned. He questioned his classroom application of it: "Bruffee talks of collaborative learning. . . . I actually gave a collaborative project during class today. . . . One of the students mumble[d] under his breath that 'you (the instructor) should do the talking; that's what I pay you for.'"

Vera, a former policewoman, had been worrying quite a bit about how differently each teacher seemed to be functioning and said: "At this stage, we don't need to be convinced to apply group work in our classrooms. We ARE going to do group work. Now, let's get on with how. What I want are some recipes. . . . I want somebody to give me their version of 'this is how to do it.' Step by step by step."

Janet pointedly said: "Why am I spending time reading Bruffee when I need the time . . . for my next hour and fifteen in front of my group? Why am I spending half an hour on a listserv entry when I don't have lesson plans done? . . . It's evident we're all feeling the same concerns. Any answers, Brad? And no, no, no—not more theory!!!"

Eulie added a very different note to the discussion, protesting: "I need pragmatics, too. [But] couldn't it be possible that we, yes we, are experiencing 'social transition . . . crises of identity and authority' [Bruffee (1996) citing Trimbur

94]? [I]sn't it fundamentally good . . . asking for help/community, stealing each other's ideas, having moments of success and . . . making mistakes?"

Eulie's comments opened the way for Brenda to talk about the theory of collaboration, pragmatics, and a moment of success—giving us all a reason to stop short in amazement. Brenda had already moved her class into a collaborative essay. The student groups had voted on topics, researched, written drafts individually and synthesized them, revised, and had then given panel presentations before turning in a final version. She reported:

> Today they finished up their panel presentations. . . . I structured this very similarly to what Brad had us do [in a pre-service project last year]. [O]ne of my students got up with her partner . . . AND she began her presentation with an anecdote: the story of a young high school girl who had been raped. . . . When she finished . . . she said 'and that is *my* story.' Well the class just went deadly quiet. . . . Her partner then gave a litany of cold hard statistics, percentages of rapes per minute, unreported vs. reported, etc. . . . The students had to comment on the panel presentations much like Brad had us do, on our class listserv . . . and another student wrote . . . 'I'm glad you spoke out because now I know that the feelings that I felt were . . . normal among rape victims. . . . I now know that I need to talk about [being raped, too] in order to understand that it wasn't my fault. The best way to come out about it is to first tell my peers and then take the next step forward.

From Boal's perspective, a discussion on the interpersonal level such as the above deals intensively with the group's overarching goals, values, or internal conflicts (134). After the remarkable but nerve-wringing job the TAs had done getting the university to respond to their call for technological support, it relieved me that the discussion had moved to this level for a while. Brenda's post highlighted the way some of the TAs were now developing their narratives of individual, teacherly identity in terms of interpreting and adapting what everyone was exploring collectively. And it was gratifying to see how successfully they were experimenting.

The one thing that alternately alarmed and calmed me was the way they saw my function in it all. On the bad days, I became an antagonist, someone who was withholding vital information from them. On the good days, I became a role model (at least to the extent that some were willing to indicate where the preservice seminar had served them). And if whatever messages I posted in general to the listserv seldom received response, TAs began contacting me regularly off-listserv—or they visited my office. Could it be that they were trying to reconfigure my role as a more benevolent one? If so, a WPA might want to keep in mind that even under the most vexed conditions, there will be opportunities to intervene in the dramatic action of a theater of the oppressed—perhaps as an off-stage consultant, rather than as a director of the action.

Tensions continued, though, and I knew that I often represented a focal point for them. One indication was Brenda's frustration after I told her that legally she could not tell a student to stop coming to class, even if his excessive absences had already guaranteed that he would fail the course. Brenda consulted other comp teachers, full-time faculty, and finally the chair before she accepted what I'd said, spreading the word that I had pronounced a self-contradictory policy by announcing that students should know how absences could seriously hurt their grades. Nonetheless, the more worrisome nature of those tensions did not bare itself fully until one session of the inservice seminar when I'd asked everyone to visit another TA's class and come ready to discuss what helpful and interesting things each had seen.

Discussion was rich. For instance, Janet was teaching her students to set up their own Web pages on topics such as women's suffrage, the industrial revolution, and the Vietnam War. Kurt was getting his class to invent the biography of a superhero to fight some major social problem. Stan's students were visiting developmental writing classes and using Mike Rose's research as a model for analysis. Landi's class was investigating how well the university prepared students for the actual jobs graduates would likely obtain. When we had finished telling and questioning each other about what we'd observed, I asked each TA to take into consideration the variety of things they'd heard. I then asked them to write a brief reflection on what they'd learned about their own boundaries as teachers and how those boundaries had changed since they'd first started that semester. After that, I asked all of them to read what they'd written.

Once Vera read hers aloud, I was unable to hear what anyone else had to say. She wrote:

> I have seen that I feel screwed in regards to my training as a TA—I don't feel I was prepared this semester to teach. . . . I feel that this is unacceptable. I also feel that it would be unacceptable to take this out on my students. It is not their fault I wasn't trained properly. I have come to the conclusion that someone has to suffer here. I can teach insufficiently based on how I was trained, and then the students suffer. Or I can bend over backwards, and work my ass off to give them 100 percent of what I can give them despite my lack of training. Then I suffer. What I have learned about my own boundaries is that when I take on a commitment—any commitment, but especially one that has other people relying on me—it is part of my self-expression as a human being to take the suffering on myself. I cannot do it and I will not do it any other way.

It must have been that Vera was still feeling concerned about how differently everyone was teaching from her, even though she had no reason to believe she was off-base in any way. But when the inservice session ended that particular day, I can't remember if there was any after-class talk to that effect. I went home in a thick fog, unable to think or see straight.

Memories remain long and sharp when a WPA has been perceived as a blunderer/bungler. It follows that whenever a WPA has been so perceived, and the people who work with him/her are feeling insecure about their job performance, there may be an inevitable tendency on their part to identify the

WPA as the source of their problems. How close to the truth does such a perception come? I can't say. Unless a different kind of thinking gets in its way, bungling begets blundering begets bungling begets a wrenching perpetuity. It all becomes extremely painful for everyone involved.

As Amy Goodburn and Carrie Leverenz (1998) assert, WPAs must learn how "to foreground the inevitable resistance and conflict that result [from blundering and bungling] and to make critical reflection about that resistance as much a part of the program as a new syllabus or new teacher training" (289). A WPA must also try "to put educational decisions in the hands of the teachers and students who will live with them" (85). Merely naming these fair-minded practices is easy. Living with them is not. That's why the TAs' listserv discussions became so crucial. At first, the discussions provided practice ground for living with a critical pedagogy and learning how to exercise it. Then, as the TA training moved forward with its moments of blundering and bungling—sometimes caused by me, sometimes caused by institutional and social forces, sometimes caused by the TAs themselves—the listserv *had* to become the site where the participants could articulate their problems and find the wherewithal to resolve those problems.

I will take credit for doing my best to preserve the integrity of the listserv as such a site, where such important activity could take place. It frequently seemed that my only acceptable role was to let the listserv discussion move forward without me sounding my horn, despite my desire to speak up, justify, and defend myself. I couldn't interfere with the practice I felt the TAs needed to have, as they discovered how to assert their agency in the academic world. Accordingly, I think this approach allowed the listserv to function as one of the most powerful, illuminating, distressing, and unpredictable elements of that year's training. And all told, it turned out to be pretty interesting, too. Gail Hawisher and Pat Sullivan (1998) never spoke more truly than when they observed that we have much to discover about "the online environment as a new social and political location" (173).

Given my druthers, I would have preferred to learn as much without drawing such good, thoughtful people into the muddle with me. But a critical pedagogy is nothing if it does not make room for finding the ways and reasons to forgive and try again—blundering better as we go.

7

C-Words

Classroom, Contact, Conflict, Collaboration,
Consolidation, Colonizing, Colonialism

Frances B. Singh

1. The Incident in the Classroom

Blunders. I've come across a lot of those and added to the heap during the course of a teaching life that began a year after CUNY adopted Open Admissions in the early seventies. As the teaching tape unwinds in my head, the tape pauses in Spring 1985 when I am a tenure-track assistant professor at Hostos Community College in the South Bronx teaching a low-level ESL class. As I review that incident fifteen years later, I can see now that it was one of those pedagogic blunders which, given the circumstances of my life, was just waiting to happen. Even more importantly, it started a set of reflections going on the nature of pedagogic blundering and the implications of blundering for the teacher who is a student of herself, though hopefully not a navel-gazer.

The blunder announced itself as Everyteacher's worst nightmare: a fight in the classroom. The room in which the incident occurred was rather congenial. Students from classes earlier that day had left it clean. It was large enough for thirty students to shift their chairs and work in collaborative formations. It had two chalkboards and good ventilation. There were windows which gave you, to the north and south, a view of the Bronx's wide Parisian boulevard, the Grand Concourse. To the west, you got a slice of the Le Courbousier's George Washington Bridge and a wedge of Columbia Presbyterian Hospital, that fortress-like pile that stands, like Donne's Truth, "on a huge hill, cragged, and steep." Beyond you could see the Palisades of New Jersey, the beginning of the U.S. landmass.

I liked the room that had been assigned to this class. It evoked things I loved, like Paris and modernist architecture and the poetry of John Donne. And particularly because I was teaching an ESL class, I appreciated the fact that I could see New Jersey, too. In my mind, New Jersey was more than a state. It was a figure of speech, a metonymy by which a part stood for the whole. The whole, of course, was the United States. This was a room with a view, indeed. What scope I had to effect change! As the child of immigrant parents, I had been put in speech classes in elementary school because my accent was not American enough. As an academic in India, I had to seek clearance from the Ministry of Education in New Delhi in order to teach because as an American passport holder, I wasn't Indian enough. Personal experience had made me acutely aware of the negative polarity of the education/politics nexus, and I imagined this room as the site where I was going to change that orientation.

Back in the early eighties, the buzzwords were *community* and *construct*. The class was defined as a community of learners who constructed knowledge, who could construct knowledge because knowledge itself was a social construct. The students were, to use Kenneth Bruffee's (1984) memorable phrase, "a community of knowledgeable peers: equals" (644). Ergo, the teacher's responsibility was to use classroom space so that it potentiated the development of knowledge.

So at Hostos sometime around 1985, the discrete grammar-based syllabus was suspended. We were told to give up our teacher-centered ways of teaching, become student-centered, and consider ourselves "facilitators." We were told that students who work collaboratively in small groups learn to develop ideas and organizational strategies as they put together the pieces of knowledge that they had brought to and on the table. We were told that collaborative learning brought individuals together, and that this coming together led to sharing, and consciousness-raising, and consensus-building, all of which would empower or enable our students to take control of their lives and effect social change.

I felt like I was at the epicenter of national change. In reality, since the Freierian pedagogy we adopted gave students voice and awareness but didn't give ethnicity and gender their due as elements in classroom dynamics, the stage was being set for the blunder that took place.

The books that were prescribed for the course didn't tell you how or prove that a composition produced through the methodology of collaborative learning would transform society, but the spate of books that glutted the textbook market and espoused this connection left no doubt that this pleasing but theoretical cause-and-effect relationship had been accepted by large numbers of faculty in composition and ESL (Mincock 1994, 154–155) as a magic bullet against previous pedagogies that focused on students' lacks, or saw knowledge as so many pieces of information to be deposited in the student, or regarded students themselves as assembly-line products of GE (General Education). I suppose it was just assumed in the mid-eighties that classes would function in the same way that rowboats cut through water, by a continuously smooth and synchronized pulling of the oars, everyone working together for a common good and common goal.

No workshops were offered and there were no teacher guides or textbook caveats about taking into account large cultural determinants like ethnicity and gender, so it is only with 20/20 hindsight that I could say that the situation that developed in my ESL classroom could have then been avoided through teacher training apparatuses. Nor were there any teacher narratives/ethnographies out that problematized this new approach, showing that in the crucible of the classroom, the collaborative learning methodology sometimes led to students' exhibiting behaviors not just hostile but aggressive and offensive in the norming and socializing context of the classroom; they, too, came later (Friedman 1985, 203–205; Culley 1985, 212–213; Jarratt 1991, 111–112; Payne 1994, 103–108; Miller 1998, 16–17). In fact, for a long time, I thought that the story of the fight that erupted in my class was mine alone, too personal to have relevance to other instructors. Nobody realized then that between the collaboration and the composition would fall the shadow, that eight-letter *c*-word, *conflict*.

What a change, I think, *from what I've been used to. Here I am, only two years back in New York after nine years of teaching in India where I lectured standing on a dais and students stood up when I entered the room and remained silent and immobile during the class period. There, the classroom reproduces the colonial paradigm in which the one who is deemed to know has status, authority, and power, where the gaze of the one in power takes in all, where the others are subordinate because they are deemed lacking in knowledge; here is the classroom democratized, where the others are granted status, authority, and power, in a nutshell, voice, and the one who was historically deemed the one who knows now serves those historically denied access to higher education.*

I think: *ideologically, this latter scenario is very appealing. First, it is a translation and implementation of democratic American principles in accordance with the civil rights movement that had shaped my teens and twenties. Second, it is a translation and implementation of the Gandhian principles that I had come to know during the ten years I spent in India, that partnership can only be called such if it is based on equality and the voices of the historically mute need to be undumbed, heard, and taken into account. Third, now I am in a position, thanks to this pedagogy, to unite two parts of my own history and do my bit, in my own little sphere of influence—the classroom—to dethrone a colonial model that privileges the sight of one individual and is predicated on inequality and to replace it with a structure that privileges voices from the community and is predicated on equality. Ah,* I think, *ah, my America, ah, my newfoundland, thanks, for giving me this opportunity.*

In my euphoria, I had forgotten that both the civil rights movement and the struggle for Indian independence were a series of confrontations and conflicts.

The students, all thirty of them, in the low-level ESL course I was teaching in the spring 1985 semester were all Spanish-dominant. There might have been a few from Ecuador or Salvador, but the bulk of the class—let's say, twenty-six students—were evenly split between two birth places, the Dominican Republic and Puerto Rico. Like all classes at Hostos, this one was predominantly female, but there was at least one Dominican and one Puerto Rican male in the classroom.

Educationally speaking, they were quite homogeneous. Most of them had dropped out of school in their native countries in their teens, the men to take up jobs, the women because they became mothers. According to the deficit model of education, they were lacking in Spanish reading and writing skills, study skills, numeracy, cultural literacy, academic etiquette: in short, all the knowledge a student acquires as a result of a traditional education.

In terms of their social background, most of the students had family responsibilities. A lot of the women worked after school. Others sold Avon products. They were having a difficult time juggling the demands of home, school, and work. They differed, I think, from many other nontraditional students in having high self-esteem. They took pride in their appearance and their apartments and their children. They were proud of being Dominican or Puerto Rican. They believed, too, that they could "make it" in America if they kept on trying and struggled. They believed in themselves; they believed in the American Dream.

This is a class in which the focus is on writing, and there is a composition to be begun in class today based upon some material that has been previously covered. I cannot now say what the specifics of that material were, but I do not think that it was exceptional. Most low-level ESL reading matter tends to be innocuous. Banal or boring rather than incendiary would probably describe the material that would be serving the students as a springboard for their own writing.

Okay, I say, *today we're going to start working on a composition based upon the material we finished reading in the textbook. Before you write your individual compositions, you are going to work in groups so your classmates can give you feedback and help you develop your ideas and vice versa. So let's begin by forming small groups so you can talk about the material and share your thoughts and point of view.*

I have set the stage in motion for collaborative learning, for community empowerment through classroom dynamics.

Chairs scrape, irregularly shaped circles appear. Books open to the chapter in question as the groups warm to the task. In some groups the students are taking turns reading the material while in others they are talking. One group is already exchanging pieces of paper, though I can't tell what is written on them. Avon orders? Verb forms? Supporting details? Vocabulary? In Spanish? In English? Standing off to the side, literally de-centered, I feel good about what I am looking at: communities, collaborating, critiquing. Time passes. I circulate among the groups, facilitating by offering suggestions regarding vocabulary, writing small notes to improve organization, responding to grammar questions. I do not see myself as authoritarian though I am no longer off to the side and am clearly regarded as the one-who-knows.

Does the origin of the blunder lie in the mismatch of my self-perception and their perception of me?

The class period is eighty minutes, and after about thirty minutes I say: *Okay, group work time now is over. Let's have quick oral reports on what you discussed and accomplished today in your groups.* I am feeling pretty good about this whole process and the way the class had gone because everything had gone according to theory. The groups had formed after I had told the students to get into groups. There had been discussion and sharing, reading and writing in the groups. It had seemed to me that the students were focused and had concentrated on the assigned activity. True, I was a little concerned that more Spanish had been used in class than I would have liked, and the writing, despite my feedback, was still qualitatively unsophisticated and the same grammatical errors kept on appearing, but *it's okay: learning to write, writing to learn in a communal, collaborative setting takes time, takes even more time when the writing to be generated is in another language, maybe when the act of writing is itself another language. Focus on the engagement that took place, the way the students interacted with each other to construct meaning. Their collaboration, their writing mattered to them. Did you not see how they were. . . .*

And then all hell breaks loose. A shouting match erupts between the Puerto Rican male and the Dominican male, both of whom are in the same group. They are trading insults (in Spanish) of a political and sexual nature. This is the gist that I remember. The Dominican called Puerto Rico a U.S. colony and said that Puerto Ricans were under the U.S. thumb whereas Dominicans were independent. The Puerto Rican told the Dominican that for an independent country the Dominican Republic had been invaded a lot and asked why more and more Dominicans were coming to New York if they were so independent.

As the class is over for the day, the other students walk away from the arguing men. I watch the men leave the classroom and take their dispute to the Grand Concourse. For a few minutes the fight becomes physical and disrupts traffic on the wide Parisian boulevard I am so fond of. I do not remember how the pair is separated, but the police are not called. The two students come to class the next day. I never discuss the incident with them or with the other members of that group, and I never again do group work with this class.

My overt response to the incident was classic: total denial that it ever happened. Looking back on the incident, I realize now that while the students could have been hauled up on disciplinary charges, it was actually I who had acted inappropriately in the pedagogical context. The students were using an alternative discourse to say that something had happened in the class that had stung them to the quick, and I, who was supposed to analyze and reflect and had been on the receiving end of the educational apparatus as well, denied their discourse. I refused to probe the causes of the fight, to examine its meaning for them and for me. I'm not a bad teacher. I don't cut my classes or give multiple choice tests. I don't inflate grades. But on that occasion, I was a very bad teacher for I denied my pedagogic responsibility to examine students' responses to a classroom situation that I had created.

In my own defense, I can only say that I was quite shaken up by the confrontation. Its rapid escalation into a fistfight on a major arterial road of New York City was frightening. I was afraid for the students and afraid for myself as an untenured faculty member who needed that job. But it was more than self-interest that rendered me passive and quiet. I felt betrayed by a theory of critical pedagogy. I had set up a scenario for empowerment, and it had generated instead a display of power that left me feeling angry and powerless. Where was Paulo Freire when I needed him? I had, I thought, decentered myself, been a facilitator rather than an authority figure, treated the students with respect, and my "reward" for implementing this aspect of critical pedagogy was a verbal and physical confrontation and a feeling that as a woman, I was being put in my place, told that I had no authority to tell men what to do. The room with a view had turned into a site of betrayal.

What had or hadn't I done that these students felt unable to resolve difference except through coming to blows? No book I had read about group work in the classroom community mentioned conflict; struggle was external to the classroom. This fight was not supposed to have taken place, and it did, in a classroom that I had self-consciously set up according to the socially and politically correct paradigm, to construct knowledge and meaning, to implement and practice collaboration and community, to transform society. To borrow another memorable phrase, this time from the anthropologist James Clifford (1988), something went very wrong in my "scriptorial workshop" (25). Later, if not sooner, I knew that I would have to reflect on this incident. Why did it happen? Could it have been prevented? What pedagogic value did it have? What were the students telling me that I needed to hear? In the form of these questions, the incident became a permanent resident of my mind and acquired a legitimacy it did not have earlier.

2. The Classroom: Community or Contact Zone?

Community as a pedagogic principle is directly related to open admissions as a higher education policy (Gale 1996, 7–8). It was the way by which colleges sought to meet the educational needs of the great numbers of students who came from diverse backgrounds and were now in the classrooms. Indeed, open admissions led to the setting up of many *community* colleges, one of them being Hostos Community College, where I have been teaching since 1983. Put another way, community has always been a highly politicized concept, one which supports, nurtures, valorizes identity politics, one whose goal is to provide a model of a functioning, complexly plural American society. But because *community* as a keyword carries no negative connotations, and in academia the term *politics* is associated with decisions made for the wrong reasons and conflict with dysfunctional behavior, many teachers prefer not to think about the close connection between community and politics for fear that the negativity of *politics* will contaminate the beauty of *community* (Harris 1989, 15). So when teachers structure a class according to the community model, there is a strong tendency for a "do-good" feeling to overwhelm the critical consciousness that the teaching of English is a politically charged activity, as explosive as a land mine. I suspect, too, that Freire's (1970) influential and demonizing characterization of teachers who do not teach according to his political ideology as "steerers, conquerors and invaders" has ironically contributed to the lulling of the critical consciousness (155). So terrifying is the portrait that many in our ranks — by many, I mean others like me — chose to focus on the sweeter elements in his pedagogy and downplay the harsh role of politics in consciousness shaping.

Fifteen years ago I had a scorching experience in a classroom at Hostos because my understanding of the political base on which the pedagogic concept of community rests was rather naïve. Filtered through images and developed through black and white contrast, I saw a beautiful and distant goal: Donne's Truth. The truth of the matter was that I was imposing rule through methodology *(Okay, class, form groups and share; Okay, class, now group time is over)*. I hadn't calculated the resistance the pedagogy would provoke, though looking back, it seems obvious that when you put a teacher who comes from one background together with students who come from another in the same classroom, you are creating a potentially unstable brew of subjectivities (Weiler 1988, 125). Given that knowledge is socially constructed, that race and gender shape people's ways of creating meaning and responses and expressing authority, why not a fight on the Grand Concourse in response to a classroom strategy? If, for example, I — and this *I* is a white female — regard the classroom as a site for implementing pedagogic strategies that foster cooperation and offer an alternative to competition and dictatorship, but I have students who don't perceive cooperation in the classroom setting as a good and competition and authoritarian rule as no-nos, and who are not accustomed to women being in positions of authority, then there is bound to be conflict between me and them. But what appears so logical to me now didn't appear at all in my mind in spring 1985.

In retrospect, the spectacle — the verbal confrontation, the fistfight — was a wake-up call to reexamine my self-representation and the pedagogy I was employing. I had thought I was validating the students' knowledge and meaning-making powers by decentering myself and having them form groups; the two men, however, may have perceived the arrangement as a denial of their identities as politically independent and gendered subjects. I would say now that in orchestrating the disposition of people I was acting like a minor Prospero, but this being the post-colonial world, I was no longer in control of the situation. My students were more conscienticized than I thought they were or maybe even wanted them to be; I was less so. Shakespeare's Prospero caused a tempest; I was the recipient of one.

Their response suggests to me that what I was calling community was, from the two students' point of view, code for colonialism. As Edward Said (1993) has noted in *Culture and Imperialism,* colonialism is about implanting territorial settlements, and what was I doing if not forcing them to live in particular settlements by working in small groups in the classroom? You could even say that the fight that erupted between two members of my *polis* was between two versions of cultural history: the culture of the North American (classroom), the culture that I was imposing (the community model, felt as Yankee colonialism), and their cultures, the histories of the places they came from, one of which has commonwealth status but was perceived as a colony, the other of which was independent but had been invaded a number of times by the United States and looks to it for economic well-being even as it cherishes its independence.

The political language of the fight made it very clear to me that for the two students the imposition of community was politically unacceptable in that it locked or inscribed them into regressive historical narratives of their birthplaces. Subsequently, I came to construe the fight as an act by which they attempted to liberate themselves from the history into which I had written them. By saying this, I do not mean to glorify their violence, only to show that the ideal of the classroom as harmonious community, of a pedagogy that puts emphasis on resistance to imposed practices, and of the power of human agency to produce new meaning, has its limitations as a strategy for teachers and students and needs to be supplemented by teaching practices that allow for the exercise of authority (Friedman 1985, 206–208; Weiler 1988, 120; Jarratt 1991, 113). It needs to be recognized that while we may support disruption as a narrative strategy by which the disempowered can talk back or find voice or break into a dominant structure (Ritchie and Boardman 1999, 600), disruption actualized as a physical and verbal fight, while also a strategy for talking back, achieving voice, breaking into a dominant structure, is, in a practical sense, a counterproductive classroom mechanism.

The classroom is always a site of conflict, a "contact zone" rather than a community, the ESL classroom particularly so. The phrase "contact zone" is Mary Louise Pratt's (1991). It describes the space where "cultures meet, clash, and grapple with each other, often in contexts of highly asymmetrical relations of power" (34). Conflict is intrinsic to the contact zone. Pratt uses words like "clash," "grapple," and "oppositional discourse" to describe some of the ways conflict is perceived, experienced, or manifested in the contact zone, and I had all three in my classroom.

Contact zone theory offers an explanation for what happened in that ESL classroom that takes gender into account as well. I had, of course, two male students with strongly developed political sensitivities. Each considered the other's place of birth to be dominated by the U.S. Colonialism is a form of domination; in the iconography of colonialism, the ruled are frequently presented as women or in some way feminized. The two male students were now being placed in a setting that assumed and demanded collaboration and sharing. These are the nonhierarchical, counter-hegemonic bedrock principles of feminist teaching, and the male students, who came from male-dominant cultures, may have picked up the nonpatriarchal vibes and felt uncomfortable with the sexual politics I was projecting. Could it be that a relationship of coequality was now insidiously stripping them of their maleness and their culturally sanctioned male prerogative to act independently? Thus, the demand for group work by a female American teacher appears to have been perceived as a powerful sexual affront that had to be resisted—and was—by a display of machismo. The combination of the sexual with the politics caused the fight to break out, explains its intensity, and perhaps, explains why the Hispanic women in the class did not get involved. (The group work was threatening the men's sexual identity and status, not theirs.) By fighting, could it be that they were asserting their maleness and their male power in order to prove that they had not been colonized, i.e., feminized, by a female?

Perhaps, too, because I was demanding that they generate a composition that was informed and correct (according to the level), they may have seen me as a masculine woman, who had discarded the traditional nurturing mother-schoolteacher persona and appropriated the role of the stern father-disciplinarian-professor. Thus, the fight that broke out could also be explained in psychological terms. The male students were expressing their anger over the loss of teacher as the nurturing mother and her self-displacement and reappearance as stern father-professor (S. Miller 1991, 47), and their fear of being perceived as female by an act of verbal and physical violence. Sexual crossovers, mothers into fathers, men into women, women into men, particularly symbolic and culturally transgressive ones, are inevitably sources of anxiety, and anxiety begets conflict. I had opened a Pandora's box.

The above explanation makes sense to me, situated as I am as a female, fifty-something American academic who knows some theory and has taught abroad, but since this moment of discord took place in the mid-eighties, I have deliberately used tentative language for conjecturing meaning out of it. Indeed, by my waiting so long to probe the incident, it has attained a kind of ghostly status in my mind, compounding the blunder. Substance is now shadow, and I have gotten myself into the meretricious position of reconstructing a scenario whose authenticity cannot be questioned except by me. Hence, the use of tentative, qualifying language to analyze the incident. Since I cannot go backwards and undo the incident, this speech that acknowledges that the analysis does not take into account of perspectives of others is the closest I can come to saying "*mea culpa.*"

If my reading of the incident does make sense, though, it offers a cautionary message to those who consider themselves critical pedagogues. It is: To what end are you putting collaborative methodology? Critical pedagogy would say that the end is in some way related to transforming capitalist society, but to tell the truth, despite my rhetorical bluster, my end was quite supportive of capitalistic structures. I wanted my students to learn English so that they would be able to get decent jobs and housing and enjoy the benefits of material success. I thought that a nonauthoritarian collaborative methodology would create the right environment for this learning to take place. But instead I tapped into deep and vital cultural "stuff" that two students found impossible to deal with constructively through the medium of the English language. According to my reading of the incident, frustrated by the socio-political structure foisted on them, they forsook English altogether and resorted to body language in order to restore themselves to a sense of power and pride in their most fundamental identities.

And they rent the veil off my illusions, forcing me to see them as they construed themselves. They forced me to recognize that their hostile, aggressive, and intimidating behavior was personally crucial, culturally, and politically meaningful. However, given that their purpose in taking the course was to learn English and that I was supposed to be helping them meet this goal, this particular class where the teacher got taught and the taught were the teachers, benefited me more than them.

There have to be better ways for this lesson to be taught.

3. Conflict and Consolidation

If the problem with the community model is that conflict is unpresented, the problem with conflict in contact zone theory is that it requires further problematization. Pratt acknowledges that conflict in the classroom puts all students' "ideas and identities on the line," causing all of them to experience rage, incomprehension, pain, suffering and horror, and the hostility of others. But as Pratt feels that the benefits of contact—"moments of wonder and revelation, mutual understanding, and new wisdom"—outweigh the disadvantages, she calls for the development of the pedagogical arts of the contact zone, one of which she identifies as collaborative work (38–40). In other words, Pratt assimilates community into her model, making collaborative endeavor one of the pedagogical arts of the contact zone and seeing it as site where learning is maximized.

Most of the articles in *College English* that describe classrooms that function as contact zones present the students' interactions with each other and their professors in positive terms. Students' conflicts lead, in the end, to better understanding and mutual respect (see Soliday 1994; Lu and Horner 1998). But there are also a number of studies of writers in collaborative settings that suggest that conflict is not helpful and can become detrimental "if it escalates beyond initial causes, takes on a life of its own, drains a group of needed energy, or motivates any of the involved parties to try to destroy the other" (Wall, Galanes, and Love 1957, 33). Wall, Galanes, and Love also make the interesting observation that while groups that reported very little conflict did not necessarily produce higher-quality outcomes, the 120+ participants in their study nonetheless regarded conflict as bad and a form of dysfunctional behavior (52).

In the same vein, Geoffrey Cross' (1994) ethnographic study of a corporate work group whose task was to produce a letter revealed that this group, composed of highly literate and well qualified professionals, ended up taking more than two months to generate an unsatisfactory letter because the members of the group suffered from miscommunication regarding the delegating of writing tasks, lack of communication with top-level management, and the absence of a high-ranking executive in the group who would have provided leadership. They had different perceptions of audience and didn't want to give up their versions of the letter, while the process of working together also brought gender differences to the surface. Cross' conclusion is that "a conflict over ideas can enhance group-writing processes, but . . . that for this conflict to be productive, it must occur in an environment that fosters sound decision making. This environment includes (a) functional communication channels, (b) groups unanimously committed to the project and well equipped with rhetorical and linguistic strategies, and (c) a culture that capitalizes on dissensus" (133).

This research on conflict in writing groups, though done in the business world and based on participants who were white, well-educated, and middle-class, sheds light on conflict in the contact zone that is the classroom, even when the students in that classroom are diverse and nontraditional. The point is that conflict is productive only when certain factors come into play, and even then, even when it leads to a quality product, it is still regarded as a form of dysfunctional behavior.

If I had known then what I know now about conflict in small groups/collaborative settings and its relationship to quality outcome, I would not have implemented it in my ESL class, for the odds were against the conflict becoming productive. If the professionals working on the letter felt that the absence of a top-level executive in the group handicapped them, didn't I handicap my students by limiting my involvement and the nature of my communication? If a homogenous group of professionals had gender-related problems, shouldn't I have anticipated a serious gender-related problem in my classroom since the males in my classroom would not have been used to an order-giving female, perhaps even construing her as an aberration, a masculine woman? If highly literate professionals with rhetorical and linguistic strategies at their disposal weren't all committed to the project and couldn't pull along together, why should I have expected students with very limited English and antagonistic cultural histories to be able to work together? If successful collaboration requires "a culture that capitalizes on dissensus," whatever I knew about my students' background should have warned me to test the waters before making them work collaboratively. A taste for dissensus is an acquired one, and students who have had limited contact with books, newspapers, and schools, who did not grow up with religious, ethnic, or gastronomic diversity, are going to have trouble functioning positively in an environment that sees dissensus as an engine of growth. No wonder that the land mine I had planted in the form of a collaborative methodology caused two students to come to blows.

The blunder, then, was not the fight between the two students but the moves that led up to it and my inability to see or use it as an opportunity for growth at the time. I was naïve and simple-minded with respect to history, gender, and ethnicity issues. I wanted to "do good" *for* my students rather than *with* my students (Freire 1970, 33), with the result that I felt betrayed and hurt when the "reward"

I got for my effort was a fight. I imposed a colonial paradigm thinking that I was liberating them from one. I demanded that they work in collaborative settings for which neither they nor I was ready. Because I denied the fight, it took a long time before I saw that it was a mode of discourse, a strategy through which the students were communicating important matters to me about themselves and their self-representations. That denial led to the incident becoming a ghost in my mind, a shadow whose substance can never be fully reclaimed or recovered.

Had I broached the incident in the next class, however, I wonder how well I would have been able to teach this conflict. Would I have been able to exercise authority so that the discussion did not get out of hand? Would the male students have listened to me? As a female and a North American, to what extent would/could I have been able to divest myself of my culture/gender blinkers and dispassionately listen to their presentation? And how productive would it have been to teach this conflict, anyway? Critical pedagogy tells me that exploring conflict, contending with words, is the "starting point for creating a consciousness in students and teachers through which the inequalities generating those conflicts can be acknowledged and transformed" (Jarratt 1991, 119), but unless prepared for and handled skillfully, with respect for the students' expressed desires, couldn't this kind of teaching generate more heat than light and become the opposite of education, namely indoctrination?

In "Work, Class, and Categories: Dilemmas of Identity," Shirley Brice Heath (1996) recounts that when a group of black low-level female employees at a Midwestern university were denied a wage increase during a period of fiscal exigency, they asked for and got a special literacy course instead. The course was taught at the university according to Freirian pedagogy, but when the instructor suggested that they press the university for job-related improvements, they rejected the idea, saying they were content with their work situation and just wanted to be able to meet and share their thoughts and feelings with each other. Saying "no, not for me," these workers rejected their instructor's political orientation. They didn't see the classroom as a site for resistance and revolutionary struggle but as a place where they could develop their expressive skills and a sense of community. This was agency enough for them.

The moral of the story is clear. If we respect our students and believe in their critical consciousness, their ability to articulate their goals and their understanding of the world, then we need to listen to them. We should not assume that because they are nontraditional or minorities, they don't know what they want. We should not push them in a certain direction because we believe an ideology based on opposition and resistance is somehow superior to a position that does not challenge the status quo. The reaction that I generated suggests a pedagogy based upon an ideology that fosters resistance to capitalistic structures can be as coercive as that which it is trying to replace (Newkirk 1997, 90).

I think it behooves us to problematize critical pedagogy. Richard Miller (1998) is on the right track when he says that although we think of ourselves as liberators, the fact is that we are primarily "functionaries of the administration's educational arm" (18). Rather than deny our primary role, we should fill it intelligently; as Miller says, teach the students to succeed in business and get them to think about the effects of discriminatory business practices (25). Miller's pragmatic approach might make Freire roll over in his grave a few times, but after thirty years, isn't *Pedagogy of the Oppressed* due for an update?

At the risk of proving that fools do indeed rush in where angels fear to tread, I want to begin the revisionary process by revisiting the concept of "banking." Freire presented banking as a completely top-down process. It didn't take into account all the kinds of thinking people do while listening, and it didn't acknowledge that teachers use narrative and explanatory strategies to present their positions. My sense is that educational banking is a far more complicated transaction than what Freire made it out to be, and that there is something called good banking that pays the students compound interest in later life.

When I was in elementary school, our principal Mr. Karow made all students in the fourth, fifth, and sixth grades learn the Great Documents of American History by heart. He came around personally to each class to hear every single student recite, in whole or in part, those documents—Patrick Henry's speech to the House of Burgesses ("Give me liberty or give me death."), Daniel Webster's on the preservation of union ("liberty and union, now and forever, one and inseparable"), Abraham Lincoln's Gettysburg Address and Second Inaugural, and so on. This was clearly education according to the banking model, but much good came out of it. Here are some of the things I learned. 1) Vocabulary. Even now, I remember some of those words and the straightforward definitions Mr. Karow provided for them. *Supine*—flat on your back. *Self-evident*—plain as the nose on your face. *Inalienable*—can't be taken away from you. 2) Rhythm and cadence. Those dead white males are behind many a paper I've written. 3) The ability to speak in public. That's a useful quality in one who chooses to profess English. 4) Critical thinking skills. In order to be able to speak them eloquently, we first had to grapple with the ideas contained in those documents.

To those who would argue that Mr. Karow was indoctrinating us, I will only say that it was he who got me out of the speech classes I was routinely put into because I sounded "foreign." Through the example of Mr. Karow, I learned that a good banker really cares and takes tremendous personal interest in students. I believe that we all have stories of teachers like Mr. Karow, and I believe that by pooling these stories we can come up with a positively nuanced depiction of the educational banker.

About ten years before the incident in the ESL classroom took place, my husband and I were living in Shillong, the capital of Meghalaya, a state in Northeast India. We were on good terms with the Deputy Commissioner (the "DC") and his wife, and one Friday Vinay called us up and asked if we would like to go with him and Anita and spend the weekend in a small and remote but very picturesque village called Nongstoin where he had to attend to some minor administrative matter. We said yes with alacrity and were soon picked up by a Jeep. The village was indeed lovely, and I will never forget the sight of wild horses on a cliff rearing themselves on their hind legs and our Saturday picnic, but what I remember most from this trip to Nongstoin is a missing section of road.

"You see," said Vinay, who as the DC knew about these things, "the road was laid down directly on the ground so there was nothing to hold it in place. When the rains came, it just got washed away. A road only stays put if consolidation is done beforehand." I had seen women making gravel by chipping away at boulders while other men and women carried the chips on their heads in large flat baskets that were subsequently overturned and smoothed into place on road-building construction sites in many places in India, so I realized that the term *consolidation* referred to this critical preliminary of gravel-packing and placement.

For me, the story of the missing stretch of road on the way to Nongstoin, missing because of lack of basic consolidation, holds a clue as to why collaborative learning in classrooms imagined both as communities as well as contact zones doesn't always take place. A road won't stay in place unless there is something that has been consolidated beneath it. By the same token, new learning will not stick in a student's mind unless there has been consolidation of prior knowledge. Students such as the two I had in my ESL classroom—and there are many such in the community colleges of New York City—had not had the cognitive equivalent of gravel deposited or banked in them by a good, caring banker, and I did not address their needs, either. Lacking the foundation and the preparation, the prerequisites required for successful collaboration, i.e., functional communication channels, unanimous commitment to the project, excellent rhetorical and linguistic strategies, an appreciation for dissensus, the collaborative scenario self-destructed on the Grand Concourse. It was washed away, like the missing stretch of road on the way to Nongstoin, and I was left feeling the way I looked by the time we reached Nongstoin—dirty—because consolidating, banking, had not taken place.

4. Colonizing and Colonializing

At the end of the twentieth century, no teacher wants to consider that the pen with which she writes grades in her roll book or on opscan sheets destined for a Registrar's Office cuts a swath worthy of a finely-tempered sword, killing some, sparing some, wounding others, some seriously and some hardly at all. At the end of the twentieth century, no U.S. teacher wants to consider herself a colonialist imposing her practices and her knowledge on those over whom she has power. So she makes the class student-centered to show that she is not a colonialist, but in the process she abdicates her colonizing function, which I see as the settling and consolidation of matter and ideas.

Students who have immigrated here from countries as diverse as the Dominican Republic and India were educated according to a paradigm that regards the teacher as the primal settler and schooling as a process by which the ignorant and undisciplined are converted to civility by a master (Cheyfitz 1991, 113–114). They know and accept that it is the teacher who submits the grades that determine their fate. I am sure, like me, many of you have been told of teachers who shouldn't have had this power, but the point of these students' anecdotes is not to question the investing of teachers with the power of the phallic pen, its colonizing or civilizing function. It is, rather, an expression of a desire on their part for us teachers to use our power and authority in such a way that we become colonizers rather than colonializers. We need to use those pens—but wisely.

My sense is that the student doesn't care that the teacher may feel that exercising power in this context feels politically wrong for her because she likens herself to a colonialist taking up "the white man's burden." The student makes a distinction between colonializing, which is takeover, appropriation, and colonizing, which is the settling and consolidation of matter and ideas and the transfer of the knowledge that is power, authority used for the good. The student's attitude is: *Teacher, I am your responsibility. Teach me as you are supposed to do. Impart that knowledge and bring me to the level I am supposed to be at so I can become a productive member of the society in which I am living. Accept that the classroom has the structure of a colonizing encounter. Don't feel guilty about it. Just don't reproduce the old colonial paradigm when you go about colonizing me.*

The internal dialogue continues. It's my turn now, and I reflect: *Maybe this is where I went wrong. As a female and a feminist, I was averse to acting according to the traditional colonial paradigm. I did not want to show my power, control and dominate the class. So I established and gave the power over to the student groups in what I thought was a counter-hegemonic move. But in going to the other extreme, I did not so much establish a counter hegemony as present myself as the soft-sell crypto-colonial teacher. As a teacher, my responsibility was to get them to contend with words, not with fists, so obviously the way I perceived and modeled decentering needed to be revisited. Just standing off to the side with occasional forays to the groups is not a satisfactory enabling methodology.*

A few semesters back, I taught a section of Basic English. One of my students had come from the U.S. Virgin Islands. She was sharp and funny and hated to see her papers marked up. One Monday, I came to class with a bunch of essays and said, before returning them, "My pen and your papers have had an intimate relationship this weekend." It was meant to be a droll remark, and I did elicit a few smiles, but this student's reaction was, "Professor, don't write all over my paper. Just let me know briefly what the problem is so I can fix it." Colonialism as takeover, as sexual appropriation of body (my remark as well as her reaction had implied that I was treating their texts as penetratable body) is out, but colonizing as knowledge transferred from the one who knows to the one who wants to know is responsible behavior on the part of all teachers, and it is a lesson that female/feminist teachers particularly need to learn for they, more than male teachers, have traditionally had problems claiming and exercising authority, and it is in their classes that male students have tended to act up, sometimes striking out in extreme responses (Culley 1985, 212).

Fifteen years ago, I caused two students to come to blows. I've implicated my naïveté and the political and psychosexual dynamics of the classroom as causal factors. There is another factor as well that went into the making of this disruption. The students who composed that classroom had not had much formal contact with educational institutions prior to their registering at Hostos. To use my (perhaps unfortunate) terminology, their minds still needed to be settled and disciplined. Because they were in need of colonization, they were unprepared for the collaborative learning scenario that I had set up. So what I came to see long after the event was that, with respect to the ESL students I teach (who may be different from the ESL students you teach), I needed to do more preparation and training before moving on to group work. My first task had to be the settling of the students' minds, the imparting and consolidation of knowledge: banking, but done so that it would develop the students' minds, ideally pay them compound interest in later life, similar to the way Mr. Karow's banking of the Great Documents of American History did for me. Speaking personally, I have come to believe that the teaching of English as a second language is, at heart, in essence, a colonizing job, with the teacher, particularly at the lower levels, in something of the missionary posture *vis-à-vis* the students. At the same time, because colonizing and colonializing are not unrelated phenomena, and the missionary posture does connote dominance, I have to be ever vigilant that I exercise authority and transfer knowledge without imposing the colonial paradigm. A delicate balance, but one worth struggling for, I think.

5. Conclusion

And so, in the final analysis, I got a lot from the mistake I made. I learned that the colonial paradigm can be nourished by a pedagogy that critiques it, and the reverse, that a pedagogy that is supposed to support it can serve students' needs. I realized that I was a key player in their acquisition of language and that *pace* Freire and his intellectual heirs, I had to do some cognitive banking before I got ESL students to contend with words. But I had to be a good banker if I wanted to empower my students. I learned that nobody checks his or her politics at the classroom door. I learned that gender roles were a source of conflict in the ESL classroom, and that conflict was not necessarily productive, *pace* Pratt et al. I learned that students who had been pedagogically degendered would find a way to reposit their sexual identity. I realized that disruption as a narrative strategy and disruption as a classroom practice allow dissenters to find voice and express agency, but I came to the conclusion that what was appropriate in a text was counterproductive in a classroom. At the same time, I realized that I, a female, could do to men what men had historically done to women. And so I came to write a critical ethnography called "*C*-Words" by which I have tried to make sense of an experience that was a blunder—and more.

8

Hero or Villain, Blunderer or Bungler?
Caught in the Middle Pedagogically

Jeff Sommers

1

A long time ago, I published a short story about teaching in which the climactic moment occurs when the young professor—a stand-in for me—discovers his prized student Katherine is out at a party instead of preparing for a final exam in his literature course. Disillusioned, he realizes that her commitment to his class isn't nearly as intense as he had thought; he has deluded himself, and to some extent, she has led him to flatter himself. She subsequently visits his office to get her grade and chats briefly with him before rushing off to meet her friends. The story concludes:

> He knew she would probably never become an English major, but it troubled him only slightly, and more he knew for his own sake than hers. He hastily pushed aside the final exams and his grade book. Squaring his shoulders, he faced his desk and took out the buzz group plans. If he could get the students to choose a story they liked, maybe even that Schwartz story, and then break them into groups. . . . He excitedly grabbed a stray piece of paper and began writing down some ideas, under the incantatory power of new plans. In his excitement, he did not notice until later that he was writing on the back of Katherine McArthur's exam (Sommers 1980, 41).

My alter ego was energized, reflective, naïve, and, in a sense, under a spell, but not particularly self-critical. That's a good characterization of my teaching at that point.

I've been postponing the writing of this essay for about seven years now. It's a story, at least nominally, about a blunder (or perhaps a bungle) I committed (performed? engaged in?) in a composition course I taught. My block about writing the piece isn't connected to the fact that I made some kind of teaching error in that course; I don't mind talking about my mistakes and have done so on a number of occasions. No, my delay is part of a larger admission (confession? "truth"?)—I'm not sure whether I'm a liberatory pedagogue or an unreformed expressivist or just what I am nor where I am with my own teaching. This collection of essays positions its contributors as teachers committed to "liberatory" pedagogy, but for me that is not a particularly informative label. I've always been committed to "liberating" my students, as far back as my current-traditional teaching days. What teacher with any degree of altruism at all would ever plan to be anything but "liberatory"? The question now is whether I fit the definition implied by the label.

But I'm going to muddle through this in an effort to reflect upon where I was, am, and might be now. In the mid-seventies, I began teaching composition without any training either as a teacher or in composition, without even having had the experience of taking a composition course myself (given the literature-oriented study I had followed as an undergraduate and graduate student). Simply presented with a composition handbook by my department chair, I began trying to figure out how to teach something I initially thought was unteachable: People either knew how to write or they didn't, I believed. But as I struggled, I grew more interested. My thinking led me to one particularly significant breakthrough: I resolved never to teach anything about writing that I didn't know through my own experiences as a writer to be "true." Eventually, after reinventing the wheel a number of times, I encountered Donald Murray and Peter Elbow and not only received validation but learned quite a bit about pedagogy. And I continued to write about my teaching.

Refraction

Good teachers are invisible
not absent. (The others are
opaque.) For they cannot
avoid being present.

But not really invisible either.

When the light is refracted just so,
we glimpse a sharp elbow or a
grizzled beard.

They say they are invisible—
we see through them.

Through the mid-eighties, I would have described myself as thoroughly immersed in an expressivist model of teaching composition, inviting students to discover their unique voices through the use of a writing workshop format. As I abdicated overt control of the classroom, paradoxically, I felt increasingly powerful because I knew that my class was helping students write with greater authority and ease, providing those who had often been silenced in school with a site to be heard.

Beginning in 1987, I started teaching our department's summer seminar for incoming teaching assistants, a course I would teach for eight years, and as I prepared each summer, I read and learned more about social constructionist pedagogy, and my thinking changed. Not surprisingly, as even my fiction and poetry evidence, I focused on the position of authority held by the instructor, which is more complicated from a social constructionist perspective. I had already discovered that the notion of the self-effacing teacher who serves as a guide was somewhat disingenuous, so I was drawn to the conversation about how we wield authority in the classroom, especially in a "decentered" classroom. (I believe decentering the classroom was—and remains—a radical move for teachers. Only last week I had yet another unpleasant interaction with a colleague in a social sciences discipline who castigated me in writing for leaving the desks in our shared room in a "willy-nilly" arrangement [his description of my approximation of a circle] instead of in the rows they "belonged in.")

I was particularly influenced by the work of Dale Bauer (1990), a colleague at that time, which caused me to think more about my own role as an authority figure. Citing Freire, Shor, Giroux—the icons of this book—she argued that it was impossible for a classroom to be value-neutral and the stance of the objective, disinterested coach was nothing more than a pose. "[I]t's clear"—she writes, in a passage I underlined in 1990—"that there is no way not to accept this authority: Anything less ends up being an expressivist model, one which reinforces, however inadvertently, the dominant patriarchal culture rather than challenges it" (390).

At that time—and still, to some extent—I rejected the depiction of expressivism as reinforcing the dominant culture. That's what the current-traditional pedagogy was doing; my teaching, by encouraging students to write about what mattered to them personally, was "liberating" them. As a teacher on a two-year campus, I had seen student after student whose stories had never been encouraged or permitted to be written before blossom when given the opportunity to write them in my classes. But I also, thanks to my new reading, began to see that things were more complicated than they appeared.

Accepting Credit

I am shooting hoops when Jenny
stops by. She was in my class for
a year, one of those gifted writers,
glistening with talent. She said
hello and thanked me for our year
together. And I laughed, bouncing
the ball all the while.

I always take too much credit
and puff with pride when my
students succeed. I always
buckle under my guilt over
their failures. Except with the
Jennies.

> What did I have to give her, she
> who had so much when she
> arrived? So I laughed and told her
> I had done nothing.
>
> She looked surprised. "You read
> my writing for a whole year. You
> read it with respect, you treated it
> with care, you shared with me
> honestly. I needed that." And she
> walked away.
>
> I bounced the ball and
> drove to the basket. Then
> I smiled to myself.
>
> Even Michael Jordan needs a coach.

So that's where I was coming from at the time of my blunder/bungle. I was in transition from one kind of teacher to becoming another kind. Frankly, I remain in that transitional stage all these years later, and therein lies my quandary. At any rate, in one composition class, I encountered a problem that I had faced before, but in the midst of reformulating my own ideas and approaches, I was not certain about how to proceed.

2

In my course at the time, I routinely used volunteered student drafts in class in two different ways. On some occasions, the class would critique and interrogate the student author, who would respond and ask questions of his readers. These "full-scale workshops," as I called them, fit into the course emphasis on the writing process. However, several times each term, I also set aside a "safe" class period to allow students to read drafts in progress to the group, not for critique, but simply to acknowledge ownership of their own work and to share it with the community, to "publish" it, in good expressivist style. We listened attentively and applauded when the author was finished, not to signify that the project was completed in any sense, but to honor the effort already expended in both working on the writing and then claiming it publicly by sharing it with the group. Students often read first drafts, even journal entries during these sharing days. What they read was not as important as the fact that they had "published" a piece of their own work.

My students, at a two-year branch campus of a four-year state university, often had not been successful in their past writing courses. My objective was to help them become more confident in their ability to write effectively, so I constructed a course where they could meet with success by discovering that the stories they had to tell were stories worth telling. These sharing sessions were one of the strategies I employed toward that end. While I continue to devote class time to public critique/discussion of student drafts, I have discontinued the public readings as I rethink how to provide the public space for sharing without critique in a way that does not close off discussion of the written content.

At the time of my blunder, I became aware that at our next public sharing, one of the students, a young man named Elliott, planned to read his satirical piece about flight attendants. While the readings I had been assigning in class did not focus explicitly on social issues, I had begun to move the ensuing class discussions into talk about the selections' social implications. For instance, one piece we read was a student essay that satirized "brown-nosing" for grades. That discussion had been a lively one with criticism directed at teachers and students alike. The author was female, a factor that I pointed out to the students, leading to a discussion of gender and brown-nosing. I suspect the satirical approach had appealed to Elliott and the observations about gender struck a chord in him. He created a character named "Jane," whose misadventures he mocked. I recall that he routinely referred to her as "a stewardess, oops, flight attendant" and that the piece emphasized her struggles to be attractive enough and thin enough to entice male passengers while also suggesting that her intelligence was quite limited. The snide tone resembled the popular rightwing radio talk show hosts of that era. While I found the piece to be cleverly written, no surprise since Elliott was among the more accomplished—and vocal—student writers in the class, I also felt it was offensive in its misogynist attitudes.

I was troubled. Elliott's essay would have been problematic earlier in my career as well, no matter what pedagogy I was professing, because his attitude in the draft would have appeared just as misogynistic to me then. In the past, I had always been firmly committed to the idea that I was not only a teacher but a human being myself, a person with rights that might, at times, supersede my obligations as a teacher. I had never accepted that I was to silence my own responses as a reader in order to play the role of supportive writing coach at all times and in all situations. I would not ignore or overlook writing that I thought was offensive by shifting the focus to grammar or technique; I always spoke with the student-author about my own personal reaction to his or her work. In light of my growing understanding of the complexities of teacher authority, however, this response no longer seemed adequate, grounded as it was in my own personal response rather than in my objectives for the course. I saw several choices available to me: I could refuse Elliott the opportunity to read the piece, since I knew what it contained; I could allow him to read it without comment, our established procedure; or I could allow him to read it and then respond in some way. In the past, I most likely would have permitted Elliott to read his paper and then spoken to him in private to let him know of my personal reaction and concerns. At this point in my development as an instructor, however, I decided to be more forthright and, as I understood my decision at that time, exercise my authority publicly instead of pretending I had divested myself of it. This decision represented a definite move away from my earlier expressivist methodology. Although I was uncomfortable with this choice, not being certain that it was the right one, I did view it as the best option. I was aware of the risks here. I had not raised any public objections to a student's work before, and I knew that the class would probably pay close attention to my comments. As a result, I spent the better part of the weekend carefully composing my own written response to his satire. My goal was to open a discussion of Elliott's piece that would not be personally damaging to him since he had every reason to expect that his reading would be greeted only by applause, not critique. I was trepidatious that my actions might seem a betrayal to Elliott and to the class itself, but I was certain that I could not let his draft go without a critical response.

In class the next day, Elliott read his piece, and we applauded, as we usually did. But then I announced that I had something to read also, not unusual as I had previously on occasion taken my turn in reading a personal essay during a sharing session. I followed Elliott's satire by reading my carefully crafted response: I praised his skill as a writer but acknowledged my personal discomfort as a listener. I articulated my understanding that as the teacher of the course, I had to accept responsibility for everything that transpired during our time together, and I asserted that I wished to make public that I did not endorse or approve of what he had written because of its potentially offensive nature. The emphasis in my commentary was not to critique Elliott so much as to explain my own responses as a reader and teacher and to clarify why I felt compelled to share those responses. I had labored hard on that response because I did not wish to belittle Elliott, but as I read my essay, I could see Elliott visibly wilting, my impression then—and still—is that he was genuinely shocked that his essay offended me. I don't believe he set out to challenge me in the piece so much as he tried to be funny and clever, most likely having been rewarded for such writing in the past, most likely figuring that satire was a welcome vehicle for his ideas in my class.

When I finished reading my piece, I asked the class to reflect in writing about the situation and to submit anonymously their responses to me, if they chose. Many did; Elliott did not. A number of students said they were relieved I had spoken out because the piece had bothered them, and I recall that one student, who identified herself as female, wrote about her anger over Elliott's actually thinking the piece humorous. A few students expressed surprise at my concern, having found the piece inoffensive and funny. The only signed response came from a friend of Elliott's, who accused me of sandbagging and sabotaging Elliott unfairly. As I read Elliott's friend's response, I was stung by his words because I thought—and still think—his observations were accurate. Elliott left the room that day quite obviously shaken by his experience; as I read through the class comments later in my office, I too was shaken.

Elliott was silenced that day and never participated in class again, although he and I continued to discuss his work in conferences. In fact, the class limped along for the rest of the semester. At the end of the term, during our final conference in my office, I asked Elliott not to include the satire in his portfolio as I felt I couldn't evaluate it. I offered to find another faculty member to grade his work, if he felt he wanted to include that piece. Convinced that the satire was his best writing of the term—and perhaps by this point a bit rebellious—he insisted upon including the piece in his portfolio. So a colleague of mine graded his writing (and assigned him a grade lower than I would have, as I recall). Elliott was the only student in the class who refused to sign a waiver allowing me to use his writing in my research; thus I do not have a copy of his essay. Why I no longer have a copy of my written response to his essay is less clear to me: I save such materials as a matter of course, usually on a disk if not on my hard drive, almost always in hard copy in a folder. That I can't locate my own essay suggests, perhaps, how painful the interaction had been.

What then should I have done, could I have done, that would have been a more productive response? What has been clear to me almost from the outset is that the choice I made was not a good one: Elliott learned nothing after that from me except to acquiesce enough to complete the course. What did the other students learn? Judging from their later silence, apparently I had cowed them too. While some appreciated the stance I took, I cannot point with confidence to any evidence that they acted upon that appreciation; they, too, chose silence and acquiescence. As the term continued, the students' willingness to participate in class discussions of the assigned readings faded. The kind of lively give-and-take we had had about the brown-nosing piece, for example, no longer took place; students' willingness to extend the discussions of the reading into more socially critical venues, as had happened with the brown-nosing essay, also ceased. The reader we were using was one I had published, and in the early part of the term, some class members had on occasion criticized the reading selections as "boring," suggesting that they felt safe enough to criticize my book in my presence. However, later in the semester, such good-natured criticism stopped. At midterm, I asked a colleague to visit my class and conduct a course evaluation, as I hoped to learn more about what I might do to resuscitate our dying class. After speaking to the students, she reported that while they alluded to the incident, their primary impression was that "Mr. Sommers doesn't like us." Incidentally, based on his body language, my colleague correctly identified Elliott as the "victim" of my "persecution," even though the class never pointed him out.

In retrospect, then, what should I have done differently? While I did not make a good choice, I did reject other worse choices: cancelling the reading or prohibiting Elliott from reading his essay would have had fewer repercussions for the rest of the class but would have violated my own beliefs as a teacher by censoring him. Letting him read without any follow-up at all might have suggested to the class that "anything goes" as far as their writing, that there are no consequences to publication of their ideas, perhaps even that I wasn't listening very closely to what they said, just to how well they said it, lessons I certainly did not want to impart.

Another choice would have been to delay the reading, giving me the opportunity to speak with Elliott and allow him to read my written response before I shared it with the class. I am surprised that I did not consider this alternative. Why did I overlook it? What I was thinking, I suppose, is that I had never before postponed a student's reading, and I felt delaying Elliott's while allowing the other students to go ahead with theirs would have unfairly singled him out and, ironically, in light of what I actually did, bring undue attention to him from the class, which might make him uncomfortable. I could have run copies of Elliott's piece and mine, asked the class to read both, and then perhaps have engaged in a discussion of the issue, but that didn't occur to me either.

3

Not long after my blunder/bungle, Richard Miller's (1994) "Fault Lines in the Contact Zone" examined the challenges presented to teachers who "read and respond to the kinds of parodic, critical, oppositional, dismissive, resistant, transgressive, and regressive writing that gets produced by students writing in the contact zone of the classroom" (394). He describes responding to such writing as "uncharted territory" where "we often find ourselves at a loss, not knowing what to do, where to go, or what to say once we cross this line" (395). Later he suggests that treating such essays as anamolous is a misreading of their "cultural significance and pedagogical possibilities" (397). He critiques taking offense at such writing as "exactly the wrong tactic" (405) and concludes that teachers who believe in education "as a force for positive social change" must not "exile students to the penitentiaries" for writing such papers nor "give free rein to one's self-righteous indignation." (408). Unfortunately, Miller's article was not published until after my interaction with Elliott.

Miller's comments are useful and thought-provoking obervations, but how to apply them in the situation in which I found myself? In their introduction to this book, the coeditors comment that "the cause of most blunders, then, is often hard to pinpoint, as a network of factors contribute to these difficult and challenging occurrences." In my own case, the primary cause of the blunder was that I was attempting to make a transition in my own teaching and, simply put, was not up to speed at that point; I was not ready to engage in the kind of negotiation Miller advocates. For a number of years, I had incorporated dialogic features into my course: Students and I exchanged Dialogue Journals in which we discussed the course; students wrote Writer's Memos to me about each draft they submitted. At that time, however, I was using those communicative vehicles as a way of expanding the students' comfort zone so that they could produce more writing. Because many of my students had been unsuccessful in previous writing courses, I was attempting to demystify the writing process, the writing classroom, and the writing professor by interacting in a personal way on a regular basis. I used the journals and memos to initiate what I saw as a helpful dialogue, one that would provide students with the reassurance that they could succeed. Negotiating tough issues did not fit the model for me at that time, although I can now see how they might have.

However, I do not accept Miller's characterizations of my choice: I did not sentence Elliott to the "penitentiary" as I offered him the opportunity to respond that day in class and subsequently spoke with him in my office. I did not give "free rein to . . . self-righteous indignation" as my response to his draft was leavened with praise for his ability as a writer and couched in nonaccusatory prose. My only defense is that I was sincere and was thinking about what was right for the whole class at that point. Not very satisfactory, I know.

In an effort to see how other instructors have dealt with the exercise of their authority in class, I turned to a more recent blunder narrative: John Clifford's (1997) "Testing the Limits of Tolerance in the Democratic Classroom." Clifford tells a story about a graduate seminar with an outspoken, oppositional student. The student challenged Clifford's liberatory teaching by accusing him of being unethical in emphasizing subjective truths instead of focusing on the objective truth presented by literature. Clifford silenced her by ignoring her comments, a choice approved of and readily accepted by the other graduate students who collaborated to make the student (ironically dubbed "Constance") invisible. Clifford concludes his tale with a *mea culpa.*

> Although I surely want to, I cannot yet write this narrative with myself as the hero. Constance somehow should not have felt alienated in my classroom; the rest of us should not have felt superior. Constance tested the boundaries of my tolerance. Somehow, these inevitable limits should be written into all our narratives about school, about authority. (172)

Clifford rejects himself as a hero figure, but then offers no critique of what he might have done differently. Perhaps it is the venue in which he relates the story that leads to this conclusion; his contribution to the volume lies in his assertion that all of our stories need not, perhaps should not, depict us as heroic, an important assertion, one I can assent to. But where does that leave me *vis-à-vis* Elliott? Clifford did indeed sentence Constance to the "penitentiary" by consciously choosing not to hear her. Although I made an effort to provide Elliott with a space to speak after my blunder, he felt he could not or ought not use that space. Perhaps I had sentenced him, albeit inadvertently, to a similar penitentiary?

In a 1998 article, Richard Miller continues to examine the complications of liberatory pedagogy, focusing on the role of the teacher in that pedagogy and raising a troubling question: "[I]s the appeal of the image of teacher as liberator itself proof that liberatory teachers are, in fact, filled with the very false consciousness that they're determined to eradicate in others?" (15). What Miller is grappling with is the notion that liberatory teachers may well fall into a trap of presenting themselves as having all the answers, and thus the liberation of their students, in a sense, comes when the students learn to be like the teacher, casting the teacher in the familiar role of hero (see Helmers 1994). Using James Scott's concept of the "hidden transcript" (15), the discourse that takes place out of sight of those holding the power, a concept that reminds me of Robert Brooke's (1987) notion of the "underlife" in every classroom, Miller notes that students always know exactly where the power in the classroom resides, even if teachers manage to ignore it as they teach (18), and he observes that the teacher's goals, even the liberatory teacher's goal, "more often than we care to admit . . . is to restore order, return to the lesson plan, get the hidden transcript back offstage and out of sight." (21). His description captures Clifford's crisis very aptly as Clifford opts to restore order and then critiques his own choice.

In Miller's analysis, I see some of my own behavior: I chose to restore order, return to the lesson plan. Miller's forthrightness appeals to me because it acknowledges that the teacher has responsibilities for order. While liberatory pedagogy should engage the students in creating the course, it also cannot sit back waiting for them to do so only if the mood happens to strike. I seized control in my classroom at a moment when, I remain convinced, I needed to do so. Yet the means of doing so are still at issue for me. While I needed to make a decision and move the class in a productive direction, in all honesty, order hadn't been disrupted. After all, most of the students apparently were not disturbed by Elliott's essay. The "lesson plan" for the day was, as I described earlier, to continue the process of honoring students' writing efforts in a noncritical atmosphere, in hopes of continuing to encourage them to write and rewrite their work. Elliott's essay, in my judgment at that time, disrupted that order because, for lack of a better description, it was "unpleasant." While I interpret my choice at the time as exercising my authority, it is clearer in retrospect that I functioned in an authoritarian manner, imposing my own judgment of the piece on the class. Such a choice would not have been consistent with my expressivist approach as it undercut Elliott's sincere efforts as a writer, but it was also not consistent with the liberatory approach I was trying to adopt as it killed any potential discussion of what "misogynist" might mean and whether Elliott's essay deserved such a label. My confusing an authoritarian move with an exercise of authority defines the choice as a blunder.

Was I, in reading my impassioned response to Elliott, trying to force the students to quickly convert to my view? They would certainly have had some incentive to do so: Loyalty to Elliott was not likely to produce any gains for them while "loyalty" to me very possibly would. Although the written comments I collected were anonymous, is any such message ever truly "anonymous" in a writing class? Were some students convinced that I'd recognize their writing by the handwriting, the paper they chose to write upon, their ink choice, even their writing style? Did I get a glimpse of the hidden transcript or did that transcript, by definition, simply recede further into hiding?

I'd like to return to Miller's earlier observation about the teacher as hero. In the introduction to this book, Bill Thelin and John Tassoni suggest, "It could be argued that in exposing and in a sense creating the genre of the blunder narrative, this volume simply recasts the role of the hero: replacing the heroic virtues of action and resolution with tentativeness, doubt, sharing, reflectiveness, awkwardness, disruption." That's a refreshingly honest comment to make, but, of course, it casts doubt about my entire enterprise here: Am I trying to "salvage" my blunder by heroically doing public penance for it? And if I do that public penance, is my quashing of Elliott (and his classmates, I suspect) absolved?

4

Doctoral Orals

Doing the Dance of Theory
twirling in a ballroom of mirrors
catching a glimpse a reflection
turning to your partner who
leads you in a gavotte.

Gliding with a new partner who
leads you in a waltz
and always spinning, spinning, glimpsing
mirrored images of partner
after partner always
hoping you can lead,
that you will know how to lead.

Learning to marry the dancer
with the dance. (Sommers 1993, 187)

My difficulties reside now in trying to find my dance. When I think back to my own evolution as a teacher, I recall the strong conflicts that I felt, conflicts that, in my recollection, reflected what was happening in composition at the time. I attended the "debate" between Peter Elbow and David Bartholomae at the Seattle CCCC; I read Maxine Hairston's (1992) bitter published denunciation of critical pedagogies. The field was in conflict, and so was I. My blunder took place just at the moment when I was struggling to marry what I had learned from expressivism with what I was learning from social constructionism. Tobin and Newkirk's (1994) *Taking Stock: The Writing Process Movement in the '90s* offered a response to these conflicts in composition. In particular, Robert P. Yagelski's (1994) "Who's Afraid of Subjectivity? The Composing Process and Postmodernism or A Student of Donald Murray Enters the Age of Postmodernism" spoke to me. It's no accident that Yagelski mentions Donald Murray by name; I assume that Yagelski was responding to what at times felt like a demonizing of Murray and expressivist pedagogy by social-epistemic theorists. Expressivism, whatever its limitations, had always been squarely focused on students' writing; social-epistemic theories at times felt more interested in advancing a social/political agenda. For instance, I remember Richard Miller ruefully acknowledging that the writing his students produced in his liberatory classroom was indistinguishable in quality from the work elicited in other more traditional writing classrooms (1998, 11). I find such an admission a major concern, part of my ongoing struggle to figure out what to do, what pedagogy to embrace. Yagelski's struggles parallel my own and offer what I think is a workable reconciliation between expressivist and liberatory pedagogies.

Yagelski offers his definition of *process:* "a way of describing and understanding what writers do when they write; 'process-oriented' pedagogies grow out of that understanding." He continues by pointing out that expressivists, social constructionists, and cognitivists all see writing as a process, differing in the way they define that process (206). He concludes that while postmodern critics challenge "so-called expressivist" pedagogies and theories, the "idea of writing as a process remains essentially intact" (208). Yagelski apparently reads these critiques of process as excessive, arguing that rejecting expressivism need not, should not, constitute a rejection of writing as a process. In other words, he's arguing against throwing the baby (the writing process) out with the bathwater (expressivism). This is an argument that I find quite powerful: the label " post-process," for example, strikes me as ill-conceived and unfruitful, as well as inaccurate.

Yagelski continues by explaining that the expressivist's "apparently exclusive focus on the individual writer" appeals to many teachers who have grown "frustrated by the ways in which students' voices are squelched by traditional pedagogies" (208). Eventually, he attempts a reconciliation between the efficacy of teaching writing as a process and his growing sense of writing as a social, political, ideological act , posing the question, "[I]s it possible to retain in our teaching what is most useful about the idea of writing as a process at the same time that we account for the inherently social and political nature of writing?" (210). He reaches that reconciliation, describing a course that acknowledges the "individual and idiosyncratic process in which . . . students engage as writers" while at the same time emphasizing that the students are "socially constituted authors participating in situated discourses" (215).

I point to Yagelski's essay because it recounts how one composition instructor has successfully completed the transition I was trying to make at the time of my blunder. Because that transition for me is ongoing, because there is a tension between the pull I feel toward a process-oriented pedagogy located within the expressivist approach and the tug I feel toward a more postmodern, liberatory pedagogy, I remain conflicted. In the years since my blunder, I have continued to change. I ask my students now to interrogate the assumptions of the culture around them in their writing. They critique popular culture such as television family sitcoms; conduct classroom ethnographies, examining the ways in which gender and race affect the dynamics of those classrooms; and explore the unwritten rules and assumptions of their workplaces. We work through the process of writing these papers through conferences, dialogue journals, peer response groups, multiple revisions, and portfolios. Negotiating my own role as the instructor in such a classroom remains, of course, complicated and complex, but I also acknowledge now how necessary that negotiation must be.

5

Thus my teaching now is still unsettled and likely to remain so. But as I look back at my interaction with Elliott, I can see that it represents a key moment in my development as a teacher. How to view that key moment is something of an open question because the notion of blunder is itself problematic to me. Opposed to the concept of a blunder, which carries some significance for future change, is the bungle, a mistake that leads nowhere productive and may, in fact, have originated out of no significant pedagogical initiative. Certainly, this book argues that it is better to blunder than to bungle; in some ways, blundering may even be a postmodern route to becoming a hero.

But how do we know when we've blundered or when we've merely bungled? My experience with Elliott is a text, and like all texts, isn't a stable one. Did I blunder or did I bungle? If today I can apply Yagelski's reconciliation productively in my teaching, I can view the painful mistake I made with Elliott as a blunder because I can situate it in the context of my evolving teaching philosophy. If tomorrow, the tensions bridged by that reconciliation break down, and my course starts to resemble the expressivist one I used to teach, must I then view the mistake as a bungle because it has not produced any significant result for liberatory teaching? Can a blunder metamorphose into a bungle? Do I forfeit my hero status when it does? If in similar circumstances with another student essay, I make the same choice I made with Elliott, wouldn't that choice be a bungle, but wouldn't it also require me to define the earlier act as a bungle as well?

Our students are, we are told, in a contact zone, experiencing the conflicts caused by their attempts to cross borders between cultures. Perhaps I, like other teachers whose teaching is in flux, am also in a contact zone, attempting to cross borders between the cultures of two pedagogies. No wonder things are painful and unclear. Unlike my fictional alter ego who started writing new teaching plans on the back of Katherine McArthur's exam book, moving unwittingly and unreflectively beyond his blunder/bungle, I have been scrutinizing what happened in my very real classroom. What if I put the episode aside? Does that make it a bungle? Must I perpetually examine that choice for it to have any value? At what point can I, should I, put it aside and move on? When is it time for me to let Elliott go?

9

What *Are* We Talking About?

Re-Imagining Community in Service Learning

Kevin Ball

"So, what *are* we talking about when we say *community?*"

I never anticipated Gerald's question. I was recording notes on the chalk-board from our class discussion when Gerald, a student in my first-year composition course at the University of Nebraska-Lincoln, posed this single simple question to the entire class. Gerald didn't intend to disrupt our discussion with his question (although that's certainly what it did). Indeed, his question was genuine, stemming from a sincere desire to define our working terms. Coming when it did, however, four weeks into a semester-long course devoted to ethno-graphic inquiry into local community, it caught me off balance. What I had assumed as a foundation for our inquiries—my students' discernment of com-munity as a building block in their individual and social identity—was clearly far from a given.

As I turned slowly, mind racing, to face the classroom, several students be-gan nodding their heads sympathetically as if affirming Gerald's question. Soon most of the students were gazing at me, heads nodding, waiting. Clearly, they too wanted to know what we meant by this strange and unfamiliar term *com-munity*. While I assumed that we had established the necessary groundwork for them to begin ethnographic writing and research into their local communities beginning the following week, it was becoming quite clear that I had overesti-mated their familiarity with community investigation and its role in an under-graduate writing experience.

We backtracked. We spent the next several weeks defining and discussing community in relation to detailed examples, activities that would provide a framework for future discussions, but even then we all struggled throughout the remainder of the course to relate our differing conceptions of community. In fact, my students continued to fire questions at me throughout the semester, ques-tions that eventually provided three distinct moments that would challenge me to reread my own classroom and my assumptions about inquiry-based learning. And while questions like Gerald's stemmed partly from my naïve attempts to focus this course around the idea of investigating local communities, an approach I had not tried before, my struggle suggests just one way in which notions of community are often collapsed or under-conceptualized within composition theory and pedagogy. Addressing these misconceptions of community is imperative if we are to continue to teach writing as a meaningful negotiation between and among the "public" and "private" contexts of students' lives. With this goal in mind, Gerald's question is a question all students, teachers, administrators, and community members should be asking.

Just as Wayne Campbell Peck, Linda Flower, and Lorraine Higgins (1995) place education and inquiry at the center of "community literacy" (198), students' learning—and thus their writing—must center around and stem from their knowledge of and inquiry into those communities and cultures if that learning is to be meaningful to their lives. This is not to say that students should not critically examine larger cultural ideologies, but only that they should inquire into the nearby, reflecting on the local ideologies and forces that have shaped them to that point in their lives, simultaneous to examining a larger culture. Together, my class and I negotiated a definition of community that included geographical as well as perceptual sites, the range of groups and contexts that serve as sites of an individual's meaning-making. Thomas Bender's (1978) definition of community as an experience in the "human surround" and "a network of social relations marked by mutuality and emotional bonds" (7) allowed me to expand traditional notions of community to include geographic places and conceptual spaces, localities of reciprocal relations that sustain a voice, reinforce values, and promote socially constructive behavior. These communities may be bounded geographically, but frequently they are formed outside of locality or despite an absence of it. Members may come from separate cultures and possess a range of experience, but one set of lived, shared experiences and understandings—a way of knowing—connects each group of individuals in a unique relationship and forms the common denominator.

Gerald's question reveals just one of the areas in which critical pedagogies and the politics of location remain under-conceptualized within composition. It can be a common experience for students to enroll in universities only to have their communities and cultures erased, neglected, or forgotten in the process of gaining an "education." Radical educators such as Henry Giroux (1997a) continue to call for educators' pedagogical practices to transgress the rigid division between academic culture and popular culture in order to make all knowledge subject to serious analysis and interrogation. Giroux asserts that educators need to provide the opportunities for students to learn that their histories and experiences matter: "[E]ducators need to argue for forms of pedagogy that close the gap between the university and the everyday life. Their curriculum needs to be organized around knowledge of the communities, cultures, and traditions that give students a sense of history, identity, and place" (266). Yet while radical educators seemingly never fail to invoke Freirean pedagogy[1] when describing their projects, they often fail to observe one of the most fundamental tenets regarding students' communities. Paulo Freire (1973) reminds us in *Education for Critical Consciousness* that the basic content of education "springs from the peasants themselves and their relations with the world, and transforms and broadens itself as the world becomes revealed to them" (159). The most basic component of Freire's literacy method requires the use of students' generative words and themes—the language and subjects drawn from the students' lives—as the material for critical inquiry. By participating in this inquiry, learners become subjects of their own destiny, and they realize their roles as Subjects in the World and with the world (46). Far too often, critical pedagogies focus on larger cultural critiques while neglecting individual and local issues, thereby silencing those students meant to be empowered. As a result, many students enter the university mistakenly conceiving of themselves as cultural peasants, unaware of (and therefore unable to draw upon) the extremely rich and diverse communities and cultures of their lives as sites worthy of investigation.

"Can We *Do* That?"

When I first began planning an inquiry-based composition course, I realized that my students would need models for the kinds of investigative research I wanted them to attempt in their writing for the class. I stumbled upon these models while working with the Nebraska Writing Project (NeWP), a five-week summer institute that I was helping to facilitate at UNL. The NeWP, a workshop for K–12 teachers modeled after the National Writing Project, is an association of teachers devoted to the improvement of writing instruction at all levels from kindergarten through post-secondary education. During the summer session, I worked closely with two local elementary school teachers who were already doing writing projects with their students similar to the kinds of writing I envisioned for my students. These teachers, Tom and Tami, gave a brief presentation during the institute describing the community inquiry writing projects they were doing collaboratively in their fifth-grade classes at Devaney Elementary School, a multi-racial school in one of the older neighborhoods in Lincoln. Tom and Tami were teaching their students about writing—among many other subjects—by actively engaging them in inquiry projects requiring fieldwork within the neighborhood surrounding their homes and school and research into this community and their lives within that community. The previous year, students had researched such various sites as a nearby funeral home and the bell tower at a nearby church and topics ranging from gender dynamics in a neighborhood restaurant to health conditions and policies at local tattoo parlors. Their students wrote extensive field notes, synthesized their findings, and revised their final reports before sharing their writings with their classmates and the members of the communities they researched. These community inquiry writing projects engaged the students in actual experiences of writing and thinking *in* and *about* those community settings, prompting them to examine and analyze those settings more critically and reflectively through observation, interview, and research in addition to personal experience.

When I discussed with Tom and Tami the idea of our classes working together in the fall, we were all excited about the potential benefits for everyone involved—for students and teachers alike. Rather than simply copying Tom and Tami's inquiry strategies in my own classroom, I believed pairing our classes and causes could create a reciprocal relationship between the students. We conceived of the relationships as partnerships rather than mentorships, striving for a community of writers invested equally in the projects. I hoped that my students' experiences with the Devaney students' community inquiry projects would provide them with the confidence and expertise necessary to use their writing in my course to begin investigating their own communities.

We kept the project simple at first, establishing one-to-one writing partnerships between the university students and the fifth graders that would last the entire semester. The partnerships would then choose their sites, determine what they would research and write about that site, and decide how they would write about those topics together. The students in my class who were interested agreed to volunteer for one hour each week to work with their writing partner at Devaney Elementary. At the initial meeting, we did some brief introductory writing and then Tom, Tami, and their students talked briefly about the previous year's projects. We tried to stress, without overwhelming my students with the concept, the untapped potential sites of study in the community within walking distance of the school.

The next day, when my students actually worked one-on-one with the Devaney students, proved to be quite bewildering for my students. Tom and Tami's class members, most of whom had done community inquiry writing the previous year, appeared much more comfortable with the arrangement. As their writing partners arrived, they came out of their classrooms carrying clipboards and pencils, ready to start brainstorming and writing. My students hesitated and clustered together, looking at me for direction about where they might write. It was amazing to see the stream of African American, Asian, and Native American fifth-grade students blending with my predominantly white, middle-class university freshmen. "Let's go write in the media center," one Devaney student called out to her university partner, who looked befuddled at the celerity with which the partnerships were proceeding. "Last year we investigated First Plymouth Church, the tattoo parlor, and a Vietnamese market," said a Devaney student, rattling off past fieldwork as an introduction. Once they were paired, the partners seemed to mesh quickly, though, and the Devaney students led their university partners off to various hallways, lounges, and library tables to begin writing, my students trailing slightly behind in their wake.

A frustrating (although not unanticipated) routine developed almost immediately. As I roved from group to group to see how they were progressing, each of my students would look at me in confusion (and a touch of panic) and ask, "What are we supposed to do with them?" They wanted a set agenda, an outlined plan for every group to follow, rather than the responsibility of brain-storming their topic and the appropriate method of researching that topic. The idea of doing what for them were nontraditional types of "academic" writing must have been challenging. David, a UNL student, was paired with a Devaney student who had already rattled off a list of potential community research sites including the capitol and stores in the area as well as interviewing officials in her mother's office, members of the UNL women's basketball team, and local officers of the police force.

"Can we do that?" David asked me while eyeing the list they had gener-ated. "Can we go places with them?"

David's question became a litany as I moved from group to group. The first question on each of my student's lips seemed to be, "Can we do that?" or "Can we actually *leave the school?*"

Later that day, I mentioned my students' need for assurance to Tom. He, too, had been observing the partnerships. "You know, Kevin," he said after pausing, "in many ways, it's like our students are teaching your students."

The problem was not that my students were not engaged; their interest was just outweighed by other considerations. Their questions and surprise reflect traditional assumptions about rule-governed institutional situations that do not permit students to leave the school building, in addition to practical concerns for responsibility and liability. Their comments also reflect an ingrained sense of traditional "schooling," a set of socialized assumptions about what educa-tion is and the unspoken rules by which it operates. Tom's comment made me realize that my students had been socialized to think in many of the ways Kurt Spellmeyer (1996) suggests when he describes the peculiar and "disembodied" character of knowledge in the modern world. Spellmeyer notes: "Just as the survival of the modern nation depends on the persistent suppression of regional allegiances and 'provincial' traditions, so what qualifies as 'knowledge' is al-most always removed from experience at the local or personal level" (42). In contrast to earlier societies where knowledge was inseparably tied to the tasks and processes of everyday life, the modern assumption that the pursuit of knowledge must begin with an act of voluntary alienation and radical, Carte-sian detachment causes knowledge to become disembodied and removes it from the local contexts of its origin: "In our world, the modern world, whatever remains 'particular,' whatever fails to claim the status of universality, gets dis-missed as special pleading, ignorance, or empty sentiment" (42).

My students' assumptions about knowledge and learning were limited to experiences within the walls of the school. One student responded in his jour-nal: "The thing that I find interesting about the class is how they get so involved in the city they live in. I would die to find out that there is a world outside my yard." This student, like many of his classmates, commented on the contrast be-tween the writing (especially the worksheets) he had done in fifth grade com-pared to the writing Tom and Tami's students were doing. Overwhelmingly, my students endorsed the opportunity to write about subjects and sites that interest the individual writer. Another student wrote, "I would have liked to have had this opportunity while I was in school," a wistful comment echoed by many of his classmates in their journals and during classroom dialogues. When we discussed the best ways for students to learn to write, the students expressed admiration for the creativity of such a curriculum as well as the writing it produced. The same student who wrote about dying to find out about the world outside his yard noted, "The only trips that we went on was to the zoo and you could see an alligator like he would be in the wild, laying down in a swimming pool having chickens thrown at him for dinner."

Paul Theobald (1997) argues that students' inability to "see" the value of their communities results from a deliberate erasure, not a natural process. In *Teaching the Commons: Place, Pride, and the Renewal of Community,* Theobald condemns the cultural constructions of schools and the ways school curricula tend to devalue communities within the studies of the classroom. Arguing that schools must attend more consciously to their physical place on earth and the social, political, and economic dynamics that surround it, he states: "Doing so would render the entire school experience more meaningful and, in the process, would contribute in a small, though not insignificant, way to a cultural healing desperately needed in American society. We need to foster a sense that community is a valuable asset, something to be promoted rather than destroyed" (1). While Theobald provides systematic attention to the circumstances faced by rural schools, his analysis illuminates and directs educational work in other contexts as well. Theobald illustrates how notions of rural backwardness (and thus of rural community) have flourished ever since the Enlightenment philosophers set in motion a cultural propensity to ridicule what to them was rural parochialism or downright foolishness (17). This cultural propensity to ridicule anything considered local or nonacademic thus carries over into the classroom, leaving students with no way of thinking about their communities other than in negative or devalued terms. Wherever a school exists, Theobald argues, the professionals who work within it must focus their pedagogical energy on the unique geographic place inhabited by the school, fostering the sense that community is a valuable societal and educational asset.

Tom and Tami foster this sense of community within their students by actively engaging the personal as a primary source for making sense of the world. Their students had not yet been taught to limit their thinking about the possibilities and potential sites for writing and thus did not assume that knowledge must be removed from the local or personal level to be valid or significant. Most, if not all, of my students were the recipients of an entire "education" consisting of a traditional, institutionalized approach to writing that had constricted not only their writing but their thinking about that writing and its relation to their lives. While naturally familiar with their communities and hometowns, my students were clearly unfamiliar with the concept or significance of "community" within an academic setting. Gerald's question, and the other students' equal degree of unfamiliarity with the concept of community, reveals the condition of many students for whom local knowledge is devalued or elided within the university setting.

"So, What *Are* We Talking About?"

With the Devaney writing partnerships in mind, I had selected course texts that explored the role of community in individuals' lives to help my students conceive of community from their own perspectives. We read and discussed these texts while students were participating in the writing partnerships at Devaney. One of those books, Teresa Jordan's (1993) *Riding the White Horse Home: A Western Family Album,* chronicles Jordan's family's ranching heritage rooted in the Iron Mountain country of southeast Wyoming and the struggles against cultural and economic pressures that have made ranching a dying way of life. The book celebrates the communities of Iron Mountain and the West in addition to the people who have shaped and continue to shape it. While education removed Jordan from her community when she left for college, her writing about Iron Mountain and the American West saved her. Jordan writes, "My mother was dead and the ranch was for sale, but in the study of the American West, I had found a way to come home." For Jordan, education is the key: "Education has given me a road back to my people, but it has also kept me apart" (82). Jordan does not question the significance of her education, only the ways in which her education seemed to devalue not only her Iron Mountain community, but also its community-based ways of knowing: "I don't question my desire for education—I can't imagine it otherwise. But I do question the inevitable course that education seemed to dictate, as if it could have no application within the community that bred me, as if it would be wasted were I to return" (79). This passage about the "inevitable course" of education led to a class discussion of the students' own educations at UNL and the effect of education on their perspectives toward their home communities. In the midst of our discussion of the conflicts between communities, Gerald asked his question: "So, what are we talking about when we say *community*? What do we mean?"

Gerald's question changed the course of what had been a very hesitant, sputtering class discussion. It was not until we had defined *community* and listed several forms of communities on the chalkboard that the students could begin to imagine the multiple communities in their own lives. We began with Nebraska listed at the top of the chalkboard, then branched out into hometowns—Aurora, Beatrice, Waverly—and the public schools inhabiting those hometowns. "What about ranchers in western Nebraska?" one student proposed, expanding our sense of community beyond physical boundaries. "The ranching community is a lot different than the farming [community] of eastern Nebraska." It was not until we had covered the chalkboard in possibilities that I realized I had assumed an understanding of *community* from the beginning of the course without prompting my students to conceptualize or imagine the multiplicity of such spaces within their experience. My syllabus was especially vague and broad in its conception of their project: "One of the main focuses for this class will be the idea of Community Inquiry and Cultural Exploration. In other words, what I want us to do as a class is get outside of the classroom and explore the surrounding communities and diverse cultures of the university, the city of Lincoln, and the state of Nebraska." From the description in my syllabus, it sounds as if these "communities" are arranged neatly outside of the classroom, lined up like tangible objects to be picked up and examined. Since that semester, I've added a list of my own communities—from the small, rural town in Missouri where I was raised to my present "place" within the university and the city of Lincoln—as an example to outline the multitude of contexts I could explore.

One reason that *community* remains so foreign to students is that compositionists themselves continue to struggle to define it. Raymond Williams (1976) reminds us of the warmly persuasive nature of the term and the way it can be used ambiguously to denote a range of relationships,[2] while Joseph Harris (1984), Mary Louise Pratt (1991), and Kurt Spellmeyer (1996) have all argued that oversimplified, naïve representations of community ignore cultural, political, and ideological realities. Harris' essay "The Idea of Community in the Study of Writing" perhaps best reflects the work of teachers and theorists of writing who see the idea of community as somehow central to their work. His description of his transition from a working-class home in Philadelphia to college and his realization of a "sense of difference, of overlap, of tense plurality" between his multiple communities reminds me of my students' negotiation between the university and their home communities (11). While Harris argues that theorists have erred in treating community as a monolithic construct, he never addresses *students'* constructions of community. Similarly, the concept of the "discourse community" has enabled compositionists to conceive of the teaching of writing in new and imaginative ways, but the concept also presents a danger of becoming so abstract and theoretical within scholarly discourse that it never enables students to reflect critically on their communities or the discourses of those communities, preventing them from connecting the literacies of the university with the daily world they also inhabit.

And although Iris Marion Young (1990) and Gregory Clark (1994) focus on the political assumptions that underlie the rhetoric of the discourse community, they leave the pedagogical applications to others. Their writing, like Harris' essay, is intended for a professional audience of theorists, scholars, and perhaps some teachers, and ultimately their concern is more with how *teachers* as professionals conceive of and construct community in the classroom than with how we foster or challenge our *students'* constructions and realizations of community. In many ways, the language of community has remained *our* language of community.

Although this abstract discussion is necessary in order for theorists to gain a "fuller picture of the lived experience of teaching, learning, and writing in a university today" (Harris 21), our discussion of community within professional journals and at conferences often neglects attention to students' "pictures" of that experience. We have argued the pros and cons of the metaphors of community while neglecting the development of a pedagogy that helps our students to write about and realize their positions as members of communities and the ways their interactions, relationships, and ways of knowing are bounded by the landscape against which their interactions occur. Because I am now several semesters removed from the community inquiry projects, I am unable to coauthor this essay with my students; ideally, such an essay should integrate their "pictures" and conceptions in order to better represent their realizations. As a discipline, we need a fuller picture within the classroom of students' conceptions of community and their continuing struggles to reconcile membership in a plurality of communities—especially their newfound position in the university classroom. As nebulous and complicated as the concept of community is for Harris and the other theorists attempting to define it, we have not imagined what it must be like for students unfamiliar not only with the concept but the territory within which they are considering it. Students come to the university expecting to sacrifice (or at least to compromise) their community in relation to the perceived sophistication and culture of the university. Most are willing to assimilate into the university community and scholarly culture in order to achieve an "education." Unless that education values communities outside as well as inside the university, and unless we recognize the significance of those communities, we have not really taught them—or perhaps we have not taught them to ask the appropriate questions.

Much of the challenge of getting students to see the interconnectedness between their community and the writing they do in a composition course results from cultural conventions figuring "public" and "private" writing. Students may fail to recognize the connection between home and school because they have been socialized to view the classroom and their community as separate and nonintersecting spheres. While my students' writing partners at Devaney Elementary were accustomed to writing stories about their homes and reading those stories at school to their peers (as well as writing stories about school and reading them at home), my students had been socialized to distance themselves from such boundary-free movement, learning to value only the writing of the academic setting *in* the academic setting. It was not that my students did not *want* to conduct community investigations; it was that they could not imagine a personal application of writing in the ways they were being asked to imagine writing with their Devaney writing partners.

"What Is There to Value About My Community?"

This doctrine of separate spheres often limits students' appreciation of community. Even when students recognize their community, they may fail to see its relation to the academy. After all, what does the Hispanic community or the rural community or the ranching community (concepts that are tossed around by everyone from politicians to reporters) have to do with what students are learning at the university? To them, community and the academy remain separate spheres and separate communities, a fact which another student, Drew, revealed during one of our class discussions of *Riding the White Horse Home*. Obviously frustrated by examples of Jordan's appreciation for her Iron Mountain community, Drew finally blurted out his question. "What is there to value about my home community?" he asked, genuinely puzzled. "Seriously, I don't value anything from there." Many students, especially freshmen like Drew, find it hard to value a community they have spent their entire lives attempting to escape. They seek desperately to flee that community and all it represents in order to define themselves.

"My new life and my old one are at odds" (84), Jordan writes, capturing perfectly the position of students as culture straddlers between "old" and "new" worlds. One of the challenges of community investigation with first-year students is that they are in transition. While they are highly invested in moving away from home community, community investigations ask them to return to "home." After only several weeks at college, students discover that returning home (either literally or figuratively) is a much more complex experience than they had previously imagined. One of my students confessed in his journal, "The one thing I am still having trouble with is what to do my community inquiry on. I have been breaking away from my community and I do not know what is going on back home. I have many confused thoughts about my home." His confession reveals how his previous dichotomies of "home" and "college" no longer encompass his lived experience. Another student commented, "I don't understand this whole 'finding your place' thing because no matter where I am, I am in my place. I don't feel that the dorms or even this University is even in the slightest way my place or community. Yes, I live here and go to school here and work here, but I am not comfortable enough to call this my place." Her remarks reflect an assertion of a sense of place coupled with the simultaneous confusion caused by her awareness of her situatedness between a previous sense of place or "home" and her new "home" at the university.

The goal of our pedagogy should be to help students negotiate that transition back and forth, and part of that negotiation involves developing a language of possibility, as Henry Giroux (1997a) terms it, to describe their home community beyond the limiting dualism of unexamined critique or unrestrained nostalgia. Central to the construction and perception of reality, this language enables students to discuss local sites of knowledge in far more complex and meaningful ways. A language of possibility also enables students to utilize their own language(s) to imagine an audience beyond the boundaries of the discipline's discourse.

While it is challenging to ask first-year college students to research their communities as mini-ethnographers, I have also realized that there can be negative consequences from emphasizing marginalized or "other" cultures in a way that makes students' own experiences appear less significant as sites of study. One of the most ethnically diverse schools in the state, Devaney Elementary represented a separate community for my students, the majority of whom were white, middle-class Nebraskans.[3] Patricia Stock and Jay Robinson (1990) identify a margin as "a generative site for building knowledge with the potential to benefit all of us wherever we reside" (273). Since most of my students came from far different communities in terms of race, culture, and economic and social class than those represented at Devaney, the elementary school represented an unexplored and unexamined margin for them.

What I had not anticipated was the way my students' experiences in the "margins" would leave them with nothing to say once they began investigating their own communities. "The community around Devaney elementary is so much more interesting and diverse than my podunk town," one of my students wrote in her journal after working with her writing partner one day. Many of my students echoed similar sentiments throughout the semester in their journals, equating racial and social class diversity (commonly defined as minorities and the poor) with the only kind of communities worth investigating. Meanwhile, these students were struggling to imagine sites within their own communities that might "compete" with their work at Devaney Elementary. Margaret J. Marshall (1997) provides one explanation for students' inability to "see" their community with her idea of "marking the unmarked" and examining statements that position students as already belonging to a set of culturally hegemonic literacy practices. Marshall writes, "Being already central, these students are positioned as if they were already known, and, therefore, not worthy of our scholarly attention" (231–232). I realized from reading my students' journals that many of my mainstream "unmarked" students felt like they came from categories that are already constructed in the center, as if they and their communities are already known (after all, *they* aren't from the margins) and, as a result, are not worthy of scholarly attention. Rather than privileging their experiences, as such an assumption might imply, this perspective actually reflects a devalued experience as students are lulled by an apparent homogeneity into ignoring distinctions. They cannot see or imagine anything worth knowing or communicating and thus assume they have to sacrifice their community or culture. Questions such as "What is there to value about my community?" suggest that students must learn to look beyond the obvious markers of their experience and to "mark" their communities by writing and reflecting critically about their communities. Students and teachers alike must continue to question the very idea of a "center" and the assumption that center implies of a homogeneous community.

By exoticizing the communities my students perceived as marginal through our readings and discussions, I limited my students' imagination of the potentials of their own communities. One student, Angela, responded to Jordan's book in her journal by writing: "It makes me sad to read about how their ranch was sold and how she misses the ranch and the land. If I were her, I would be the exact same way. I love the country and the outdoors and would be just as sad to see it go! Especially if I grew up in a picturesque, history-filled, interesting area like the one she came from." Framing our discussions of community and culture with Jordan's book as the "official" class text encouraged students to exoticize the Iron Mountain community and ignore their own areas as significant communities and sources of meaning. I even showed slides of Iron Mountain taken during a recent vacation, overlooking the fact that we were using Jordan's text as *an* example of community investigation, not *the* model. Angela, like many of my students, fantasized about these ideal, picturesque communities ("if I grew up in . . ."), while overlooking the history, beauty, and significance of her own personal picturesque community. Other students complained in their journals that they would have had much more to write about if they had grown up in such interesting areas as Iron Mountain. Although many of our class activities and discussions encouraged students to examine the types of knowledge and ways of knowing constructed by their communities, we obviously needed to devote more time to viewing their sites as equally valid and significant as the "margins."

Such a shift is subtle yet significant. Instead of showing slides from Iron Mountain, I should have been encouraging students to take their own pictures of their communities to share with the rest of the class. In addition to reading about Jordan's relationship with her community, I could have prompted students to bring in more of their writing about their communities for class discussion. While I talked with students about their community investigations during workshops and writing conferences, their investigations rarely received the entire class' attention, seeming to imply by omission that the investigations did not merit time or attention. Understanding the connections and relationship between fieldwork, course reading, or service learning projects and investigation of one's own community is often the key to avoiding the dualistic marking of homogeneity and exotic. At the beginning of the writing partnerships, I prompted my students to consider these connections. As part of their first journal prompt, I asked them (among other questions), "What does your work with your writing partner make you think about your respective communities as well as the similarities and differences between your cultures?" After that first journal, however, I only required them to respond to their weekly interactions and experiences with their writing partners. Had I consistently revisited that initial question through a series of journal prompts or class discussions throughout the semester, rather than assuming they would continue to explore the connections on their own (an assumption of which I never made them aware), my students might have been better prepared to relate to and understand the barrage of communities they were being exposed to in their reading and in their writing partnerships at Devaney.

Compositionists often tout the value of students' experiences in the margins through the metaphor of the contact zone. Cynthia Cornell Novak and Lorie J. Goodman (1997) even suggest that service learning projects create a "safe/r contact zone" of critical thinking and writing. I had envisioned the Devaney writing partnerships as a space where my students, especially those students who normally would not have ventured into such a community on their own, could enter into and engage with a contact zone of difference. Yet, what are the implications for community investigation when the only way we can conceive of studying community is through the examination of difference in the "margins"? Elizabeth Chiseri-Strater and Bonnie Stone Sunstein's (1997) *Field-Working* engages students in the research process by teaching them to "observe, listen, interpret, and analyze the behaviors and language of the 'others' around them" (vii). What does such an emphasis on the "other" imply for students still struggling with a conception of their own community? Can students even investigate the "other" without first interrogating their own communities? If the only way teachers can conceive of studying communities is by going to the margins (as we define them—as other) and thereby othering its members, then naturally students will believe they must write about Otherness in order to have anything significant to say—at the expense of the communities they know best and the contexts that are most meaningful to them. By neglecting their experiences within their own communities while focusing so intensely on their work at Devaney Elementary as a site of inquiry, I actually made it *more* of a challenge for my students to imagine their own sites as worthy of scrutiny; instead of inspiring my students to write about their communities, I was silencing them. Given the drastic contrast in communities, it should come as no surprise that students like Drew couldn't apply their experiences at Devaney as a model for inquiry into their own home communities.

Ethnography and Service Learning as Critical Pedagogy

The recent trends in composition toward the integration of ethnographic writing and service-learning projects within writing courses reflect an attempt on the part of many teachers to bridge the perceived gaps between the university and everyday life and to connect communities and classrooms by representing and addressing the realities of daily life within the intellectual work of the composition classroom. Linda Adler-Kassner, Robert Crooks, and Ann Waters (1997) even deem the trend toward service learning in the last five years as a "microrevolution" in college-level composition. Their collection, *Writing the Community: Concepts and Models for Service Learning,* explores the ways implementation of service-learning projects fosters a radical transformation of experience and understanding of education and its relation to communities outside the campus for both teachers and students. Other scholars such as Aaron Schutz and Anne Ruggles Gere (1998) further address bridging these gaps by interrogating the theoretical grounding of the terms *public* and *private* as they are applied to service learning, while Ellen Cushman (1996) calls for scholars in rhetoric and composition to move beyond their roles as classroom teachers and to become activists within communities outside of educational settings. And texts such as Chiseri-Strater and Sunstein's *FieldWorking* prompt students to consider research topics beyond the classroom. Yet if students struggle to apply their experiences in the margins or their research into the "other" to their inquiries into their own communities, and if their appreciation of community does not necessarily transcend inherently from one site to another, then what are the ramifications of these trends for our students?

In "Work, Class, and Categories: Dilemmas of Identity," Shirley Brice Heath (1996) predicts one future of service learning, asserting that composition and other university courses must respond to the changing demands in community and work settings: "Postsecondary choices will consequently have to look very different from their current configuration, for they will need to be much more tightly tied to vocational, personal, and community-building goals than the current four-year college norm" (234). Heath's discussion of the ways composition courses will be forced to adapt relates to Robert Connors' (1987) point that the question of personal writing is uncomfortable for many teachers because it presents such a clear mirror of one's individual philosophy of education, forcing teachers to take an implicit stand about what we think is important, for students and society. Connors notes how it is easy to feel that one's teaching is not striking well the balance between "making writing meaningful to the student and making the student meaningful to the community," a tension that creates a divide between advocates of "honest, personal writing" and advocates of "writing that gets the world's work done" (180). It is significant that many educators view this as an either/or decision between two choices at seemingly opposite ends of the spectrum rather than aspects of the same process of individual meaning-making. Writing about communities prompts writing that is meaningful to both the student and to a variety of academic and nonacademic communities. The fluidity of the definitions of public and private makes facilitating such meaningful writing more complicated and challenging. How can we as teachers strike this balance effectively within our curricula when *we* haven't even defined the concepts satisfactorily?

The perceived divide between public and private creates barriers to such local meaning-making, just as the growing doubt about the worth of the baccalaureate in our culture encourages efforts to try to make composition more responsive to a "larger community" through service-learning projects and writing that "gets the world's work done." Ultimately, such "worldly" efforts privilege the public over the personal in their definitions of community. Anne Ruggles Gere (1996) notes, "[H]igher education has responded to the questioning of its worth with increased attempts to demonstrate the value it adds to students' lives, ultimately compelling higher education to justify itself to the larger society by showing how it enhances the literacy skills of future citizens and workers" (122). Increasing efforts to link university courses to job settings or specific communicative situations define students as meaningful only within the larger business and economic community. While I do not think this was Heath's agenda behind her remarks about responsiveness to vocational, personal, and community-building goals, teachers and administrators can go to such extremes in making students meaningful to "the community" (meaning: the community where work gets done) that ultimately there is no meaning for students in community apart from that communicative or functional situation—and certainly no room for writing about place-based ways of knowing. And once again note who defines *community*. In these discussions, ideological factions, such as the "business community" define *community for* students. In my syllabus, I attempted to counter this narrow focus on the business world by encouraging students to define and explore community in ways that are most meaningful to them. "In this course," my syllabus states, "we'll use writing to explore our thoughts and reactions as we work on these projects in order to make meaning out of our experiences and out of our worlds."

Although they do not address service learning directly, Giroux and Roger Simon (1989) warn of the dangers of linking schooling to the demands of a technocratic and specialized literacy. They observe that educational reform has been linked to the imperatives of big business, with schools serving as "training grounds for different sections of the work force" (236). Rather than only preparing students for the community they will join upon graduation, teachers should appreciate the communities of which students are already members. Students become truly meaningful to their communities when they can recognize their places within those communities. Sadly, we are far better at making students meaningful to their communities than we are at helping them recognize the communities of which they are members. James A. Berlin (1996) noted that our colleges are "much better equipped to prepare workers for the new job market than they are to prepare citizens for the cultural conditions of our new economy" (224). We rarely, if ever, encourage students to trace place-based ways of knowing to those geographical, cultural, and cognitive roots. When service learning and writing about community serve merely as means of higher education justifying itself to "the public," we move further from the education endeavor and closer to Giroux's scenario of writing as specialized training into a technocratic world. It should come as no surprise that students like Drew value nothing about their communities when the utilitarian criteria we supply them leaves no room for a meaningful personal connection.

Talking About Community

The challenge for composition teachers in bridging the public and the private is to provide meaningful settings where students can make connections between classrooms and home communities. Community is not a concept we can just introduce to students and expect them to explore immediately in depth, and it requires more than one heuristic to conceptualize the complexities of context, place, and perception. Freire's literacy programs always began with learners defining their communities in their own terms and on their own terms; my experience with my students emphasized how even that "simple" act is a highly charged action loaded with the politics of location. Although compositionists are reluctant to admit it, depictions of community in academic journals, at professional conferences, and even in composition classroom syllabi reflect the ideological ways in which they represent, define, and thus limit the communities within which students exist.

I am continually amazed at how our students succeed despite the obstacles we unwittingly provide. I thank my students for being patient and willing when confronted with an intimidating experience. I like to think that their willingness to participate stems from something more than a crass desire for a good grade in my class and that they found something about the idea of community compelling. They persisted despite their questions.

Our students' questions remind us of the boundaries of cultural conventions limiting what can and cannot be imagined in the classroom as well as where students can and cannot go when they are "in" school. Ultimately these conventions dictate what kinds of writing "count" in the composition classroom. If we ever hope to generate a discussion within the discipline about these conventions rather than assuming community has already been fully conceptualized, perhaps the best thing we can do is listen to our students' questions.

Notes

1. See "Education as the Practice of Freedom" in *Education for Critical Consciousness* for further discussion of Freire's literacy method.

2. Williams notes, "What is most important, perhaps, is that unlike other terms of social organization (state, nation, society, etc.), it seems never to be used unfavorably and never to be given any positive opposing or distinguishing term" (66).

3. According to Earl Hawkey, Director of Registration and Records, 93 percent of the undergraduate student population during the fall semester of the 1995–96 year were Nebraska residents ("Teaching at UNL." University of Nebraska-Lincoln. 18.1 (1996): 1). Of the 469 students enrolled at Devaney Elementary School, 35 percent were white, 28 percent were black, 22 percent were Asian, 10 percent were Spanish surnamed, and 5 percent were American Indian (Ethnic Counts Summary Report. Lincoln Public Schools. October 14, 1997). Of all first-time freshmen at UNL in 1997–98, 93 percent were white (Enrollment Information, Institutional Research and Planning. University of Nebraska-Lincoln. Fall 1997).

10

Learning to Write with a Civic Tongue

Elizabeth Ervin

Unlike some pedagogical innovations, service learning in composition came on strong—so strong, in fact, that some proponents have elevated it to the status of a "microrevolution," one which has engendered "radical transformations" of our experience and understanding of education (Adler-Kassner, Crooks, and Watters 1997, 1). Service learning holds that by doing community service and writing about it—or, alternatively, by doing writing that serves the needs of community agencies or that attempts to influence authentic public concerns—students develop a greater sense of commitment to the world beyond the classroom and come to see themselves as agents who can transform oppressive social institutions. These are laudable goals, but also problematic ones, as recent critiques of service learning have uneasily revealed. As Wade Dorman and Susan Fox Dorman (1997) have acknowledged, "Service learning is not . . . a wonderland from which alienated students emerge transformed into literate, responsible citizens" (131). Bruce Herzberg (1994), for example, recounts a conversation overheard between two students engaged in service learning at his university: "'We're going to some shelter tomorrow and we have to write about it.' 'No sweat. Write that before you went you had no sympathy for the homeless, but the visit to the shelter opened your eyes. Easy A'" (309).

Such critiques represent inevitable counterbalances to the almost uniformly optimistic and inspiring early accounts of service learning projects that have appeared in our professional literature—accounts that have largely been accepted as, in the words of Mary Ann Cain (1998), "necessary fictions" (9). I've contributed to these accounts, and in this essay would like to offer something of a critique—not of service learning *per se,* but rather of the ways in which we tend to write about it and other kinds of teaching that manifest an explicitly democratic agenda. Specifically, I suggest that narratives describing "civic-minded" teaching seem to support democratic ideologies more than democratic practices, and that being a good citizen in our profession, like being a good citizen in our larger society, demands more honest narratives, full of inconvenient and even troubling detail about the challenges new pedagogies pose and the incongruities that exist between our practices and our ideologies. Because it immerses us in the discourses and behaviors of civic participation, service learning provides us with a case study of what it means to write with a civic tongue—that is, to write truthfully and responsibly in ways that are consistent with the democratic processes our profession purportedly values.

A model for this kind of narrative can be found in "A Multivalent Pedagogy for a Multicultural Time," James J. Sosnoski's (1994) teaching diary that became a wide-ranging written dialogue with David B. Downing. In this essay, Sosnoski "confesses" to a variety of problems and doubts in creating a classroom organized around "different kinds of work environments, different kinds of intellectual spaces . . . [and] different [work] expectations" (313). He suggests at one point—parenthetically—that "I think I might have to burn this diary lest it disqualify me from writing the essay. After all, I can't talk about my failures in print, can I?" (319). Downing responds:

> Sure you can. (With some risk, of course.) We have to be able to do this. . . .
> In disciplinary work "error" is bound up with the principle of falsification—
> if we can prove this claim or theorem false, we have advanced our inquiry. Thus
> errors are to be avoided and eliminated as quickly as possible from the relevant disciplinary regime. So in that sense the disciplinary protocol is always
> one of effacing error in the name of knowledge, which is supposed to be somehow error-less by definition. (320)

Downing continues by suggesting that refuting error in "the usual academic ways" probably isn't the most productive way of thinking about "postdisciplinary" pedagogies such as those represented by service learning. I agree.

And yet, attempting to speak honestly about our teaching can leave us vulnerable, particularly when we choose to do it in professional forums; it can, furthermore, upset our notions of what experiences are appropriate to write *about*. From an epistemological perspective, publicly telling tales of teaching struggle and failure seems to violate the still-widespread belief that failure interferes with knowledge creation. From a rhetorical perspective, such narratives run the risk of being dismissed as the distasteful airing of dirty laundry. As Mary Rose O'Reilley (1993) observes in *The Peaceable Classroom,* we tell the stories of our classrooms in certain ways "not only because it's hard to be honest but also because our minds keep trying to create order." Because rendering our experiences "faithfully" might be the best we can achieve, says O'Reilley, "it's important to sketch the details as precisely as one can" (10). That's what I'd like to do here: talk faithfully about some of my own efforts to incorporate service learning components into my classes, including the problems, blunders, and downright failures that resulted. My purpose in doing so is not to diminish the vitality or importance of service learning or critical pedagogy, but to raise some questions about the most ethical and professionally beneficial ways to write about them.

Service Learning: The Varnished Truth

I'll start by revisiting an earlier published narrative in which I glossed over the problems of a service learning project, conducted several years ago in an honors section of first-year composition. The "honors factor" presented some predictable problems as well as several significant advantages: I didn't have to justify the unusually high grades for the class, a perennial sticking point for teachers attempting nontraditional course structures (see, e.g., Sosnoski and Downing 1994, 320); and the students themselves, ambitious and eager to succeed, demonstrated minimal overt resistance to the service learning orientation of the class. Perhaps more importantly from my perspective, these students took classes together, went on university-sponsored field trips together, and even lived together in the dorms, thus having more occasions than many of their university peers to see our class as what Robert Putnam (1995) calls a "secondary association"—groups like bowling leagues, gardening clubs, and PTAs in which people come together not just to advance private interests, but to create and foster interpersonal commitments. According to Putnam, such efforts increase social and civic "capital" and thus positively influence civic engagement, an outcome I assumed would enhance the agenda of the class.

The most graphic way to illustrate what was left out of my original narrative is to cite it directly (see Ervin 1997, 396–397). It read like this:

Last year, an article appeared in our city's newspaper soliciting volunteers to contribute to the local history project of Sunset Beach, a small neighboring town. When I suggested to my first-year composition students that it might make a rewarding class project, they agreed to write a detailed timeline of the town's thirty-some years of existence. This involved a Saturday field trip to Sunset Beach (about 50 miles away), during which each of us—including me—would take notes from a year's worth of Town Council records and compile them as a class.

A more faithful account would have acknowledged that I didn't really "suggest" this project to my students; the opportunity "introduced itself" in the spring, and that summer I arranged for my class to do it during the following fall semester. This process was itself frustrating, for I was frequently at odds with the local coordinator, a Sunset Beach resident whom I'll call Mr. Edwards. For one thing, Mr. Edwards behaved condescendingly toward us throughout the project—as, for instance, when he called to make sure there would be female students coming to take notes on the town records, because "women are really better at that sort of thing." For another, he insisted that we focus our history on events like road construction and land annexation, even though more interesting stories were available to us in the form of controversies over coastal development, radically changing local demographics and social mores, and an organized secession movement. Students insisted upon addressing some of these issues in our final timeline—by chronicling, for example, a lengthy public debate over whether swimmers should be allowed to wear thong bikinis on the beach strand, which we gleefully dubbed "the thong ordinance."

Our task sounded straightforward enough, but problems arose immedi-
ately. Several students were ill or had other commitments and thus could not
participate on the weekend excursion; the class had to come up with different,
but equivalent, ways for them to contribute—in this case, gathering references
to and pictures of Sunset Beach from regional newspapers. Then, at the last
possible minute, the reservation for one of our vans was usurped by the athletic
program, leaving us without enough space to accommodate the remaining stu-
dents; by executive decision, the "overflow" was reassigned to do background
research on coastal development at our campus library. And finally, the Town
Council records documented fiscal rather than calendar years, so no one was
solely responsible for any given year; everyone worked with at least two years
simultaneously, and every year involved the efforts of at least two people.

The project was difficult to coordinate—not to mention evaluate—and
thoroughly disrupted students' expectations about, among other things, "equal
workload." It was also, I think, successful. By design, it fulfilled two elements of
my conceptual framework: my students and I produced public discourses for au-
thentic audiences, while simultaneously practicing legitimate college writing
tasks (e.g., taking notes from primary, archival materials; writing summaries
and annotations; devising organizational schemes and codes by which to or-
ganize data). But it was ultimately the messiness of the project that enabled us
to form secondary associations, perhaps the most challenging feature of the
civic classroom. Simply put, no one could do this project alone. We were com-
pletely dependent on each other, as well as completely responsible to each other
and to the citizens of Sunset Beach. Though students found the situation chal-
lenging, Ginger spoke for many when she wrote, "It was fun to go to Sunset
Beach and spend time with the class out[side] of class. I think . . . the people in
Sunset Beach will be pleased with our efforts. . . . [Although] I wish I could have
gone back and studied the documents more carefully and clarified things. . .
[o]verall, I think that I did a good job and so did the class." This is what can hap-
pen when we recognize and nurture our students' desires for social connected-
ness, their latent inclinations toward "doing something beneficial for society."

In fact, neither the decision making nor the work itself was as blithely democratic as I let on in my published narrative. When problems occurred, I alone
came up with solutions; these decisions did not meet with universal approval,
and indeed some students complained bitterly about what they saw as a "very
tedious" (Jason) and purposeless undertaking. For example, when we encountered transportation problems, I asked Bridget, who owned a car, if she would
drive a group of four students to the sole library in Brunswick County, where
Sunset Beach is located. She agreed, but when the students arrived they discovered that the library closes at noon on Saturdays. By that time the students had
little time to work, so two of them made subsequent trips to the Brunswick library during the next week, and the other two tried unsuccessfully to do their research at the campus library, which doesn't carry the county newspaper. In short,
this group did a lot of running around but found little useful information. They

felt frustrated and aimless, and I felt derelict in my duties to lead them in some clear direction. This haphazard and autocratic brand of problem-solving seemed, ironically, the best way to keep alive the democratic potential of service learning in the face of daunting logistical and pedagogical obstacles.

Although quoting appreciative student feedback—or better yet, "before" and "after" testimonials—is a familiar strategy for illustrating the positive impact of critical pedagogies, it can also be a deceptive one. As Cain explains, such practices "trap" students in the teacher's quotation marks, subjecting them to "a heroic narrative that they have no stake in authoring" (17). Moreover, it makes it easy to forget about those dissatisfied or bewildered students who aren't quoted, probably because they raise uncomfortable questions about our teaching. In the case of the Sunset Beach project, for example, students' self-assessments contained an unusually high number of "I hate group work because not everyone does their share" comments—and even a fair number of "I didn't do my share" comments—as well as some more pointed criticisms. Katie, for example, wrote: "Why we were assigned this project is a question I cannot answer. I know you said it was to learn paraphrasing, but why Sunset Beach? Why town records from before we were born?" Katie's concerns were legitimate, but I resented her for raising them after the fact, and so chose to attribute the project's failings to willful and mutinous students rather than to my own mistakes or flaws in the pedagogy I had adopted. I was able to maintain this fiction largely by suppressing critique.

The Sunset Beach project never really concluded to my satisfaction. We didn't hear a word from Mr. Edwards until several months after we had sent the finished timeline, and only after I wrote to remind him that my students and I had spent a beautiful Saturday in the Town Hall taking notes on the history of a community where none of us even lived. His penitent response was followed by a letter from the Town Manager expressing the town's appreciation for our contribution. The letter was complimentary enough, but the fact that the Town Manager had misspelled my name left me feeling rather deflated and forlorn—sorry for myself, in other words—which in turn made me feel guilty for wanting to receive public recognition.

It's not difficult to identify which parts of my service learning experience I was less than honest about in my original narrative: those in which I might appear overly autocratic or teacher-centered, disorganized or lacking in vision, or ineffective in communicating with students; in which I disliked or became frustrated with my students or the people on whose behalf we were writing; in which students resisted or openly spurned our work, slacked off, or behaved in less than democratic ways; and in which I came off as an opportunistic publicity hound rather than a committed citizen-teacher. Such details complicated the veracity of my own published theories about the civic classroom and, moreover, conflicted with much of what our profession values these days in terms of sound pedagogy and appropriate political attitudes. All teachers know that there are moments in the classroom when actions must be taken and decisions must be made *immediately,* without cumbersome negotiations, and in such moments, principle often yields to expediency. But these practical truths seemed so inconsistent with the potent ideological impulses of both service learning and student-centered classrooms that I kept my errors and my uncertainties to myself.

Do-Goodism Gone Bad

Deliberately or not, this first service learning narrative concealed, or at least minimized, the complications of the Sunset Beach project—perhaps out of fear of unflattering comparisons to more worthy colleagues, perhaps to convey my allegiance to what I thought was a suitably democratic ideology, perhaps because facing the disappointments that frequently accompany civic classrooms was simply too much to bear. Now I'm going to describe a second service learning project conducted with the same group of students, only this time I'll try to construct a narrative in which the complications are more faithfully integrated.

This project involved creating a sourcebook for the study of African American history, and was proposed to me and my students by a colleague in sociology, whom I'll call Professor Miller, on behalf of the residents' organization of a local public housing community, which I'll call Jefferson Homes.[1] Members of this group—all African American women—were organizing a resource center in a vacant apartment and wanted to develop a self-study program that focused on African American history and culture. Their previous efforts to initiate such a program had been plagued by misplaced materials, lack of dependable transportation to obtain library books, erratic levels of commitment, and various other problems. Working in their favor, though, was the fact that they had a computer with Internet access and—courtesy of a local Internet service provider and volunteers from Professor Miller's urban sociology class—an elaborate homepage. The plan, then, was for my students to create a sourcebook and present hard copies to the Jefferson residents and our university's African American Cultural Center, and to provide disk copies for a sociology student who, as part of an independent study project supervised by Professor Miller, would transfer the data to the Jefferson homepage.

Our first step as a class was to figure out what a sourcebook is and decide what kind of sourcebook we wanted to create. This was an exciting phase, for in our class brainstorming session, students seemed to envision the sourcebook as an *activist* document, complete with a political agenda; a directory of area political, social service, and African American cultural organizations and contact persons; sample copies of petitions and citizen action letters; and addresses of Congressional representatives—*in addition to* the annotated bibliographies and other reference materials that I recommended. Needless to say, not all of these made it into the final document, but I was hopeful at this early stage of the project.

The students, however, were not quite as optimistic as I was. On the day I introduced the project, they left the classroom wearing expressions that ranged from skepticism to alarm; one student, Jason, later admitted that he had considered dropping the class at this point. Not wanting the project to be doomed before it started, I considered ways to explain to my students the rationale for its design. At our next class meeting, I described to them ways I *could* have organized an honors writing course—more reading and writing than a "regular" course, for example—but that I had settled on the idea of a qualitatively different kind of classroom with ambiguous assignments because I believed they would be more challenging and would better prepare them for future writing tasks, and also because they promoted the kinds of civic behaviors I considered valuable. This explanation seemed to satisfy my students, but set into motion a cycle that would characterize our work on the sourcebook: foot-dragging followed by cheerleading followed by brief periods of routine teaching and learning.

Our next step was to discuss the rhetorical situation that lay before us: Who is this audience and how do they want to use this document? What kinds of source materials will be most appropriate for this purpose? How does a sourcebook differ from, say, a textbook? How much original writing will we need to produce and of what kinds? How might we divide the workload among ourselves for optimum fairness and efficiency? It was during this process that we nearly aborted the project. Simply put, these very talented, very motivated eighteen-year-olds were ill-equipped to devise their own assignment—particularly one as complex as this, and even *more* particularly since none of us had more than a sketchy knowledge of African American history. To assist us, Professor Miller visited our class and guided us through the Jefferson homepage, which included historical information, pictures, and plans for future renovations to the homes there. He told us about the Jefferson Residents Organization (JRO) and its primary concerns and functions—how, for example, members log on to the Federal Department of Housing and Urban Development Website every day so that they can print out and post flyers with current HUD announcements for other residents to read.[2] He told us that the majority of the Jefferson residents were high school graduates, and that many had some advanced education or were attending college.

In spite of these insights, students' discussions of audience remained awkward throughout the semester. Comments like "Our sourcebook has to be easy to read, because *these people* . . ." would trail off, unfinished, forcing us to spend two weeks candidly confronting our prejudices about public assistance, poverty, and race. Even after we had completed the sourcebook, many students persisted in their belief that our audience was not only uneducated but perhaps simpleminded (not to mention lazy, undisciplined, and all the other stereotypes that go along with being poor in an urban area). Certainly, there exists a tension between our students' goodwill and the sense of condescension that can develop in the context of community service writing projects, a tension that teachers must actively address. I'll say more about this below.

To bring the sourcebook together, my students worked in five groups of three or four, divided along chronological and thematic lines; for example, one group focused exclusively on the complex history of African Americans within our town (which included a still-controversial race riot in 1898), while another focused on the Civil Rights era. They conducted extensive research in our campus and local libraries and consulted experts on campus and in our community. They wrote letters, outlines, timelines, and essays; they compiled directories and bibliographies; they took photographs and created maps and visited museums and arranged interviews. Jason, the student who had contemplated dropping the class, even enrolled in a weekend-long local history class offered through the African American Cultural Center on our campus. The final product—a five-volume sourcebook—was truly impressive, and we celebrated it with a "publishing party" at the African American Cultural Center that was attended by various campus and local supporters and covered by the local media.

Although the sourcebook project was eventually—and apparently successfully—completed, this process was far from painless. The most serious setback came when a student named Erica (a member of the group exploring the history of slavery in the United States) unexpectedly withdrew from the university about a week before the first full draft was due. When her partners tried to retrieve Erica's notes, they found out that her husband had burned them and the rest of her school materials. I, meanwhile, learned that Erica had basically done all the work for her group so far, which meant that her partners, Cindy and Katie, needed a deadline extension if they were to turn in anything at all. Cindy and Katie had plenty of excuses for why they hadn't been able to assist Erica with their project, as well as for why they needed an extension and, later, an extension on their extension. I quietly seethed about the situation, but felt that I had to honor their requests because I didn't want to derail the other groups' progress—or their morale. I recognized the "teachable moments" inherent in these problems, of course; but once again, expediency held sway. Simply put, there were times when getting my students to "like" service learning, and hence to go along with my curriculum with a modicum of enthusiasm, seemed more important than demonstrating the finer points of democratic process. Thus I tried to shield them from the major hassles.

When teachers try to establish a different kind of classroom, with different kinds of work and different expectations for how that work is done, students behave unpredictably. This has been a well-established phenomenon at least since Robert Brooke (1987) published his influential essay on student underlife, and yet I was so busy keeping up with the organizational details of service learning that this predictable unpredictability took me by surprise. The result was a teacher and students who found themselves in unfamiliar classroom roles and who thus tried to behave, and tried to force one another to behave, in the same old ways. O'Reilley (1993) writes:

> One of the teacher's hardest jobs is to break conditioning. You can't just open
> the cages, as do some of my friends in the animal liberation movement, and

hope the poor beasts will run free. They will cower on their familiar newspaper, by their dish of Kibbles and Bits. Set free in the wide world they will
desperately try to run mazes. (69)

I knew from their journals and discussion comments that, like many honors students, Cindy and Katie had learned to presume the trust and goodwill of their
teachers; they believed (or so I imagine) that because they were capable writers who would eventually meet the obligations of the assignment, I should honor
their schedules. And truthfully, these expectations were reasonable within a
"radically democratic" classroom, a term coined by Herzberg (1994, 317):
Cindy and Katie had learned that writing is a messy, chaotic undertaking and
that people can fulfill their obligations to a project in different but equivalent ways.

Could it be, then, that *I* was the poor beast cowering on my familiar newspaper? After all, I became a teacher during a period when the advantages of
student-centered composition classrooms were all but taken for granted, and
I was neither comfortable nor particularly skilled in the role of commander-
in-chief. In other words, I would have preferred to occupy my familiar position
at the classroom margins while my students navigated this extremely difficult
project. And in fact, this is basically what I did—that is, until contingencies
such as Erica's demanded immediate intervention and I found myself slapping
together rickety "Plan Bs" that affected the entire project. This in turn caused
many students to lose confidence in what we were doing and my ability to guide
them through it. They felt cynical about the possibilities of the radically democratic classroom, and who could blame them? I was naïve to think that sus-
pending some conventions of classroom life wouldn't disrupt others, that compelling changes in students' behavior would have no effect on my own. I
attribute this error in judgment to the faulty assumption that "all critical pedagogies look alike," and more specifically, that they depend fundamentally upon
decentered classrooms.

Even after the publishing party, several disappointments lingered in my
mind. Most disheartening was the JRO's lack of participation in our project.
My students and I had set aside several class days for representatives of the organization to visit the class and give us feedback—at our convenience, admittedly—but transportation and scheduling problems repeatedly thwarted our
plans. We offered to bring our drafts to the residents, but their liaison, whom
I'll call Ms. Walters, was running for mayor during the crucial drafting stage of
our project, an endeavor which consumed not only *her* schedule but also those
of other JRO members. Eventually, my students and I stopped trying to arrange
a meeting and in the end, wrote and revised the entire document without any
input from our supposed audience. The real blow, however, came when nobody
from the residents organization attended the reception to celebrate the completion of our project, despite their RSVPs and our offers of transportation (which
were declined). I was, frankly, mortified by this unexpected turn of events. Other

African American faculty and community activists attended the reception and graciously praised our efforts, but I couldn't help but wonder whether our project was an authentic contribution to a community-defined need, or simply a hollow gesture tainted by what Ellen Cushman (1996) has called "a here-I-am-to-save-the-day air" (20). My question was answered when I delivered the sourcebooks to the JRO resource center at the end of the semester and Ms. Walters—with whom I had spoken several times—appeared not to know who I was. Seeming vaguely confused by what I was offering her, she thanked me and said simply, "Oh, we'll be able to show these to our high school students when they work on papers for school." With these words, our project was reduced from a tool of grassroots empowerment to something far less grand. Or perhaps more accurately, the sourcebook of our imaginations had been humbled by the reality of how far we'd missed the mark.

Another frustration was that the sourcebook project didn't get posted on the Internet as originally planned—first because Professor Miller's student graduated before preparing our materials, and later because Professor Miller himself accepted a position at another university and took our computer disks with him. For a while I received hopeful e-mail missives from my former students, "just wondering when the sourcebook is going online," and in response I offered them not only explanations of what had happened, but also solemn reflections on the messy, sometimes ineffectual, but ultimately worthwhile nature of democracy. I didn't want them to feel discouraged or duped by this experience, but the fact is that I, too, wondered what we accomplished. Two years after I taught this class, Cindy approached me about creating a Website based on the sourcebook for independent study credit. This was a gratifying development, as Cindy had been one of the more resistant students in the class. But while she worked hard tracking down the original documents, converting them to HTML, and designing the Web page, even I had lost interest in the project by the time she was finished.

The final blow came several months after the completion of the sourcebook, when I happened to read a notice in the newspaper that our county library had

> received a $19,000 Local Historical Organizations Grant to publish a full-length history of black life in Wilmington . . . from Emancipation to 1948—through the history of its schools, churches, civic and social clubs, politics, businesses, military companies, community affairs and leaders. . . . *Strength Through Struggle* will be the first full-length compilation of black life in Wilmington to be published. ("Grant" 1996, 4D)

Having managed to forget some of the more disconcerting details of my first foray into service learning, I was again forced to confront the question of whether our sourcebook had ever had an "authentic" civic purpose or public audience—those rhetorical features that had been, even in its more befuddled moments, the project's saving grace. And I was reminded of the character Mr. Casaubon in George Eliot's *Middlemarch* ([1872] 1977), who devotes his life to researching "The Key to All Mythologies"—a manuscript that, he realizes too late, simply replicates existing scholarship and thus will be of no use to anyone. Rather than abandon the project or make appropriate adjustments, the sickly Casaubon tries to induce his wife Dorothea to carry on with the project in the event of his death, but Dorothea's reluctance to accept responsibility for the "Key" so upsets Casaubon that he has a heart attack and dies. Were the efforts of my students and I, like those of Mr. Casaubon, laughable—"got by groping about in woods with a pocket-compass while [others had already] made good roads" (Eliot 144)? Was our sourcebook as ill-conceived as the "Key," "withered in the birth like an elfin child" (331)? And did my students labor over the project only to spare me a heart attack?

I had to face the fact that although the sourcebook project *had* invigorated our class with the spirit of collaboration and civic purpose (if only in spurts), it took an unexpected shape: do-goodism, ranging from the "merely" liberal variety to the more unctuous self-promoting kind. A newspaper article describing the project generated some good university publicity for me, and my students and I were all so excited about seeing ourselves on the evening news that we watched the videotape twice. Because I wanted to believe that students had embraced the challenge of influencing public debate through language, I didn't see the reality: that many of them (or should I say many of *us?*) were so busy patting themselves on the back for being noble that they saw little reason to explore critical or activist roles of citizenship—for example, to consider the racially marked relationship that existed between the members of the residents organization and us despite the fact that we'd never even met, and indeed *contributing to* the fact that we'd never met. After all, inequities of income, housing, and educational access are monumental, downright depressing problems, but believing that we've "helped the poor and unfortunate" makes us feel good. Many of us long to "make a difference in the world," and hey, if it fulfills my honors requirement, too. . . . (Or in my case, if it attracts the attention of the Provost. . . .) I unintentionally encouraged this paternalistic attitude: hypersensitive to every lag in energy or enthusiasm, I constantly reminded my students of the importance of their work. In such an atmosphere, arrogance thrived.

Oh, I could go on. For these two service learning projects provided enough examples of pedagogical blunders—both exotic and garden variety—to fill this book. What was ultimately more frustrating than the problems themselves, however, was the fact that I had no context for understanding or assessing them, and hence narrating them. Was the sourcebook project an "inauthentic" exercise in civic participation simply because it didn't fulfill the purpose we had originally envisioned? Did it fail because it replicated (at least in part) a well-heeled local project that was already in the works, and because my students and I didn't interact in any meaningful way with our audience? Or was it enough that we *did it*—that we opened our energies to such a complex project in the first place, that it led to frank discussions of difficult issues and prejudices, that we produced a document of potential use to someone other than ourselves, that we turned in disks as we were asked and tried to use computer technology to expand our audience, that we waived traditional writing-class luxuries like working alone and choosing our own topics, that we learned the conventions of researching and writing for publication? In short, was our muddled *attempt* at civic writing—like Ms. Walters' failed bid for mayor—enough to make the project successful?

I don't know the answers to these questions. But what I was certain of even then was that my efforts did not live up to those air-brushed images of collaboration, democracy, and consciousness raising that I'd read about in other service learning narratives, and that any public acknowledgment of this hard truth threatened to expose me either as someone who didn't know what she was doing or whose version of a democratic classroom was shockingly inadequate. So for years I've dutifully encouraged others to plunge into service learning while brooding silently on my own failures to realize the democratic ideology I championed.

The Importance of Being Honest

Reflecting upon my service learning projects, I've found consolation in O'Reilley's rather unorthodox claim that "certain people have to undertake experiments and live out the consequences of ideas for the benefit of the rest, even if the ideas turn out to be wrong—especially if they turn out to be wrong" (36). But as Judy Z. Segal (1996) points out, when pedagogical experiments come "from good intentions rather than good theory, it can be hard even to find a language to discuss [their] failure" (174). What we need, Segal suggests, is a "discourse of failure" that can help us to avoid the discourse of blaming (blaming the student[s], the teacher, the institution, the theory), move us away from self-aggrandizement or self-flagellation, and lead us in the direction of improved teaching. Developing such a discourse should be a high priority, if only because, as O'Reilley suggests, what *we* learn from our teaching is at least as important as what students learn (71).

I'd be a liar if I said that I'm grateful for the mistakes I've made in my service learning experiments, or that I'm glad I didn't have the knowledge or judgment to deal with them more effectively at the time. Like everyone, I want my teaching to run smoothly, to "work." But as we know from studies of language acquisition and basic writing, getting it wrong is often how we get it right. That is, errors serve a useful heuristic function: As catalysts of critical reflection and action, they can bring us to the brink of new understandings. If we are serious about teaching and learning—within our professional communities as well as our classrooms—we must treat *our own* errors as generously as we treat those of our students. And toward that end, we must consciously resist the desire for "order" that O'Reilley describes, and the desire for heroism that Marguerite Helmers (1994) identifies in *Writing Students,* both of which can induce us to create less-than-truthful pedagogical narratives in the first place.

But there is also that little matter of "living out the consequences" of our teaching blunders. Although exposing our shortcomings can be painful under any circumstances, writing about our failures as critical teachers seems especially fraught with hazards. For like democracy itself, democratic classrooms are experiments that manifest themselves both in theories and in practices, and writing about our flawed approximations of them can feel like inscribing the deficiencies of a cherished ideal. Stakes this high must be taken seriously.

David Nyberg (1993) suggests that glossing over inconvenient truths is such a widespread, complex, multiform, and *useful* practice that we can't take for granted its moral—nor, presumably, its professional—offensiveness. Asserting that "a fundamental purpose of language . . . is to regulate relationships among individuals and groups of people by maintaining surveillance over information revealed and concealed," Nyberg concludes that ideological interests might be better served by deception than truth-telling (114). Having seen our best professional efforts publicly caricatured by the likes of George Will (1995) and John Leo (1997) in recent years, it's easy to understand why composition teachers might be reluctant to lay bare our classroom practices in their flawed complexity. But while concealing our blunders might indeed help us to "maintain surveillance over information" about our profession, this practice also threatens the utility and credibility of our scholarship—and thus the efficacy of our teaching. Stephen M. North (1985) has questioned whether composition practitioners "have become too sophisticated to air our doubts in public, to expose the complex and not always well-disciplined processes that lie behind the new self-image we seem bent on creating." Lamenting what he perceived as a decline of published essays whose authors seemed "unafraid of confusion or failure or students . . . or, for that matter, one another," North argued that "no journal can afford *not* to publish such [essays]" (98; ellipses and emphasis in original).

Certainly, honest discussions of pedagogical error should amount to more than the celebration of failure or cheerless confessionals. But they should likewise amount to more than the kind of ideological pep talks I felt compelled to offer my students when our forays into civic writing went awry. More honest narrative practices also have consequences for democratic teaching. As Sandra Stotsky (1992) observes, writers have obligations to their readers "independent of the reader[s'] needs," and one of these is the disclosure of "all relevant information" (799), including problems. Sissela Bok (1978) argues, furthermore, that in the case of professional research, it is actually preferable to forgo certain kinds of knowledge than to conceal the dissonant details of our work. Such deceptions, however trivial they may seem, are rarely "openly debated and consented to in advance," she says, and thus undermine professional trust (181, 188). According to Bok, when we believe we need to deceive in order to advance knowledge or what we perceive to be the "public good"—for example, a theory or political ideology—we enter into a morass of antidemocratic and ethically ambiguous practices (166). "[T]he filters through which we must try to peer at lying are thicker and more distorting than ever" under such circumstances, Bok warns, making such lies seem not only harmless, but noble (166–167).

A few years ago I watched a documentary about the 1989 Tiannamen Square massacre in China. As the pro-democracy rallies wore on, conflicts erupted among the student demonstrators: Some wanted to "impose" democratic practices in order to sidestep the difficult process of negotiating a political system that they had never actually experienced; others wanted to establish democracy in ways that were more ideologically consistent, even if that meant it never got established at all. This dilemma provides a useful analogy for our own political work in the classroom. Truths are multiple and complicated, to be sure, but as John Clifford and Janet Ellerby (1997) observe, "all discourse, especially narrative, enacts ethical choices, is imbued with values, and asserts implicit positions on the big questions of ethical theorizing" (11). Narratives that make deliberate use of dissembling and prevarication ultimately cannot sustain successful democratic experiments. And while restoring the messy realities of our teaching might expose us to criticism or negative judgment, it also allows us to practice "radically democratic" teaching—teaching whose ideals may never be fully realized, but which nevertheless unfurls in full view of a constituency to whom such ideals continue to matter.

Notes

1. In the interests of full disclosure, let me point out that although the timeline was arranged first, the sourcebook project was technically the first service learning project my class undertook. After the initial drafts of the sourcebook were completed, we took a three-week break in order to recharge our batteries and reflect on our progress, and it was during this sourcebook hiatus that we completed the timeline project in full.

2. Some background is needed here. Several years ago, the JRO received a HUD grant to use at its discretion for the improvement of the residents' conditions. Instead of spending it on drug-prevention or job training programs—"recommended" government programs in which the residents had little faith—the JRO purchased computer equipment. Part of the reasoning was that Jefferson is scheduled to be razed and rebuilt in the next few years, and the JRO wanted to participate actively in the plans for redesigning a new housing facility to better meet the needs of residents. It believed that a computer with Internet access would be the most effective tool for communicating with architects, city planners, and government officials; studying building codes; and mounting grassroots support. So far, the JRO has been effective in establishing itself as a knowledgeable voice in this renovation process—although not without significant resistance from local and federal officials.

Works Cited

Adler-Kassner, L., R. Crooks, and A. Watters. 1997. "Service-Learning and Compo-
sition at the Crossroads." In *Writing the Community: Concepts and Models for
Service-Learning in Composition,* edited by L. Adler-Kassner, R. Crooks, and
A. Watters, 1–17. Washington, DC: AAHE.

——, R. Crooks, and A. Watters, eds. 1997. *Writing the Community: Concepts and
Models for Service-Learning in Composition.* Washington, DC: AAHE.

al-Shaykah, N. 1992. *Women of Sand and Myrrh.* Translated by C. Cobham. New
York: Anchor Books.

Anderson, B. 1992. *Imagined Communities: Reflections on the Origins and Spread
of Nationalism.* Revised Edition. London: Verso.

Anderson, M. 1956. *My Lord, What a Morning.* New York: Avon.

Angelou, M. 1971. *I Know Why the Caged Bird Sings.* New York: Bantam.

Bakhtin, M. 1987. *Problems of Dostoevsky's Poetics.* Edited and translated by C. Emer-
son. Minneapolis: University of Minnesota Press.

Barret, L. 1994. "Institutions, Classrooms, Failures: African American Literature and
Critical Theory in the Same Small Spaces." In *Teaching Contemporary Theory
to Undergraduates,* edited by D. Sadoff and W. E. Cain, 218–232. New York:
Modern Language Association.

Bartholomae, D., and E. Petrosky, eds. 1993. *Ways of Reading: An Anthology of Writers.* Boston: Bedford/St. Martin's.

Bauer, D. 1990. "The Other 'F' Word: The Feminist in the Classroom" *College English*
52(4): 385–96.

Bender, T. 1978. *Community and Social Change in America.* New Brunswick, NJ:
Rutgers University Press.

Berlin, J. A. 1996. "English Studies, Work, and Politics in the New Economy." In *Composition in the Twenty-First Century: Crisis and Change,* edited by L. Z. Bloom,
D. A. Daiker, and E. S. White, 215–25. Carbondale, IL: Southern Illinois University Press.

Bérubé, M. 1997. "The Blessed of the Earth." In *Will Teach for Food: Academic Labor in Crisis,* edited by C. Nelson, 153–78. Minneapolis: University of Minnesota Press.

——, S. Molloy, C. N. Davidson, and D. Palumbo-Liu. 1996. "Four Views on the
Place of the Personal in Scholarship." *PMLA* 111(5): 1063–79.

Bishop, W. 1997. "What We Don't Like, Don't Admit, Don't Understand Can't Hurt Us.
Or Can It? On Writing, Teaching, Living." In *Narration as Knowledge: Tales of*

the Teaching Life, edited by J. F. Trimmer, 191–201. Portsmouth, NH: Boynton/ Cook.

Bizzell, P., and B. Herzberg. 1996. *Negotiating Difference: Cultural Case Studies for Composition.* Boston: Bedford.

Bloom, L. Z. 1997. "Subverting the Academic Master Plot." In *Narration as Knowledge: Tales of the Teaching Life,* edited by J. F. Trimmer, 116–26. Portsmouth, NH: Boynton/Cook.

———. 1996. "Freshman Composition as a Middle-Class Enterprise." *College English* 58(6): 654–75.

———, D. A. Daiker, and E. S. White, eds. 1996. *Composition in the Twenty-First Century: Crisis and Change.* Carbondale, IL: Southern Illinois University Press.

Boal, A. 1985. *Theatre of the Oppressed.* Translated by C. and M-O. Leal McBride. New York: Theatre Communications Group.

Bok, S. 1978. *Lying: Moral Choice in Public and Private Life.* New York: Pantheon.

Bonk, C. J., E. Hansen, M. Grabner-Hagen, S. Lazar, and C. Mirabelli. 1998. "Time to 'Connect': Synchronous and Asynchronous Case-Based Dialogue Among Preservice Teachers." In *Electronic Collaborators: Learner-Centered Technologies for Literacy, Apprenticeship, and Discourse,* edited by C. J. Bonk and K. King, 289–314. Mahwah, NJ: Lawrence Erlbaum Associates.

Bordo, S. 1997. *Twilight Zones: The Hidden Life of Cultural Images from Plato to O. J.* Berkeley: University of California Press.

Brock, M. A. B., and J. Ellerby. 1997. "Out of Control: TA Training and Liberation Pedagogy." In *Sharing Pedagogies: Students and Teachers Write About Dialogic Practices,* edited by G. Tayko and J. P. Tassoni, 114–28. Portsmouth, NH: Boynton/Cook.

Brooke, R. 1987. "Underlife and Writing Instruction." *College Composition and Communication* 38 (2): 141–53.

Brooks, G. 1953. *Maud Martha.* New York: Harper & Row.

Brown, W. W. [1853] 1989. *Clotel; Or, The President's Daughter.* New York: Carol Publishing Group.

Bruffee, K. 1996. "Collaborative Learning and the 'Conversation of Mankind.'" In *Composition in Four Keys: Inquiring into the Field,* edited by M. Wiley, B. Gleason, and L. Wetherbee Phelps, 84–97. Mountain View, CA: Mayfield.

———. 1993. *Collaborative Learning: Higher Education, Interdependence, and the Authority of Knowledge.* Baltimore: Johns Hopkins University Press.

———. 1986. "Social Construction, Language, and the Authority of Knowledge: A Bibliographical Essay." *College English* 48 (8): 773–90.

———. 1984. "Collaborative Learning and the 'Conversation of Mankind.'" *College English* 46 (7): 635–52.

Cain, M. A. 1998. "What's Missing from this Picture? The Absence of Teacher 'Error' in Representations of Praxis." *Composition Studies* 26 (1): 7–20.

Cary, L. 1991. *Black Ice.* New York: Vintage.

Cheyfitz, E. 1991. *The Poetics of Imperialism: Translation and Colonization from the Tempest to Tarzan.* New York: Oxford University Press.

Chiseri-Strater, E., and B. S. Sunstein. 1997. *FieldWorking: Reading and Writing Research.* Upper Saddle River, NJ: Prentice Hall.

Clark, G. 1994. "Rescuing the Discourse of Community." *College Composition and Communication* 45 (1): 61–74.

Clee, P., and V. Radu-Clee. 1997. *American Dreams.* Mountain View, CA: Mayfield.

Clifford, J. 1997. "Testing the Limits of Tolerance in the Democratic Classroom." In *Narration as Knowledge: Tales of the Teaching Life,* edited by J. F. Trimmer, 164–72. Portsmouth, NH: Boynton/Cook.

———. 1988. *The Predicament of Culture: Ethnography, Literature and Art.* Cambridge: Harvard University Press.

———, and J. Ellerby. 1997. "Composing Ethics." *Composition Studies* 25 (1): 8–20.

Colombo, G., R. Cullen, and B. Lisle, eds. 1992. *Rereading America.* Boston: Bedford.

Cooper, R., and R. Lewandowski. 1997. "Voices of a Student and a Teacher: Freedom Versus Forced Education." In *Sharing Pedagogies: Students and Teachers Write About Dialogic Practices,* edited by G. Tayko and J. P. Tassoni, 13–24. Portsmouth, NH: Boynton/Cook.

Connors, R. 1987. "Personal Writing Assignments." *College Composition and Communication* 38 (2): 166–83.

Crenshaw, K. W. 1997. "Color-Blind Dreams and Racial Nightmares: Reconfiguring Racism in the Post-Civil Rights Era." In *Birth of a Nation'Hood: Gaze, Script, and Spectacle in the O. J. Simpson Case,* edited by T. Morrison and C. B. Lacour, 90–111. New York: Pantheon Books.

Cross, G. 1994. *Collaboration and Conflict: A Contextual Exploration of Group Writing and Positive Emphasis.* Cresskill, NJ: Hampton.

Crow Dog, M., and R. Erdos. 1990. *Lakota Woman.* New York: Harper Perennial.

Culley, M. 1985. "Anger and Authority in the Introductory Women's Studies Classroom." In *Gendered Subjects: The Dynamics of Feminist Teaching,* edited by M. Culley and C. Portgues, 209–16. Boston: Routledge and Kegan Paul.

———, and C. Portgues, eds. 1985. *Gendered Subjects: The Dynamics of Feminist Teaching.* Boston: Routledge and Kegan Paul.

Cushman, E. 1996. "The Rhetorician as an Agent of Social Change." *College Composition and Communication* 47 (1): 7–28.

Daniel, B. 1999. "Envisioning Literacy: Establishing E-Mail in a First-Year Program." In *Kitchen Cooks, Plate Twirlers, and Troubadours: Writing Program Administrators Tell Their Stories,* edited by D. George, 150–61. Portsmouth, NH: Boynton/Cook.

DeBruyn, R. L. 1996. "You're Always Communicating." *The Professor in the Classroom* 3(4). Manhattan, KS: The Master Teacher.

Demos, J. 1986. *Past, Present, and Personal: The Family and the Life Course in American History.* New York: Oxford University Press.

Dorman, W., and S. Fox Dorman. 1997. "Service-Learning: Bridging the Gap Between the Real World and the Composition Classroom." In *Writing the Community:*

Concepts and Models for Service-Learning in Composition, edited by L. Adler-Kassner, R. Crooks, and A. Watters, 119–32. Washington, DC: AAHE.

Dubois, W.E.B. [1903] 1990. *The Souls of Black Folk: Essays and Sketches.* New York: Vintage Books.

Durst, R. 1999. *Collision Course: Conflict, Negotiation, and Learning in College Composition.* Urbana, IL: National Council of Teachers of English.

Echols, A. 1989. *Daring to Be Bad: Radical Feminism in America, 1967–1975.* Minneapolis: University of Minnesota Press.

Ede, L. 1995. *Work In Progress: A Guide to Writing and Revising,* 3d ed. New York: St. Martin's.

Eliot, G. [1872] 1977. *Middlemarch.* New York: W. W. Norton.

Elliott, M. 1996. "Coming Out in the Classroom." *College English* 58 (6): 693–708.

Ervin, E. 1997. "Encouraging Civic Participation Among First-Year Writing Students; or, Why Composition Class Should Be More Like a Bowling Team." *Rhetoric Review* 15 (2): 382–99.

Faigley, L. 1992. *Fragments of Rationality: Postmodernity and the Subject of Composition.* Pittsburgh: University of Pittsburgh Press.

Fox, T. 1990. "Basic Writing as Cultural Conflict." *Journal of Education* 172 (1): 65–83.

Friedan, B. 1963. *The Feminine Mystique.* New York: Dell.

Friedman, S. S. 1985. "Authority in the Feminist Classroom: A Contradiction in Terms?" In *Gendered Subjects: The Dynamics of Feminist Teaching,* edited by M. Culley and C. Portgues, 203–208. Boston: Routledge and Kegan Paul.

Freire, P. 1973. *Education for Critical Consciousness.* Translated and edited by M. B. Ramos. New York: Continuum.

———. 1970. *Pedagogy of the Oppressed.* Translated by M. B. Ramos. New York: Continuum.

Fulwiler, T. 1997. "Telling Stories and Writing Truths." In *Narration as Knowledge: Tales of the Teaching Life,* edited by J. F. Trimmer, 84–97. Portsmouth: Boynton/Cook.

Fuss, D. 1989. *Essentially Speaking: Feminism, Nature, and Difference.* New York: Routledge.

Gale, X. L. 1996. *Teachers, Discourses and Authority in the Postmodern Composition Classroom.* Albany, NY: SUNY Press.

Gallop, J. 1997. *Feminists Accused of Sexual Harassment.* Durham, NC: Duke University Press.

Gere, A. R. 1996. "The Long Revolution in Composition." In *Composition in the Twenty-First Century: Crisis and Change,* edited by L. Z. Bloom, D. A. Daiker, and E. S. White, 119–32. Carbondale, IL: Southern Illinois University Press.

Giroux, H. A. 1997a. *Pedagogy and the Politics of Hope: Theory, Culture, and Schooling.* Boulder, CO: Westview Press.

———. 1997b. "Racial Politics and the Pedagogy of Whiteness." In *Whiteness: A Critical Reader,* edited by M. Hill, 297–304. New York: New York University Press.

————. 1993a. "Academics as Public Intellectuals," *Minnesota Review* 41/42: 314–16.

————. 1993b. *Living Dangerously: Multiculturalism and the Politics of Difference.* New York: Peter Lang.

————. 1992. *Border Crossings: Cultural Workers and the Politics of Education.* New York: Routledge.

————. 1988. *Schooling and the Struggle for Public Life: Critical Pedagogy in the Modern Age.* Minneapolis: University of Minnesota Press.

————, and R. Simon. 1989. "Popular Culture and Critical Pedagogy: Everyday Life as a Basis for Curriculum Knowledge." In *Critical Pedagogy, the State, and Cultural Struggle,* ed. H. A. Giroux and P. L. McLaren, 236–54. Albany, NY: SUNY Press.

Goodburn, A., and C. Leverenz. 1998. "Feminist Writing Program Administration: Resisting the Bureaucrat Within." In *Feminism and Composition Studies: In Other Words,* edited by S. Jarratt and L. Worsham, 276–90. New York: Modern Language Association.

Gordon-Reed, A. 1997. *Thomas Jefferson and Sally Hemmings: An American Controversy.* Charlottesville: University Press of Virginia.

Goshgarian, G. 1997. *Exploring Language.* 8th ed. New York: Longman.

Graff, G. 1996. "Response to Mark Walhout." In *Profession 1996,* 145–48. New York: Modern Language Association.

————. 1992. *Beyond the Culture Wars: How Teaching the Conflicts Can Revitalize American Education.* New York: W. W. Norton.

"Grant to help publish local black history." 1996. *Wilmington Star-News,* 17 June, 4D.

Haggerty, G. E., and B. Zimmerman, eds. 1995. *Professions of Desire.* New York: Modern Language Association.

Hairston, M. 1992. "Diversity, Ideology, and Teaching Writing." *College Composition and Communication* 43 (2): 179–93.

Harkin, P., and J. Schlib, eds. 1991. *Contending with Words: Composition and Rhetoric in a Postmodern Age.* New York: Modern Language Arts.

————. 1991. "The Postdisciplinary Politics of Lore." In *Contending with Words,* edited by P. Harkin and J. Schilb, 124–38. New York: Modern Language Association.

Harris, J. 1989. "The Idea of Community in the Study of Writing." *College Composition and Communication* 40 (1): 11–22.

Hawisher, G., and P. Sullivan. 1998. "Women on the Networks: Searching for E-Spaces of Their Own." In *Feminism and Composition Studies: In Other Words,* edited by S. Jarratt and L. Worsham, 172–97. New York: Modern Language Association.

Hayden, D. 1995. *The Power of Place.* Cambridge: MIT Press.

Heath, S. B. 1996. "Work, Class, and Categories: Dilemmas of Identity." In *Composition in the Twenty-First Century: Crisis and Change,* edited by L. Z. Bloom, D. A. Daiker, E. S. White, 226–42. Carbondale, IL: Southern Illinois University Press.

Helmers, M. 1994. *Writing Students: Composition Testimonials and Representations of Students.* Albany, NY: SUNY Press.

Herzberg, B. 1994. "Community Service and Critical Teaching." *College Composition and Communication* 45 (3): 307–19.

hooks, b. 1998. "Writing Autobiography." In *Women, Autobiography, Theory: A Reader,* edited by S. Smith and J. Watson, 429–32. Madison: University of Wisconsin Press.

———. 1996. *Black Bone: Memories of Girlhood.* New York: Henry Holt.

———. 1994. *Teaching to Transgress: Education as the Practice of Freedom.* New York: Routledge.

———, and C. West. 1991. *Breaking Bread: Insurgent Black Intellectual Life.* Boston: South End Press.

Hurlbert, C. M., and A. M. Bodnar. 1994. "Collective Pain: Literature, War, and Small Change." In *Changing Classroom Practices: Resources for Literary and Cultural Studies,* edited by D. B. Downing, 202–32. Urbana, IL: National Council of Teachers of English.

Hurston, Z. N. 1942. *Dust Tracks on a Road: An Autobiography.* Philadelphia: Lippincott.

Hyde, L. 1983. *The Gift: Imagination and the Erotic Life of Property.* New York: Vintage.

Jackson, E., Jr. 1995. "Explicit Instruction: Teaching Gay Male Sexuality in Literature Classes." In *Professions of Desire,* edited by G. E. Haggerty and B. Zimmerman, 136–55. New York: Modern Language Association.

Jarratt, S. C. 1991. "Feminism and Composition: The Case for Conflict." In *Contending with Words,* edited by P. Harkin and J. Schilb, 105–23. New York: Modern Language Association.

———, and L. Worsham, eds. 1998. *Feminism and Composition Studies: In Other Words.* New York: Modern Language Association.

Johnson, P. E. 1995. "What (If Anything) Hath God Wrought? Academic Freedom and the Religious Professor." *Academe* (Sept./Oct.): 16–19.

Jordan, J. 1994. *Technical Difficulties.* New York: Vintage.

Jordan, T. 1993. *Riding the White Horse Home: A Western Family Album.* New York: Vintage.

Kaplan, A. 1994. *French Lessons: A Memoir.* Chicago: University of Chicago Press.

Knoblauch, C. H., and L. Brannon. 1984. *Rhetorical Traditions and the Teaching of Writing.* Upper Montclair, NJ: Boynton/Cook.

Kohl, H. 1991. *I Won't Learn from You: The Role of Assent in Learning.* Minneapolis: Milkweed Editions.

Landow, G. 1992. *Hypertext: The Convergence of Contemporary Critical Theory and Technology.* Baltimore: Johns Hopkins University Press.

Lentricchia, F. 1997. "The Edge of Night." In *Beyond the Godfather: Italian American Writers on the Real Italian American Experience,* edited by A. K. Ciongoli and J. Parini, 28–48. Hanover, NH: University Press of New England.

Leo, J. 1997. "The Answer Is 45 Cents." *U. S. News and World Report* (21 April): 14.

Lewis, H. B. 1971. *Shame and Guilt in Neurosis.* New York: International Universities Press.

Litvak, J. 1995. "Pedagogy and Sexuality." In *Professions of Desire,* edited by G. E. Haggerty and B. Zimmerman, 19–30. New York: Modern Language Association.

Lorde, A. 1984. "The Uses of Anger: Women Responding to Racism." In *Sister Outsider: Essays and Speeches,* 124–33. Trumansburg, NY: Crossing Press.

———. 1982. *Zami: A New Spelling of My Name.* Trumansburg, NY: Crossing Press.

Lu, M.-Z., and B. Horner. 1999. "Conflict and Struggle: The Enemies or the Preconditions of Basic Writing?" In *Representing the "Other": Basic Writers and the Teaching of Basic Writing,* edited by M.-Z. Lu and B. Horner, 30–55. Urbana, IL: National Council of Teachers of English.

———. 1998. "The Problematic of Experience." *College English* 60 (3): 257–77.

Lyman, P. 1981. "The Politics of Anger: On Silence, Resentment, and Political Speech." *Socialist Review* (May/June): 55–74.

Lynd, H. M. 1958. *On Shame and the Search for Identity.* New York: Harcourt Brace.

Lyotard, J. 1984. *The Postmodern Condition: A Report on Knowledge.* Translated by G. Bennington and B. Massumi. Minneapolis: University of Minnesota Press.

Maasik, S., and J. Solomon. 1997. *Signs of Life in the USA.* Boston: Bedford.

Mahoney, K. 1995. "Whiteness in the Heartland: A Radical Pedagogue Running Head-First into the Walls of Privilege." Unpublished manuscript.

Malinowitz, H. 1995. *Textual Orientations: Lesbian and Gay Students and the Making of Discourse Communities.* Portsmouth, NH: Boynton/Cook.

Marshall, M. J. 1997. "Marking the Unmarked: Reading Student Diversity and Preparing Teachers." *College Composition and Communication* 48 (2): 231–48.

Marvin, C. 1995. "Bodies, Texts, and the Social Order: A Reply to Bielefeldt." *Quarterly Journal of Speech* 81 (2): 103–107.

Mayo, P. 1993. "When Does It Work? Freire's Pedagogy in Context." *Studies in the Education of Adults* 25: 11–28.

McBride, J. 1996. *The Color of Water.* New York: Riverhead.

McKay, N. 1995. "Minority Faculty in [Mainstream White] Academia." In *The Academic's Handbook,* edited by L. DeNeef and C. Goodwin, 48–61. Durham, NC: Duke University Press.

Miller, R. 1998. "The Arts of Complicity: Pragmatism and the Culture of Schooling." *College English* 61 (1): 10–28.

———. 1994. "Fault Lines in the Contact Zone." *College English* 56 (4): 389–408.

Miller, S. 1991a. "The Feminization of Composition." In *The Politics of Writing Instruction: Postsecondary,* edited by R. Bullock and J. Trimbur, 39–54. Portsmouth, NH: Boynton/Cook.

———. 1991b. *Textual Carnivals: The Politics of Composition.* Carbondale, IL: Southern Illinois University Press.

Minock, M. 1994. "The Bad Marriage: A Revisionist View of James Britton's Expressive-Writing Hypothesis in American Practice." In *Taking Stock: The Writing Process Movement in the '90s,* edited by L. Tobin and T. Newkirk, 153–75. Portsmouth, NH: Boynton/Cook.

Moraga, C., and G. Anzaldúa, eds. 1981. *This Bridge Called My Back: Writings by Radical Women of Color.* New York: Kitchen Table.

Morgan, R., ed. 1970. *Sisterhood Is Powerful: An Anthology of Writings from the Women's Liberation Movement.* New York: Vintage.

Morrison, T. 1997. "The Official Story: Dead Man Golfing." In *Birth of a Nation-'Hood: Gaze, Script, and Spectacle in the O. J. Simpson Case,* edited by T. Morrison and C. B. Lacour, iii–xxxiv. New York: Pantheon Books.

———, and C. B. Lacour, ed. 1997. *Birth of a Nation'Hood: Gaze, Script, and Spectacle in the O. J. Simpson Case.* New York: Pantheon Books.

Nathanson, D. L. 1992. *Shame and Pride: Affect, Sex, and the Birth of the Self.* New York: W. W. Norton.

Newkirk, T. 1997. *The Performance of Self in Student Writing.* Portsmouth, NH: Boynton/Cook.

North, S. 1987. *The Making of Knowledge in Composition.* Portsmouth, NH: Boynton/Cook.

———. 1985. Letter to editor of *Rhetoric Review. Rhetoric Review* 4 (1): 98–99.

Novak, C. C., and L. J. Goodman. 1997. "Safe/r Contact Zones: The Call of Service Learning." *Writing Instructor* 16 (2): 65–77.

Nyberg, D. 1993. *The Varnished Truth: Truth Telling and Deceiving in Ordinary Life.* Chicago: University of Chicago Press.

O'Reilley, M. R. 1993. *The Peaceable Classroom.* Portsmouth, NH: Boynton/Cook.

Orenstein, P. 1994. *SchoolGirls: Young Women, Self-Esteem, and the Confidence Gap.* New York: Anchor.

Payne, M. 1994. "Rend(er)ing Women's Authority in the Writing Classroom." In *Taking Stock: The Writing Process Movement in the '90s,* edited by L. Tobin and T. Newkirk, 97–111. Portsmouth, NH: Boynton/Cook.

Peck, W. C., L. Flower, and L. Higgins. 1995. "Community Literacy." *College Composition and Communication* 46 (2): 199–222.

Piers, G., and M. B. Singer. 1953. *Shame and Guilt: A Psychoanalytic and a Cultural Study.* Springfield, IL: Charles C. Thomas.

Power, B. M., and R. S. Hubbard, eds. 1996. *Oops: What We Learn When Our Teaching Fails.* York, ME: Stenhouse.

Pratt, M. L. 1991. "Arts of the Contact Zone." *Profession 91,* 33–40. New York: Modern Language Association.

Putnam, R. D. 1995. "Bowling Alone: America's Declining Social Capital." *Journal of Democracy* 6 (1): 65–78.

Qualley, D. J. 1994. "Being Two Places at Once." In *Pedagogy in the Age of Politics,* edited by P. A. Sullivan and D. J. Qualley, 32–35. Urbana, IL: National Council of Teachers of English.

Reynolds, N. 1998a. "Composition's Imagined Geographies." *College Composition and Communication* 50 (1): 12–35.

————. 1998b. "Interrupting Our Way to Agency: Feminist Cultural Studies and Composition." In *Feminism and Composition Studies: In Other Words,* edited by S. C. Jarratt and L. Worsham, 58–73. New York: Modern Language Association.

Ritchie, J., and K. Boardman. 1999. "Feminism in Composition: Inclusion, Metonymy, and Disruption." *College Composition and Communication* 50 (4): 585–606.

Rodriguez, R. 1982. *Hunger of Memory: The Education of Richard Rodriguez.* New York: Bantam.

Rorty, R. 1982. *Consequences of Pragmatism.* Minneapolis: University of Minnesota Press.

Rose, K. 1989. "Who's Bright?" In *Writing in Trust: A Tapestry of Teachers' Voices,* edited by S. Watson, 67–69. Research Triangle Park, NC: Southeastern Educational Improvement Laboratory.

Rose, M. 1990. *Lives on the Boundary: A Moving Account of the Struggles and Achievements of America's Educationally Underprepared.* New York: Penguin.

Roskelly, H. 1995. "On Becoming a Teacher." *College English* 57 (6): 713–22.

Said, E. 1993. *Culture and Imperialism.* New York: Knopf.

Sapphire. 1996. "Push." *The New Yorker* (April 29): 44–47.

Schutz, A., and A. R. Gere. 1998. "Service Learning and English Studies: Rethinking 'Public' Service." *College English* 60 (2): 129–49.

Schwarz, J. 1997. *Illusions of Opportunity: The American Dream in Question.* New York: W. W. Norton.

Searle, L. F. 1996. "Institutions and Intellectuals: A Modest Proposal." *Profession 1996,* 15–25. New York: Modern Language Association.

Sedgwick, E. K. 1997. "Paranoid Reading and Reparative Reading; Or, You're So Paranoid, You Think This Introduction Is About You." *Novel Gazing: Queer Readings in Fiction,* edited by E. K. Sedgwick, 1–40. Durham, NC: Duke University Press.

Segal, J. Z. 1996. "Pedagogies of Decentering and a Discourse of Failure." *Rhetoric Review* 15 (1): 174–91.

Selfe, C. 1998. "Technology and Literacy: A Story of the Perils of Not Paying Attention" [Preliminary Draft]. 25 March. *National Council of Teachers of English, CCCC 1998 Online.* Internet. 28 March.

————, and P. Meyer. 1991. "Testing the Claims for On-Line Conferences." *Written Communication* 8 (2): 163–92.

Shor, I. 1997. "Our Apartheid." *Journal of Basic Writing* 16 (1): 91–104.

————. 1996. *When Students Have Power: Negotiating Authority in a Critical Pedagogy.* Chicago: University of Chicago Press.

————. 1992. *Empowering Education: Critical Teaching for Social Change.* Chicago: University of Chicago Press.

Smith, V. 1998. *Not Just Race, Not Just Gender.* New York: Routledge.

Soliday, M. 1994. "Translating Self and Difference through Literacy Narratives." *College English* 56 (5): 511–26.

Sommers, J. 1993. "Doctoral Orals." *Teaching English in the Two-Year College* 20 (3): 187.

———. 1980. "Slaying Goliath." *Connecticut Quarterly* 7: 21–41.

Sosnoski, J. J., and D. B. Downing. 1994. "A Multivalent Pedagogy for a Multicultural Time." *PRE/TEXT* 14: 307–40.

Spanhauer, T. 1991. *The Man Who Fell in Love with the Moon.* New York: Atlantic Monthly Press.

Spellmeyer, K. 1996. "Inventing the University Student." In *Composition in the Twenty-First Century: Crisis and Change,* edited by L. Z. Bloom, D. A. Daiker, and E. S. White, 39–44. Carbondale, IL: Southern Illinois University Press.

Spelman, E. V. 1989. "Anger and Insubordination." In *Women, Knowledge, and Reality: Exploration in Feminist Philosophy,* edited by A. Garry and M. Pearsall, 263–73. Boston: Unwin Hyman.

Spooner, M., and K. Yancey. 1996. "Postings on a Genre of Email." *College Composition and Communication* 47 (2): 252–92.

Staiger, J. 1996. "Cinematic Shots: The Narration of Violence." In *The Persistence of History Cinema, Television, and the Modern Event,* edited by V. Sobchack, 39–54. New York: Routledge.

Stock, P., and J. Robinson. 1990. "Literacy as Conversation: Classroom Talk as Text Building." In *Conversations on the Written Word: Essays on Language and Literacy,* edited by J. Robinson, 163–238. Portsmouth, NH: Heinemann.

Stotsky, S. 1992. "Conceptualizing Writing as Moral and Civic Thinking." *College English* 54 (7): 794–808.

Tate, G., E. P. J. Corbett, and N. Meyers, eds. 1994. *The Writing Teacher's Sourcebook.* 3d ed. New York: Oxford University Press.

Tayko, G., and J. P. Tassoni, eds. 1997. *Sharing Pedagogies: Students and Teachers Write About Dialogic Practices.* Portsmouth, NH: Boynton/Cook.

———. 1992. "'I'm Not a Poor Slave': Student-Generated Curricula and Race Relations." In *Social Issues in the English Classroom,* edited by C. M. Hurlbert and S. Totten, 258–66. Urbana, IL: National Council of Teachers of English.

Theobald, P. 1997. *Teaching the Commons: Place, Pride, and the Renewal of Community.* New York: Westview.

Tobin, L. 1993. *Writing Relationships: What Really Happens in the Composition Class.* Portsmouth, NH: Boynton/Cook.

———, and T. Newkirk, eds. 1994. *Taking Stock: The Writing Process Movement in the '90s.* Portsmouth, NH: Boynton/Cook.

Tompkins, J. 1996. *A Life in School: What the Teacher Learned.* Reading, MA: Addison-Wesley.

———. 1990. "Pedagogy of the Distressed." *College English* 52 (6): 653–60.

Trimmer, J. F., ed. 1997. *Narration as Knowledge: Tales of the Teaching Life.* Portsmouth, NH: Boynton/Cook.

Veeser, H. A. 1996. *Confessions of the Critics.* New York: Routledge.

Villanueva, V. 1993. *Bootstraps: From an American Academic of Color.* Urbana, IL: National Council of Teachers of English.

Von Franz, M-L. 1964. "The Process of Individuation." In *Man and His Symbols,* edited by C. G. Jung, 158–229. New York: Doubleday.

Wall, V. B. Jr., G. G. Galanes, and S. B. Love. 1957. "Small Task-Oriented Groups: Conflict, Conflict Management, Satisfaction, and Decision Quality." *Small Group Behavior* 18 (1): 31–55.

Weiler, K. 1988. *Women Teaching for Change: Gender, Class and Power.* South Hadley, MA: Bergin & Garvey.

White, H. 1978. *Tropics of Discourse.* Baltimore: Johns Hopkins University Press.

Will, G. 1995. "Feel-Good College Fads Flush Literacy Away." *Wilmington Star-News* 2 July 1, 6E.

Williams, P. 1997. "American Kabuki." In *Birth of a Nation'Hood: Gaze, Script, and Spectacle in the O. J. Simpson Case,* edited by T. Morrison and C. B. Lacour, 273–92. New York: Pantheon Books.

———. 1991. *The Alchemy of Race and Rights.* Cambridge: Harvard University Press.

Williams, R. 1976. *Keywords: A Vocabulary of Culture and Society.* New York: Oxford University Press.

Worsham, L. 1998. "Going Postal: Pedagogic Violence and the Schooling of Emotion." *JAC: A Journal of Composition Theory* 18 (2): 213–45.

———. 1993. "Emotion and Pedagogic Violence." *Discourse* 15(2): 119—148.

Yagelski, R. P. 1999. "The Ambivalence of Reflection: Critical Pedagogies, Identity, and the Writing Teacher." *College Composition and Communication* 51 (1): 32–50.

———. 1994."Who's Afraid of Subjectivity? The Composing Process and Postmodernism, or a Student of Donald Murray Enters the Age of Postmodernism." In *Taking Stock: The Writing Process Movement in the 90s,* edited by L. Tobin and T. Newkirk, 203–17. Portsmouth, NH: Boynton/Cook.

Young, I. M. 1990. "The Ideal of Community and the Politics of Difference." In *Feminism/Postmodernism,* edited by L. J. Nicholson, 300–23. New York: Routledge.

Zandy, J., ed. 1995. *Liberating Memory: Our Work and Our Working-Class Consciousness.* New Brunswick, NJ: Rutgers.

Zawodniak, C. 1997. "'I'll Have to Help Some of You More Than I Want To': Teacher Involvement and Student-Centered Pedagogy." In *Sharing Pedagogies: Students and Teachers Write About Dialogic Practices,* edited by G. Tayko and J. P. Tassoni, 25–32. Portsmouth, NH: Boynton/Cook.

Zeni, J. 1994. "Literacy, Technology, and Teacher Education." In *Literacy and Computers: The Complications of Teaching and Learning with Technology,* edited by C. Selfe and S. Hilligoss, 76–86. New York: Modern Language Association.

Contributors

Kevin Ball's essay is part of a larger research project that examines the ways in which local and regional knowledge and literacies are erased or elided by current theoretical constructions of critical pedagogy. Kevin is also working within the fields of service learning and literacy studies. His coauthored essay in *Composition Studies* argues that current representations of service learning within the discipline often fail to reflect the voices and learning of the projects' community participants, thereby limiting the discipline's conception of "learning" for all project participants.

Elizabeth Ervin is an associate professor of English and a participating faculty member in the Women's Studies minor at the University of North Carolina at Wilmington. Her essays have appeared in such journals as *College English* and *Rhetoric Review,* and she recently published a composition textbook titled *Public Literacy.* Her primary area of interest is public discourse, and she is currently exploring the idea of whether rhetoricians might be more effective advocates of democratic projects if they embraced amateurism rather than professionalism.

Scott Hendrix is the director of writing in the English Department at Albion College. During the course described in "What Happened in English 101?" he was a graduate teaching assistant at the University of Kansas, where he completed a dissertation that examines literacy, literacy education, and local community literacy work in the U.S. His recent publications include articles on family literacy education and on labor organizing among college composition instructors.

Sarah Hoskinson, currently a junior at the University of Kansas, majors in Religious Studies and English. Sarah writes short stories, a couple of which have been published in small magazines.

Erika Jacobson is completing a master's in English at the University of Kansas. During the time of the course being discussed, she was working toward a master's in Slavic languages and literatures. Since this time she has continued to teach composition, work as a writing consultant at KU, and teach courses based on the genre of literacy narratives.

Laura Micciche is an assistant professor of English at East Carolina University where she teaches composition, rhetorical theory, feminist theory, and women's literature courses. Her work has appeared most recently in *Composition Studies/Freshman English News, Composition Forum, American Studies International,* and *Weaving Knowledge Together: Writing Centers and Collaboration.*

Brad Peters coordinates the Writing Across the Curriculum program at Northern Illinois University, where he teaches courses in cross-disciplinary rhetorics and professional writing. His interests in critical and multicultural pedagogies have led to recent publications in *Race, Rhetoric, and Composition, The Personal Narrative,* and *Stories Told in School* (forthcoming).

Douglas Reichert Powell recently completed his dissertation, "Hick Town: The Cultural Politics of American Regionalism," at Northeastern University. He is a visiting assistant professor of English at Miami University in Oxford, Ohio.

Riché Richardson is an assistant professor of English at the University of California, Davis. Her teaching interests include African American literature, American literature, critical theory, cultural studies, and feminism. She is currently working on a book-length project titled *Black Southern Masculinities and the Problem of Uncle Tom.*

Darrell g.h. Schramm's articles and essays have appeared in *A Member of the Family, Reflective Activities, Journal x, North Dakota Quarterly,* and other publications. His poetry has been published in over 100 literary journals. He teaches and directs the undergraduate writing program at the University of San Francisco.

Frances B. Singh is an associate professor at Hostos Community College (CUNY). She has published articles on Conrad and Forster as well as on the interplay between language teaching and politics. Her current research interest is in the personal narrative. Her most recent article is "A Passion for Maps: Encounters with the *Heart of Darkness,*" which appeared in *The Personal Narrative: Writing Ourselves as Teachers and Scholars,* edited by Gil Haroian-Guerin.

Jeff Sommers is a professor of English at Miami University—Middletown. He has published articles, book chapters, books, and textbooks on composition pedagogy and writing assessment. Jeff also writes approximately 1.3 poems a year.

Saira Sufi is a junior in political science at the University of Kansas and intends to receive her Ph.D. in political science. She currently works at the Watkins Community Museum of History in Lawrence, Kansas. Her interests include reading, political theorists, learning Spanish, and Kansas basketball.

John Paul Tassoni teaches composition and American literature at Miami University—Middletown. With Gail Tayko, he is coeditor of *Sharing Pedagogies: Students and Teachers Write About Dialogic Practices,* and he has published essays on pedagogy and literature in books and journals such as *Communication and Women's Friendship, Social Issues in the English Classroom, Teaching English in the Two-Year College, Journal of Teaching Writing,* and *ISLE: Interdisciplinary Studies in Literature and Environment.* He received his Ph.D. at Indiana University of Pennsylvania, where he had the good fortune of meeting his coeditor for this volume.

William H. Thelin received his doctorate in Rhetoric and Linguistics from Indiana University of Pennsylvania, where he focused his studies on the impact of politics on the field of composition. He has published articles on composition, critical pedagogy, and reading, and he works for the Conference of Teaching Academic Survival Skills in several capacities. He teaches open-access students in the Language Arts Department of the University of Cincinnati and directs the Peer Tutor Writing Center. He also is active in the Working Class Culture and Pedagogy caucus of the Conference on College Composition and Communication, directing its community-based projects.